Discovering Sexuality in Dostoevsky

Northwestern University Press
Studies in Russian Literature and Theory

Series Editors
Robert Belknap
Caryl Emerson
Gary Saul Morson
William Mills Todd III
Andrew Wachtel

Discovering Sexuality in Dostoevsky

Susanne Fusso

NORTHWESTERN UNIVERSITY PRESS / EVANSTON, ILLINOIS

Northwestern University Press
www.nupress.northwestern.edu

First paperback printing 2008.

Printed in the United States of America

10 9 8 7 6 5 4 3 2 1

The Library of Congress has cataloged the original, hardcover edition as follows:

Library of Congress Cataloging-in-Publication Data

Fusso, Susanne.
　　Discovering sexuality in Dostoevsky / Susanne Fusso.
　　　　p.　cm. — (Studies in Russian literature and theory)
　　Includes bibliographical references and index.
　　ISBN 0-8101-2107-7 (cloth : alk. paper)
　　1. Dostoyevsky, Fyodor, 1821–1881—Themes, motives. 2. Sex in literature.
　　3. Children and sex in literature. I. Title. II. Series.
　　PG3328.Z7S494　2006
　　891.733—dc22　　　　　　　　　　　　　　　　　　　　　　　2006002652

♾ The paper used in this publication meets the minimum requirements of the
American National Standard for Information Sciences—Permanence of Paper
for Printed Library Materials, ANSI Z39.48-1992.

For Joe

Contents

Acknowledgments

Many teachers, colleagues, and friends have contributed to my work on Dostoevsky over the years. It was my great good fortune to have the opportunity of studying with Robert Louis Jackson at Yale University in the 1970s, and our collegial connection has continued unbroken since then. The reader of this book will note my indebtedness to him on every page. Jackson has been an important inspiration not only in his lifelong study and profound illumination of Dostoevsky's works but in the clarity and beauty of his writing. This book is intended as a tribute to his example and encouragement.

Gary Saul Morson was never formally my teacher, but I have been learning from him for decades, both through his writing and through an ongoing fruitful dialogue. He has helped me at many stages of my own career with acts of collegial generosity that are impossible to acknowledge adequately in a few words.

My departmental colleagues at Wesleyan University have provided a stimulating intellectual atmosphere and steadfast friendship. Both Priscilla Meyer and Duffield White are experienced and insightful students of Dostoevsky's works and have provided much useful guidance and critical response. Irina and Yuz Aleshkovsky have been prized consultants on linguistic issues, as has Sergei Bunaev. My students at Wesleyan have always been among my most important sources of encouragement and perceptive feedback. I would like to thank in particular Thomas Ferguson, Noel Lawrence, Ginger Lazarus, Bonnie Loshbaugh, David Mane, Beau Martin, David Montero, Sarah Montgomery, Elizabeth Papazian, Rita Rozenblium, Jessica Sharzer, Rebecca F. Smith, John Voekel, Josh Walker, and Matvei Yankelevich. The administration of Wesleyan University has provided generous sabbatical time and financial support for scholarship. I would like to thank in particular Vice President for Academic Affairs Judith C. Brown; Dean of the Arts and Humanities Elizabeth L. Milroy; former Vice President for Academic Affairs Richard W. Boyd; and former Deans of the Arts and Humanities Carla Antonaccio and Diana Sorensen.

H. Stern of the Yale Department of Germanic Languages and Literatures has taught me a great deal about literary technique, writing, and argumentation and has offered much emotional support. Robert T. Conn, my colleague in the Department of Romance Languages and Literatures and Latin American Studies Program, helped me develop the topic for this book and has been an astute and helpful reader and tireless interlocutor all along. Special thanks are due to my dear friends and colleagues Susan Amert, Olga Hasty, Alexander Lehrman, and Nancy Pollak. Other colleagues and friends who have contributed in various ways to the writing of this book are Julia Bell, Sergei Bocharov, Catherine Ciepiela, Caryl Emerson, Carol Flath, Bruce Masters, Robin Feuer Miller, Stephanie Sandler, Gail Stern, Andrew Wachtel, and all the participants in the 1999 conference "Focus on *The Brothers Karamazov*" at Yale, organized by Robert Louis Jackson. June Pachuta Farris provided helpful advice on bibliography. Susan Betz, Rachel Delaney, and Anne Gendler of Northwestern University Press have been a pleasure to work with. Paul Mendelson provided expert editing of the entire manuscript. I am deeply grateful for his care and sensitivity.

Yury Vladimirovich Mann has offered help and support in many ways, particularly by arranging for me to meet with Liia Mikhailovna Rozenblium at the Institute for World Literature in Moscow. On visits to Moscow, I enjoyed the hospitality and good advice of Olga Monina, Sergei Semyonov, Aleksandra Semyonova, and Misha Trubetskoi.

I am most grateful to the staff at Wesleyan's Olin Memorial Library, particularly Collection Development Librarian Edwin Jay Allen; Reference Librarians Kendall Hobbs and Edmund Rubacha; Documents Librarian Erhard F. Konerding; and Interlibrary Loan staff Kathleen B. Stefanowicz and Katherine R. Wolfe. Thanks are also due to the staffs of Yale's Sterling Memorial Library and the Russian State (Lenin) Library in Moscow.

Family members have kept me going with their lively interest in the progress of my work and their thought-provoking questions about it. For this I thank my brother, James D. Fusso; his partner, Richard Barry; and my late mother-in-law, Jennie D. Siry.

H. Stern was instrumental in helping me to develop the ideas presented in chapter 3. I would also like to thank Ayşe Agiş, Ian Duncan, Irene Masing-Delic, Gary Saul Morson, Liia Mikhailovna Rozenblium, Kurt Schultz, and two anonymous readers for the *Russian Review* for their indispensable help in the research and writing of this chapter. Thanks also to the Center for the Study of Women in Society at the University of Oregon, and the Slavic departments at the University of Chicago, Northwestern University, and Yale University for the opportunity to discuss the material presented therein.

Acknowledgments

I presented part of chapter 5 as a talk in the Martin Weiner Lecture Series, sponsored by the Department of German, Russian and East Asian Languages and Literature, and Russian and East European Studies, at Brandeis University in March 2004. Thanks are due to Joan Chevalier, Steve Dowden, Robin Feuer Miller, and David Powelstock for their helpful comments on my presentation.

During the writing of this book I fell in love with and married Joseph M. Siry, a formidable scholar of architectural history. It is a cliché but nonetheless true to say that this book would never have been completed without him. He has provided intellectual companionship, a model of scholarly dedication that has shamed me into working harder than I ever have before, careful reading and criticism of the entire manuscript, and loving support.

Part of chapter 1 was originally published in *The Dostoevsky Journal: An Independent Review,* vols. 3–4 (2002–3). An earlier version of chapter 3 was previously published in *The Russian Review* 59 (October 2000). An earlier version of chapter 4 was published in *A New Word on "The Brothers Karamazov,"* ed. Robert Louis Jackson (Evanston: Northwestern University Press, 2004). An earlier version of chapter 6 was published in *The Cambridge Companion to Dostoevskii,* ed. W. J. Leatherbarrow (Cambridge: Cambridge University Press, 2002). These chapters are reprinted with permission.

Research for chapter 3 was supported by a grant from the International Research and Exchanges Board, with funds provided by the U.S. Department of State (Title VIII program) and the National Endowment for the Humanities. None of these organizations is responsible for the views expressed. Research for chapter 4 was made possible by a project grant from Wesleyan University.

In the text I have used a modified Library of Congress transliteration system, substituting "yo" or "o" for "ë" in proper names.

Introduction

The title of this book, *Discovering Sexuality in Dostoevsky,* alludes primarily to the major concern of my study, which is Dostoevsky's artistic treatment of how children and adolescents discover sexuality as part of their maturation and development. The secondary meaning, however, is that in this book I propose to discover the topic of sexuality in Dostoevsky's work in a somewhat different way than the topic has largely been treated up to now. First, my primary object of investigation is not Dostoevsky's own sexuality but his literary and journalistic presentation of the subject. Second, in analyzing sexuality in Dostoevsky's works I have tried to avoid placing it within a Freudian framework, as previous studies have tended to do. My approach is to look at sources on sexuality that were available at the time Dostoevsky was writing, with the aim of reconstructing the pre-Freudian view of human sexual development that Dostoevsky, an avid reader and observer of his own social context, imbibed and to which he reacted.[1]

The most famous investigation into Dostoevsky's own sexuality as reflected in his works was carried out by Freud himself, in a 1928 essay that attributes to Dostoevsky a variety of psychological disorders, including masochism, sadism, hysteria, a desire to kill his father which is then transferred to the tsar, and a compulsion to masturbate which is expressed as addictive gambling.[2] In his magisterial five-volume biography of Dostoevsky, Joseph Frank has shown in impressive detail that Freud's psychoanalytic edifice is built on a shaky foundation of erroneous biographical "facts."[3] Even earlier than Freud's own essay came A. Kashina-Evreinova's 1923 Freudian analysis of Dostoevsky's life and works, *The Underground of Genius (Podpol'e geniia).*[4] Kashina-Evreinova's study contains some insightful comments on the sexual theme in Dostoevsky's works, but her conclusion is marred by speculative assertions, of which the following is typical: "All the torments and cruelties scattered throughout his novels were necessary for him personally and afforded him a certain sexual satisfaction . . . All these incidents of perverted sexual attraction . . . expose in Dostoevsky such an intense enjoyment of cruelty, such an inspection of it from all sides, that it *cannot help but arouse* a certain suspicion that he received pleasure from the thought of such facts" (emphasis in original).[5] One of the most recent exercises in the genre of extrapolating a theory of Dostoevsky's sexuality from his works and from the scanty documentary evidence is T. Enko, *F. Dostoevskii—The Intimate Life of a Genius (F. Dostoevskii—Intimnaia zhizn' geniia)*.[6] The book has a frivolous cover depicting Dostoevsky kissing the foot of his lover Apollinaria Suslova and was clearly marketed to take advantage of the heady post-Soviet atmosphere of sexual freedom. In fact, however, it is a rather sober compilation of the available evidence regarding Dostoevsky's sexual experiences. Ultimately, the reader interested primarily in Dostoevsky's life experience is well advised to consult Joseph Frank's biography, in which all the relevant documented facts have been marshaled.[7] In the present study, when Dostoevsky's personal experiences are considered, it is with a view to understanding the meaning of his artistic and journalistic texts, not as a means to explain his personal sexual feelings or activity.

Among studies of Dostoevsky's writings, Elizabeth Dalton's book on *The Idiot* is probably the most consistently Freudian reading of an individual work.[8] Dalton takes Freud's theories as a given and interprets the novel using them as a guide, concluding that "the principal psychological conflict of the novel takes place at the oedipal level, between submissive and murderous wishes toward the father."[9] Few studies are as thoroughly and pervasively Freudian as Dalton's, but when dealing with sexual issues it is hard for critics of the late twentieth and early twenty-first centuries to avoid seeing through a Freudian lens. I have tried in the present book to reconstruct the ways that Dostoevsky and his contemporaries would have viewed sexual practices, so as to read his texts more perceptively and with greater historical accuracy. The immediate post-Soviet era of the 1990s saw a flowering of studies on sexuality and literature by both Russian and non-Russian scholars, many of which moved beyond a Freudian model. This is the analytical perspective developed in the following chapters, whose endnotes refer to recent scholarship in this vein.

This book is not a comprehensive study of Dostoevsky's oeuvre, but focuses on works in which his treatment of sexual issues is particularly interesting and meaningful, and where one must dig beneath the surface to derive the full significance of these issues for him as both a citizen and a literary artist.[10] The book deals mainly with sexual practices considered "deviant" in Dostoevsky's time, both because these are the practices that confront Dostoevsky's young people and because they pose the most interesting interpretive problems: due to governmental and self-censorship at the time, examination of these issues requires careful decoding by the investigator, both of Dostoevsky's texts and of their social context. I have focused almost exclusively on the mature, post-Siberia phase of Dostoevsky's career, in which his treatment of sexuality achieved its most accomplished form.

The following chapters deal with (1) Dostoevsky's search for an appropriate artistic language for sexuality; (2) the development that can be traced in his treatment of the theme of the sexually abused female child; (3) the experimentation with homoerotic desire and unconventional narrative in *A Raw Youth;* (4) the story of a young man's sexual development as told in *A Raw Youth* and *The Brothers Karamazov;* (5) Dostoevsky's complex treatment of a child's secret sexual sins in his account of the Kroneberg child abuse case in *A Writer's Diary;* and (6) Dostoevsky's conception of the ideal family, a type of family that appears in his works only by negative example.

It is not my purpose to argue that sexuality is Dostoevsky's only concern or even his major concern. I have tried here to bring out one thread in the intricate thematic weave of his novels and in so doing to illuminate his artistic process, a process that is never far removed from his moral quest.

Discovering Sexuality in Dostoevsky

Chapter One

"Secrets of Art" and "Secrets of Kissing":
Toward a Poetics of Sexuality in Dostoevsky

THE PLOTS OF DOSTOEVSKY'S great novels of the period 1866 to 1880 are moved by sexual secrets and scandals: Svidrigailov's attempt to seduce Raskol'nikov's sister, Totskii's life-crippling seduction of Nastas'ia Filippovna, Stavrogin's pedophilia, the sexual rivalry between father and son in *A Raw Youth* and *The Brothers Karamazov*. If we look back to 1861, near the beginning of Dostoevsky's reentry into Russian literary life after nine years of prison and exile in Siberia, we find him engaging in a polemic that illuminates his struggle to develop a poetics of presenting sexual material in art.[1] This chapter explores questions concerning that polemic and its connection with the novel Dostoevsky was writing simultaneously with it, *The Insulted and Injured* (*Unizhennye i oskorblennye*, 1861). Robert L. Jackson has cautioned against adopting a morally judgmental stance toward Dostoevsky's use of certain kinds of sexual material, as Turgenev did in calling Dostoevsky "our Sade." Jackson writes: "Even if we were to allow for a special personal sadistic interest of Dostoevsky in suffering, cruelty, and violence, we should in no way be making a statement on the literary and philosophical significance of his use of this material in his work. We should be making a moral judgment, and one which completely muddles the distinction between the man and the artist."[2] The present chapter has the aim not of pronouncing moral judgment on Dostoevsky but of identifying the moral problem he himself struggled with as he developed his approach for presenting sexual material in his artistic works.

In February 1861, the *St. Petersburg News* (*Sankt-Peterburgskie vedomosti*) published a description by a certain Timmerman of a benefit for an orphanage fund in the provincial town of Perm', at which the wife of a state councillor, Evgeniia Eduardovna Tolmachova, publicly recited the poem created and performed at the end of Pushkin's "Egyptian Nights" ("Egipetskie nochi," 1835) by the Italian improviser visiting St. Petersburg. This of course is the famous poetic description of how Cleopatra, at a public feast, offered her sexual favors to any man who was willing to sacrifice his life for one night with her, and how three men in the crowd came forward to accept the challenge. The enraptured journalist's description of Tolmachova's performance evoked a mocking response by the editor of the journal *The Age* (*Vek*), P. I. Veinberg, who under the pseudonym Kamen'-Vinogorov ridiculed Timmerman's account. The key moment of Veinberg's feuilleton is an attack not on the correspondent who reported the reading but on Tolmachova herself. Timmerman describes Tolmachova casting on her audience the same contemptuous and mocking gaze that Cleopatra cast on her hearers after her challenge. Vinogorov writes:

> The only thing I don't understand is what relation the audience at the Perm' literary gathering who were listening to Mrs. Tolmachova bore to Cleopatra's admirers; but they must have borne some relation, because otherwise, why would Mrs. Tolmachova have had reason to pass a gaze of "contempt and angry mockery" over the crowd? But I do not know the secrets of Perm' [permskie tainy], and therefore it's understandable that I didn't understand anything.[3]

Vinogorov's feuilleton was answered by an angry protest by M. L. Mikhailov entitled "The Outrageous Action by *The Age*" ("Bezobraznyi postupok 'Veka'"), which defended Tolmachova as a proponent of women's emancipation.

Dostoevsky entered the fray after *The Age* published an insincere and insulting "sincere apology" ("chistoserdechnoe izvinenie"). His answer, "Models of Sincerity" ("Obraztsy chistoserdechiia"), appeared in his own journal *Time* (*Vremia*) in February 1861. Dostoevsky returned to the same polemic one more time, after the conservative Mikhail Katkov, in his own contribution to the debate, in effect described Pushkin's "Egyptian Nights" as a pornographic work.[4] Dostoevsky's second essay, "An Answer to *The Russian Herald*" ("Otvet 'Russkomu Vestniku'"), published in *Time* in May 1861, contained his own well-known interpretation of Pushkin's "Egyptian Nights."

V. Komarovich has pointed out that in the same issue of *Time* in which Dostoevsky's second "Egyptian Nights" essay appeared, he also published part 3, chapter 10 of *The Insulted and Injured,* in which the evil Prince Valkovskii "bares himself" ("ogoliaetsia") verbally to the idealistic writer-narrator Ivan Petrovich.[5] The most striking verbal connection between the two texts is the comparison of both Cleopatra and Valkovskii to a "pauk" ("spider"; 19:136, 3:358), an image of bestial lust that Dostoevsky was to use again and again. As Komarovich says, "All of Dostoevsky's voluptuaries [sladostrastniki] are accompanied by the proto-image of the queen [that is, Cleopatra; proobraz tsaritsy]."[6] More broadly, the Valkovskii chapter from *The Insulted and Injured,* when read alongside the "Egyptian Nights" essays, highlights an anxiety about the presentation of sexual material in art that Dostoevsky was struggling with at the beginning of his maturity as an artist.

In the course of the "Egyptian Nights" debate it becomes clear that the public performance of a work of literary art enhances the power—one might say the danger—of any sexual material it contains. In the course of reciting the Italian's improvisation, Mrs. Tolmachova would have had to recite the following speech by Cleopatra:

> I swear . . . O mother of pleasures,
> I will serve you in an unheard-of way,
> As a simple concubine I mount
> The couch of passionate temptations.
> Hear me, O mighty Cypris,
> And you, underworld gods,
> O gods of terrible Hades,
> I swear—until the dawn
> I will voluptuously tire out
> The desires of my masters
> And I will quench them with wondrous soft pleasures
> And all the secrets of kissing.[7]

A major issue in the debate is: Does Tolmachova become Cleopatra by reciting her speech in public? Do Cleopatra's "secrets of kissing" ("tainy lobzan'ia") imply the existence of "secrets of Perm'" ("permskie tainy")?

In his first essay on the topic, Dostoevsky's answer is a firm no. He admits that it was rash for Tolmachova to recite "Egyptian Nights," not because her action was indecent but because the time was not yet ripe for it. For Dostoevsky the problem with such public behavior by a woman is a matter not of substance but of convention:

> To read an artistic work like Pushkin's "Egyptian Nights" out loud, in public, is not at all shameful, just as it is not shameful to stop enraptured before the Medici Venus in an exhibition hall, where visitors of all ages and both sexes throng. But there are many prejudices in society: it is an accepted practice to place naked statues before the public; it is also possible to read "Egyptian Nights"; after all, Pushkin's improviser read it. But if a woman reads it, people will protest. Women here do not yet have such rights. (19:102)

Dostoevsky defends Tolmachova by aligning her not with Cleopatra but with Pushkin. She was moved, he surmises, not by "voluptuous intentions" ("sladostrastnye pomyshleniia") but by "pure, lofty artistic rapture" and "artistic pleasure" ("chistyi, samyi vysokii khudozhestvennyi vostorg," "khudozhestvennoe naslazhdenie," 19:102–3).

In the second essay, responding not to Vinogorov's attack on Tolmachova but to Katkov's characterization of Pushkin's work as indecent, Dostoevsky's emphasis shifts from defending Tolmachova the performer to defending Pushkin the artist. In his contribution to the debate, Katkov had rejected Dostoevsky's comparison of "Egyptian Nights" to the nude statues of classical antiquity:

> Do the Medici Venus and the Venus de Milo really represent the same expressions of passion that sound in Cleopatra's words? Do not these Olympian types represent the most chaste images, imbued with that pure elegance that constitutes the living soul of propriety? Are not these images themselves the personification of that refined modesty, that enchanting mystery? Would the chisel not only of Phidias or Praxiteles, but even of the sculptors of the age of decadence, ever extend to depict the ultimate expressions of passion [poslednie vyrazheniia strastnosti]? (quoted by Dostoevsky, 19:134)

Katkov goes on to argue that because Pushkin's work is a fragment, it does not have an overarching artistic conception that would soften and contextualize sexual material, or what Katkov calls "that which should never become an open secret [otkrytaia taina]" (quoted by Dostoevsky, 19:134).

Dostoevsky has three answers to this argument. First, "Egyptian Nights" is not a fragment, but "the most finished work of Russian poetry" ("samoe zakonchennoe proizvedenie nashei poezii," 19:132). This point he asserts rather than argues. Second, any sexual material in the work has been transformed by a mysterious artistic process: "Here reality has been transformed, *having passed through art,* having passed through the fire of pure, chaste inspiration and through the poet's artistic thought. This is a secret of art, and every artist knows about it." ("Tut deistvitel'nost' preobrazilas', *proidia cherez iskusstvo,* proidia cherez ogon' chistogo, tselomudrennogo vdokhnoveniia i cherez khudozhestvennuiu mysl' poeta. Eto taina iskusstva, i o nei znaet vsiakii khudozhnik," 19:134; emphasis in original.) Third, if any salacious impression is received, it is the fault of the audience, not the artist. As Dostoevsky wrote in his first essay: "On an undeveloped, depraved heart even the Medici Venus will produce only a voluptuous impression. One must be rather highly purified in a moral sense in order to look at this divine beauty without embarrassment" (19:103). And, in direct response to Katkov, "The *chastity* of an image does not save it from a coarse and even perhaps a dirty thought" (19:134).[8] Finally he offers his own interpretation of "Egyptian Nights" as a work that produces not a "Marquis de Sade" effect but a shattering moral effect. Pushkin's depiction of the spiritual bankruptcy of decadent Alexandria "makes it clear to what kind of people our divine Redeemer came" (19:137). As Monika Greenleaf writes, "In the apparently pagan tale of Cleopatra's sexual bargain [Dostoevsky] discovered a kind of negative proof for the necessity of Christianity, and, by implication, for Pushkin's hidden status as a Russian Christian artist."[9]

Dostoevsky's defense of Tolmachova and Pushkin is powerful, and we can recognize in it a fairly modern attitude toward the presentation of sexual material in art.[10] But there are two moments at which his argument falters, betraying the fact that Dostoevsky has not entirely convinced himself. The first is his response, or lack of response, to one of Vinogorov's jeers. Vinogorov suggests that Tolmachova should read yet another of Pushkin's poems, "No, I do not prize the stormy pleasure" ("Net, ia ne dorozhu miatezhnym naslazhden'em," 1831): "Read it, Mrs. Tolmachova! As you read you'll be able to assume an even more *challenging* expression and make even *more expressive gestures*! If you're going for emancipation, then go all the way! Why stop halfway?" (quoted by Dostoevsky, 19:99). Dostoevsky's only response to this is "How disgusting! Doesn't it arouse your indignation!" ("Kakaia gadost'! Nu ne podymaet li eto serdtsa ot negodovaniia!" 19:99). Implicit in Dostoevsky's angry response is an acknowledgment that it would be highly improper for Mrs. Tolmachova to read *this* Pushkin poem with expressive gestures, because it is a description of the lyric speaker's preference for one type of lover (and in particular, one type of orgasm) over another. Dostoevsky is annoyed by Katkov's obsession with "the ultimate expressions of passion" ("poslednie vyrazheniia strastnosti"), perhaps because Katkov's phrase evokes the phrase in Pushkin's poem that describes the way in which the wild female lover ("the young Bacchante") "hastens the moment of ultimate spasms" ("toropit mig poslednikh sodroganii"). Dostoevsky's indignation is a sign of a logical problem in his argument. If the "taina iskusstva" ("secret of art") transforms reality, why should this bit of reality be any less appropriate for Tolmachova to read in public, provided she is moved by "artistic rapture"? Unlike Dostoevsky, Katkov draws the line between classical statues and "Egyptian Nights," but Dostoevsky apparently finds it necessary to draw a line as well.

The second moment in which Dostoevsky seems to adopt the premises of his opponents concerns the performer's relation to her audience. At one point Dostoevsky concedes that the problem with Tolmachova's performance may be not just the fact that she is violating convention, but that the reading could have a pernicious effect on a certain segment of her audience: "Of course, for adolescents [dlia otrocheskogo vozrasta] such a reading *might* even be dangerous. In adolescence a person is not fully formed either physically or morally, and the Medici Venus may not produce a full artistic effect on him" (19:103). Dostoevsky angrily rejected Vinogorov's identification of Tolmachova with Cleopatra, choosing to identify her with Pushkin instead, as one moved by artistic inspiration. But when he evokes the "adolescent" ("otrok") in Tolmachova's audience who may be harmed by her reading, one cannot help but think of Cleopatra's third and final victim, the "otrok" who comes forward to offer his life, moved by the "rapture of love" and "boundless passion," in Dostoevsky's words (19:137). "Oh, this victim promises more pleasure than all the rest!" (19:137).

The source of Dostoevsky's anxiety, betrayed in these moments of inconsistency, is not the fact that Tolmachova the performer might be mistaken for Cleopatra, but that Pushkin the artist might. Pushkin's version of this anxiety is of course reflected in the prose frame of "Egyptian Nights," as Cleopatra the queen/prostitute is bifurcated into two characters who represent two different ways of being a poet: Charskii the disinterested aristocrat, and his alter ego, the Italian mountebank who offers his divine talent for hire. But Dostoevsky's anxiety is concentrated in a different area than Pushkin's—not in a fear that the artist's audience may compromise him, but in a fear that he might abuse his audience through the presentation of sexual subject matter, a presentation that is nevertheless necessary for his own artistic mission. This anxiety becomes clearer upon examination of the scene in *The Insulted and Injured* in which Prince Valkovskii converses with the writer-narrator Ivan Petrovich in a restaurant, the scene published in the same issue of *Time* as Dostoevsky's second essay on "Egyptian Nights." Following Komarovich's hint, I would argue that the juxtaposition of these two pieces, one journalistic and one artistic, in the same publication is not fortuitous but reflects a deep connection between Dostoevsky's theorizing in defense of Pushkin and his own literary practice.

It is not necessary to rehearse here the plot complications that lead to the restaurant scene. As critics have often noted, this scene jumps out of the novel surrounding it as an apparent fragment from one of Dostoevsky's later, more mature works. What is important for the present discussion is that Prince Valkovskii's conversation with Ivan highlights some of the same issues that are dealt with in the "Egyptian Nights" debate, but from a different angle. This conversation develops in a way that is more morally compromising for the position of the artist dealing with "the ultimate expressions of passion."

Dostoevsky compared Cleopatra to a female spider that devours its mate at the moment of coitus. Ivan sees the evil Prince in similar terms: "He produced on me the impression of a disgusting creature [gad], of a sort of huge spider that I wanted terribly to crush" (3:358). Joseph Frank and others have pointed out that, beginning with *The Insulted and Injured*, Dostoevsky was drawing a parallel between the decadent classical world depicted in "Egyptian Nights" and his own contemporary Russian society.[11] As outlined in the second "Egyptian Nights" essay, the central feature of this society is sexual deviation:

[Cleopatra] is a representative of that society under which the foundations have long begun to give way. Already all faith has been lost; hope seems to be only a useless illusion; thought grows dim and disappears: the divine fire has abandoned it; society has gone astray and in cold despair has a premonition of the abyss before it and is ready to crash into it. Life is aimlessly gasping for breath. In the future there is nothing; one must demand everything from the present, one must fill life with only one's urgent daily needs. Everything goes into the body, everything throws itself into bodily debauchery, and in order to supplement the missing spiritual impressions, everyone irritates his nerves, his body with everything that can arouse sensuality. *The most monstrous deviations [ukloneniia], the most abnormal phenomena gradually become ordinary.* (19:135–36; emphasis mine)

In *The Insulted and Injured,* the word substituted for "ukloneniia" ("deviations") is "vychury" ("fancy," "mannerism," "conceit"; also an archaic word for an intricate pattern on fabric). This is the word used to describe the sexual inclinations of the obese pedophile Arkhipov: "otvratitel'no chuvst-vennaia tvar', s raznymi vychurami" . . . "strashnaia kanal'ia, griaznyi, gadkii, s vychurami i s raznymi podlymi vkusami" ("a disgustingly sensual creature, with various fancies" . . . "a terrible scoundrel, dirty, disgusting, with fancies and with various low tastes," 3:264, 273). Pedophilia is the major "deviation" depicted in *The Insulted and Injured,* but there is also the sex addiction of the Prince's son Alyosha (which would have been called "priapism" at the time).[12] Most strikingly, in the Prince's conversation with Ivan in the restaurant, he hints at having engaged in both sadomasochism and three-way sex with a high-society lady and her French maid (3:364).[13] But the most important deviation discussed by the Prince in this scene is exhibitionism, because it is a metadeviation that alludes to what the artist is doing as well as to what the characters are doing. In other words, exhibitionism implicates the artist-creator along with his creation.

The scene in the restaurant is the prototype for several important scenes in Dostoevsky's later work in which characters "bare themselves," cynically and lasciviously sharing their most intimate secrets, usually sexual secrets: Svidrigailov talking to Raskol'nikov, the *petit-jeu* at Nastas'ia Filippovna's name-day party, and the "Decameron of the dead" in "Bobok."[14] But Valkovskii is the only character to describe the baring of one's secrets on the metalevel. In discussing his pleasure in "removing his mask" before the disgusted and horrified Ivan, the Prince makes an important comparison:

There is a particular voluptuousness in this sudden tearing off of the mask, in this cynicism with which a person suddenly displays himself before another in such a way that he doesn't even do him the honor of being ashamed before him. I'll tell you a little story: there was a certain insane civil servant in Paris; later he was put in an insane asylum, when they became completely convinced that he was insane. Well, when he was going mad, here's what he thought up for his pleasure: he would get undressed at home, completely, like Adam, he

9

would leave on only his shoes, throw on a wide cloak that extended to his feet, would wrap himself up in it and go out on the street with a pompous, majestic mien. Well, if you looked at him from the side, he was a man like everyone else, taking a stroll in a wide cloak for his own amusement. But as soon as he had occasion to meet some passerby somewhere all alone, so that there was no one else around, he would silently go up to him, with the most serious and thoughtful air, suddenly stop before him, open his cloak and show himself in all his . . . sincerity [chistoserdechie]. This would last one minute, then he would wrap himself up again and silently, without moving a muscle in his face, would pass by the spectator, who was petrified in amazement, solemnly and smoothly, like the ghost in Hamlet. He did this with everyone, men, women, and children, and that constituted his whole pleasure. Well, one can find a part of that very pleasure when you suddenly discombobulate some Schiller and stick out your tongue at him when he least expects it. (3:362–63)[15]

Valkovskii the raconteur identifies with the insane exhibitionist. In other words, to tell about one's sexual deviations is itself one of the deviations.[16] The disturbing question is whether the writer who creates the confessor and the confession is complicit in the deviation as well.

The word "taina" ("mystery," "secret") is central to both the "Egyptian Nights" polemic and *The Insulted and Injured*. The operation of transforming and, by implication, neutralizing sexual material is called by Dostoevsky the "taina iskusstva" ("secret of art"). But "taina" also serves as a euphemism for sex itself: "tainy lobzan'ia," "permskie tainy" ("secrets of kissing," "secrets of Perm'"). In *The Insulted and Injured*, the latter, sexual sense of "taina" is everywhere present (perhaps an echo of one of the novel's sources, Eugène Sue's *Les mystères de Paris* [1842]). Sex is referred to as "tainy otnoshenii muzhchiny i zhenshchiny" ("the secrets of the relations between a man and a woman," 3:354). Adjectives and adverbs formed from "taina"—"tainstvennyi," "potaennyi," "tainstvenno," are also used to describe the Prince's unspecified perversions:

On . . . liubit inogda po nocham p'ianstvovat', napivat'sia kak stel'ka i potaenno razvratnichat', gadko i tainstvenno razvratnichat'. (3:354)

He . . . likes sometimes to get drunk at night, to get blind drunk and secretly engage in debauchery, disgusting and mysterious debauchery.

Ne bylo razvratnitsy razvratnee etoi zhenshchiny . . . Ia byl ee tainym i tainstvennym liubovnikom. (3:364)

There was never a woman more debauched than she was . . . I was her secret and mysterious lover.

The more elevated use of the word "taina" to refer to art does not appear in the Valkovskii scene, but the figure of the artist is disturbingly present in Valkovskii himself.

At the beginning of the scene, Valkovskii warns Ivan not to deny him any of his whims, or Ivan will not gain the information he seeks in order to aid his beloved Natasha. The Prince speaks of himself as an artist figure: "Just imagine that if I don't get what I want, all my inspiration [vdokhnove-nie] will pass, disappear, evaporate, and you won't hear anything" (3:356). Later, in response to Ivan's bewilderment that he has chosen him as "the confidant of your secrets [tainy] and erotic . . . strivings," Valkovskii says, "You're a poet, you'll understand me" (3:362). Most striking, though, is a passage that appeared in the *Time* version of the novel but was removed by Dostoevsky when the work was published separately. (No other changes of such magnitude were made in the restaurant scene.) The excised passage is a continuation of Valkovskii's speech about his mysterious sexual escapades with the seemingly virtuous society lady, escapades that "the most fevered imagination could not even dare to think of" (3:364). In the separate edition of the novel, Valkovskii's speech ends with the phrase, "That woman under-stood life and knew how to make use of it" (3:364). In the *Time* version, he goes on, saying to Ivan:

> But you—you have rented your whole life, you are having experiences that are not your own: other people have washed out their colors even before you were born—and you never once had the idea that all you have to do is want it, all you have to do is display your independence for an instant, only a tiny fraction of independence, and life will be yours, completely yours, *original, invented and composed by you* [vami izobretennaia i sochinennaia], full and rich, in which there will be a hundred times more real juices of life than in your present pitiful rented life, a life ordered by Papa and Mama. (3:477; emphasis mine)

This discourse of originality and invention, used in relation not to artistic creation but to the devising of sexual perversions, seems to have disturbed its own creator Dostoevsky enough that he removed the passage, despite its power and psychological truth. Valkovskii the exhibitionist is also, on some level, Dostoevsky the artist.[17]

Ivan, although by profession a writer, in this scene plays the role of audience instead. At the end of the conversation with the Prince, he gets to the heart of the danger posed by presenting sexual material, the danger that the artist may abuse his audience—a danger that Dostoevsky acknowl-edged in his discussion of Tolmachova's reading. After Valkovskii bares his sexual secrets, Ivan says to him: "You really did resemble that madman in the cloak. You didn't consider me to be a person [Vy menia za cheloveka ne schitali]" (3:369). In a sense, Dostoevsky presents in this scene a dialogue between two parts of the artistic self—the exhibitionist and the horrified spectator—a dialogue that we can see emerging in Dostoevsky's articles on the "Egyptian Nights" debate, at those moments when he acknowledges the dangers of presenting sexual material in art.

Yet another aspect of the artist-audience connection is Dostoevsky's location of the source of corruption in the audience itself. This same idea is present in Valkovskii's conviction that the perversions he reveals to Ivan are a universal human possession:

> If it could only be (which, by the way, can never be, thanks to human nature), if it could only be that each of us described all their intimate affairs [vsiu svoiu podnogotnuiu, literally "the dirt under their fingernails"], but in such a way that one was not afraid to set forth not only that which he is afraid to tell and would not under any circumstances tell others, not only that which he is afraid to tell his best friends, but even that which he is afraid sometimes to confess even to himself—then such a stench would rise up over the earth that we would all have to gasp for breath. (3:361)[18]

Freud claimed that "exhibitionists . . . exhibit their own genitals in order to obtain a reciprocal view of the genitals of the other person."[19] Whether clinically accurate or not, this insight does seem to apply to the Prince's exhibitionism. Although he tells Ivan that he is not asking about Ivan's own possible "secrets," "in order to vindicate myself through your secrets" ("chtob vashimi tainami opravdat' i sebia," 3:362), in fact the metaphor of the universal human stench is meant to implicate Valkovskii's audience along with himself. This aspect of the logic of exhibitionism brings us back to Dostoevsky's insistence in the "Egyptian Nights" polemic on blaming the corruption of the audience for any lascivious thoughts aroused by Pushkin's depiction of "the ultimate expressions of passion."

In defending Pushkin, Dostoevsky claimed that what saved "Egyptian Nights" from lewdness was the "point of view" of the poet—a tochka zreniia-to i glavnoe" ("and the point of view is the main thing," 19:135).[20] The "Egyptian Nights" polemic and the restaurant chapter of *The Insulted and Injured* demonstrate that maintaining the kind of distanced perspective implied by the phrase "point of view" is no easy task for the artist. Just as Tolmachova and by extension Pushkin have difficulty maintaining the boundary between themselves and Cleopatra, Dostoevsky is keenly aware of the fine line, not only between the exhibitionist civil servant and Valkovskii, but between Valkovskii and Dostoevsky himself.[21]

The "Egyptian Nights" polemic clearly indicates that, despite Katkov's disapproval of Pushkin's poem, Dostoevsky saw Pushkin as a positive model for infusing the depiction of sexual material in art with moral significance. In Dostoevsky's view, Pushkin provided the "point of view" that saves the work from producing what Dostoevsky calls a "shameful and impermissible impression," or what in modern terms would be called a pornographic impression. Dostoevsky reproaches Katkov for equating Pushkin's works with those of the Marquis de Sade (19:135). Clearly, Sade is one of Dostoevsky's negative models, although it is unclear specifically which works of Sade he actually read, if any.[22]

Jackson cites a passage from the memoirs of Dostoevsky's second wife, Anna Grigor'evna Dostoevskaia, that makes it clear that Dostoevsky took a keen interest in French erotic literature, an interest that he regarded as a professional duty. At around the time Dostoevsky was finishing *Crime and Punishment* (1866), he caught his young wife reading a French novel that had been lying on his desk. Dostoevsky took the book out of her hands, saying, "Why should you soil [griaznit'] your imagination!" The exchange that followed is most telling. Anna Grigor'evna writes:

> I protested, saying, "So why do *you* read them? Why do *you* soil your imagination?" "I am hardened [zakalennyi]," Fyodor Mikhailovich answered. "Certain books are necessary for me as material for my works. A writer must know everything and experience much. But I assure you, I do not relish risqué scenes, and they often arouse revulsion in me."[23]

Despite the occasional unreliability of A. G. Dostoevskaia's memoirs, the statement, "A writer must know everything," rings true. Dostoevsky's voracious reading of Russian and Western literature and journalism is well established. This incident illustrates that he considered it part of his duty as a writer to know "everything" about sexual matters as well. We do know of one French erotic novel that Dostoevsky most probably read, since it is mentioned both in *The Gambler* (*Igrok*, 1866) and in the notes for "The Life of a Great Sinner" ("Zhitie velikogo greshnika," ca. 1869–70): *Thérèse philosophe*.[24] This anonymous novel, published in 1748 and attributed by most modern scholars to Jean-Baptiste de Boyer, Marquis d'Argens, deserves serious scrutiny as one of the sources for Dostoevsky's views on and treatment of sexuality.

William C. Brumfield has provided the most thorough analysis of how the libertine philosophy of *Thérèse philosophe,* which at many points maps neatly onto Chernyshevskii's theory of "rational egoism," is refracted in Dostoevsky's works, especially *The Idiot* and *The Brothers Karamazov*.[25] Here I would like to focus specifically on the somewhat unorthodox way that sexuality is presented in the novel. It is unlikely that Dostoevsky *derived* his approach to sexuality from *Thérèse philosophe*, since we have no evidence that he knew the novel prior to the mid-1860s, and his own literary career began twenty years earlier. But in its embrace of the sheer multifariousness of human desire, *Thérèse philosophe* no doubt reinforced Dostoevsky's literary interest in what were then considered sexual deviations, an interest that is so clearly manifest in *The Insulted and Injured* as well as in his later novels.

The narrative of *Thérèse philosophe* takes a somewhat unexpected path for an erotic novel, due to the nature of its two main characters: Thérèse herself, who narrates the tale of her sexual development starting at age seven, and Madame Bois-Laurier, the prostitute who narrates her own story toward the end of the novel, beginning with her abduction by a procuress at age six. Thérèse is terrified of becoming pregnant because of the awful complications suffered by her own mother (a fistula that "placed her under the dire necessity of renouncing forever the pleasures that had given me existence").[26] Consequently, for much of the novel Thérèse devotes herself to the joys of masturbation, often prompted by the voyeuristic contemplation of the erotic activities of others. In fact, Robert Darnton refers to the second part of Thérèse's story as "an apology for masturbation."[27] After the death of her mother, the orphaned Thérèse, now in her early twenties, is "adopted" by Madame Bois-Laurier. Thanks to the anatomical peculiarity of an impenetrable hymen, Bois-Laurier is "neither man nor woman, neither maiden nor widow nor wife"; in the ultimate oxymoron, she is both virgin and prostitute.[28] Bois-Laurier's story is a catalog not of repetitive acts of intercourse but of the varieties of human desire. The prostitute who cannot engage in normal intercourse is called upon to participate in a range of bizarre activities and encounters a multitude of sexual eccentrics: the man whom she must fondle while his maid trims her pubic hair; the bishop who can only achieve orgasm while shouting, "Haï! Haï! Haï!"; the man who pays her to run nude through his apartments while he chases her with birch rods; and quite a few more. As Bois-Laurier says, "I would never be finished if I painted you a picture of all the bizarre tastes, all the singularities that I have come to know among men."[29] As Anne Richardot points out, Bois-Laurier's "unprecedented conformation" does not render her supernatural, like characters of a similarly "unique" vaginal conformation in Sade, but rather makes her an example "de la diversité du vivant."[30]

Thérèse refuses to be penetrated; Bois-Laurier is physically incapable of it. Thanks to the "motif of impenetrability" in *Thérèse philosophe,* standard intercourse, or what Henry Abelove has termed "sexual intercourse so-called (penis in vagina, vagina around penis, with seminal emission uninterrupted)," is relegated to the sidelines in favor of the "bizarre tastes" of a variety of men and women.[31] This aspect of the novel must have been of great interest to Dostoevsky, who devised the "fancies" ("vychury") of Arkhipov and the other lost souls in *The Insulted and Injured.* Like the decadent society of Cleopatra in Dostoevsky's imagining of it, the world of eighteenth-century France as depicted in *Thérèse philosophe* teems with examples of sexual deviation.

Dostoevsky told his wife that he was "hardened" toward novels like *Thérèse philosophe*, but that they often aroused his revulsion. He uses the same word in reference to *Thérèse philosophe* specifically, in the notes toward "The Life of a Great Sinner": "'Thérèse philosophe' disturbed Tikhon. 'And I thought I was already hardened [zakalilsia]'" (9:138; Tikhon is a monk figure). Surely there is much in *Thérèse philosophe* that even the hardened reader could find revolting.[32] Still, the model it presents of exploring the multifarious nature of human desire was one that Dostoevsky continued to follow throughout his career, and that was characteristic of pre-Freudian research on the nature of sexual desire.

In 1992 a previously suppressed passage from the memoirs of E. N. Opochinin was published, in which Dostoevsky tells Opochinin of having met a man who had what Bois-Laurier would call "bizarre tastes."[33] The man was devoted to the practice of attending the funerals of beautiful young girls in order to bestow on them a long, lingering final kiss: "I would be ready to drink it in eternally, and I find it difficult to tear myself away from her beautiful pure lips."[34] Dostoevsky introduces this anecdote of a necrophiliac by asserting the infinite variety of sexual tastes. In Opochinin's account, Dostoevsky says,

"In this respect [i.e., the sexual] . . . there are so many perversions [izvra-shcheniia] that you can't count them all. After all, there's a whole medical specialty devoted to figuring out all the different forms of this nastiness. I think, however, that everyone is subject to such perversion to a certain extent, if not in deed then at least in his thoughts . . . But no one wants to admit this: if it were otherwise, Merzheevskii [identified by the memoirist as Ivan P. Merzheevskii, but possibly V. O. Merzheevskii, who studied sexual pathology] would be able to gather a huge amount of material."[35]

Opochinin knew Dostoevsky at the very end of his life, but Dostoevsky expressed similar awareness of the diversity of human sexual desire earlier in his career, in *Crime and Punishment* (1867). In discussing "debauchery" ("razvrat") with Raskol'nikov, Svidrigailov uses the succinct phrase, "u odnogo tak, u odnogo inache" ("it's one way with one person, another way with another person," 6:362).[36] In a remarkable passage in *Notes from the House of the Dead* (*Zapiski iz mertvogo doma*, 1862), Dostoevsky's narrator describes the unclassifiability of the human personality: "Here I am trying to subsume our whole prison under categories; but is that possible? Reality is endlessly diverse compared with all, even the cleverest conclusions of ab-

stract thought, and it abhors sharp and broad distinctions. Reality strives toward fragmentation [Deistvitel'nost' stremitsia k razdrobleniiu]" (4:197).
This passage refers to the human personality in general, but it is also an apt
description of Dostoevsky's approach to the multifariousness of human sexual desire.

   Thérèse philosophe and Dostoevsky's works represent a pre-Freudian
approach to sexuality, one that makes no attempt to "subsume it under categories" or to construct a master narrative for human desire, but rather devotes itself to the exploration of "endless diversity."[37] "The writer has to
know everything," as Dostoevsky told his wife, and it follows that he has to
at least attempt to convey that "everything" in literary form. But as we have
seen from the "Egyptian Nights" polemic, such a quest is fraught with moral
risk. The writer has to find the "point of view" that saves him from becoming a Sade, a Cleopatra, or a Valkovskii.[38]

   Dostoevsky's task was complicated by the fact that his interest in sexual matters often led him into the world of children. As Brumfield points
out: "It is significant that both d'Argens and Dostoevsky . . . base the struggle between passion and restraint in the formative years of childhood, a period during which social and cultural influences determine patterns of behavior."[39] Dostoevsky himself said during the "Egyptian Nights" polemic, "In
adolescence a person is not fully formed either physically or morally"
(19:103). In Dostoevsky's works, as in *Thérèse philosophe*, the child or adolescent, not yet hardened into a prescribed form, is the perfect guide into
the diverse world of sexuality.[40] Dostoevsky's novels of the post-Siberia period, beginning with *The Insulted and Injured* and continuing through *The
Devils* (1873), indeed focus on childhood and adolescent encounters with
sexuality, culminating in the notorious descriptions of pedophilia that appear
in *Crime and Punishment* and in the censored chapter "At Tikhon's" that was
intended to appear in *The Devils*. The next chapter will examine Dostoevsky's attempts to find the "point of view" that would allow him to grapple
honestly with this subject without abusing his audience.

Chapter Two

The Insulted Female Child

BETWEEN 1861 AND 1872, in the years after his return from Siberia, Dostoevsky wrote four major novels: *The Insulted and Injured* (1861), *Crime and Punishment* (1866; separate edition 1867), *The Idiot* (1868; separate edition 1874), and *The Devils* (1871–72; separate edition 1873). In each of them, the reader encounters scenes of erotically intense and even sexually abusive relations between grown men and young girls ranging in age from five to sixteen. In dealing with this highly charged erotic material, Dostoevsky experimented with point of view, moving from a first-person account by an autobiographical narrator in *The Insulted and Injured,* to a detached, omniscient third-person narration in *Crime and Punishment* and *The Idiot,* and back to a first-person narration in the confessional document by Stavrogin that appears in "At Tikhon's" ("U Tikhona"), a chapter that was intended to be included in part 2 of *The Devils* but that was rejected by its publisher and remained unpublished until 1922. In the polemic over "Egyptian Nights," Dostoevsky asserted that "the point of view is the main thing" (19:135), the thing that saves the depiction of sexual material in art from sliding into pornography. What Dostoevsky means by "point of view" seems to involve not just the technical sense of narrative stance, but also a perceptible moral attitude toward the material being narrated. This chapter will examine the ethical significance of Dostoevsky's shifts in narrative mode as he returns again and again to the same subject matter, that of the "insulted" ("oskorblennaia") female child.

The Insulted and Injured is in a sense two novels. One of them, the story of the narrator Ivan Petrovich's unhappy love for Natasha Ikhmeneva, looks back to sentimental, dreamy pre-Siberia works like "White Nights" ("Belye nochi," 1848). It is no accident that Ivan Petrovich himself is a writer in the mold of the pre-Siberia Dostoevsky; his first novel, the plot of which is summarized in the narration, is identical to that of Dostoevsky's first novel, *Poor Folk* (*Bednye liudi,* 1846). But as R. G. Nazirov points out, *The Insulted and Injured* looks forward as well as backward: the story of Nelli, the abandoned child whom Ivan Petrovich takes into his home, offers a foretaste of the tragic nature of Dostoevsky's mature novels. This line of the plot, which

17

Nazirov labels the "tragic line" as distinct from the "sentimental line" of Natasha's story, is marked by "mystical premonitions, an atmosphere of terror and secrets, fatal inevitability in the development of events, and a catastrophic dénouement."[1] Nazirov notes the kinship between Nelli and Dostoevsky's earlier child heroine Netochka Nezvanova in his unfinished novel of the same name (1849), but explains in vivid terms how strongly they differ: *The image of Netochka is oriented toward life.* On the image of Nelli lies the stamp of tragic doom, this image is *oriented toward death.* The distance between these two 'consanguineous' images corresponds precisely to the distance between the Dostoevsky of 1849 and the Dostoevsky of 1861. Nelli in *The Insulted and Injured* is, as it were, *a Netochka Nezvanova who has gone through penal servitude*" (emphasis in original).[2] For this discussion, the most important distinction Nazirov notes between the two parallel story lines of the novel is the following: "The tragic line of the novel [i.e., Nelli's story] is constructed as a 'system of secrets [tain]'; in the sentimental line [i.e., Natasha's story], not only are there no secrets, but the prehistory of the heroes is given, their characters are described, and the realistic motivation of their actions is prepared in advance."[3] If we recall that the word "secret" ("taina"), both in the "Egyptian Nights" polemic and in *The Insulted and Injured* itself, is at times used to refer to sexual matters, Nazirov's insight takes on added significance. "There are no secrets" in the story of Ivan and Natasha, and indeed, despite the fact that Ivan claims to be in love with her, there is no erotic charge to their scenes together. The secrets and, one could argue, the sense of erotic power, are all concentrated in the narrator's relationship with Nelli. This sexual undercurrent, however, remains below the level of the narrator's consciousness and must be detected by the reader. Textual parallels to later, more explicit scenes in *Crime and Punishment* and "At Tikhon's" reveal that in *The Insulted and Injured* Dostoevsky himself was at the beginning of an artistic process of coming to grips with and taking responsibility for the true nature of a relationship such as that between Ivan and Nelli.

Ivan's first encounter with Nelli is enveloped in a mysterious terror. Ivan has taken over the apartment of Jeremiah Smith, a strange, impoverished old man whose death he witnessed at the beginning of the novel. Elena, nicknamed Nelli, is Smith's thirteen-year-old granddaughter, whose mother, rejected by Smith, has died in miserable poverty. The first encounter between Ivan and Nelli is prosaic enough: unaware of her grandfather's death, she comes to his apartment to look for him and finds Ivan instead. But Ivan's feelings surrounding the encounter are far from prosaic. As darkness sets in and he sits alone in his lodgings, he is enveloped in what he calls "mystical horror":

> It is the most oppressive, agonizing fear of something that I myself cannot define, something incomprehensible and nonexistent in the usual order of

things, but that will without fail, perhaps this very minute, be realized, and as if to mock all the arguments of my reason will come to me and stand before me as an incontrovertible fact, horrible, hideous, and implacable. (3:208)

This terrible prologue is followed by the appearance on his threshold of "some kind of strange creature": "A chill passed over all my members. To my utmost horror, I saw that it was a child, a little girl, and if it had been Smith himself he would not have frightened me as much as this strange, unexpected appearance of an unfamiliar child in my room at such an hour and at such a time" (3:208). Ivan's seemingly inappropriate horror at the appearance of Nelli is a measure of the mysterious depths of the relationship that will develop between them, as well as his fear of his own inexplicable but powerful feelings.

At their second meeting Ivan gets a better look at his child visitor, and his physical description of her is much more detailed and emotionally weighted than any of his descriptions of Natasha, the grown woman Ivan is supposedly in love with:

Small of stature, with sparkling, dark, somehow non-Russian eyes, with luxuriant dark tousled hair and an enigmatic, mute, and unyielding gaze, she would arrest the attention of any passerby on the street . . . Her pale and thin face had a sort of unnatural swarthy-yellow, bilious hue. But in general, despite all the hideousness of poverty and illness, she was actually quite pretty [dazhe nedurna soboi]. Her brows were sharply outlined, delicate and beautiful; particularly pretty were her broad, somewhat low forehead and her lips, beautifully outlined, with a sort of proud, bold slant, but pale, with just a hint of color. (3:253–54)

Ivan's remark that this exotic creature could attract the attention of a passerby on the street is most apt; as we learn later, while begging on the St. Petersburg streets she has in fact attracted the attention of the pedophile Arkhipov. The house in which Nelli is living alone after her mother's miserable death is owned by Mrs. Bubnova, who "deals in impermissible business" (3:266), and who has made an arrangement to sell Nelli's sexual favors to Arkhipov.

With the help of his friend Masloboev, a kind of freelance detective, Ivan uncovers Bubnova's evil plan. While Masloboev and Ivan distract Bubnova in her parlor, Masloboev's confederate rescues Nelli, who has been clad by Bubnova in a virginal white dress for the occasion of her deflowering: "Suddenly the door opened forcibly and Elena [Nelli], pale, with dulled eyes, in a white muslin dress that was thoroughly crumpled and torn, with hair that had been carefully dressed but seemed to have come loose during a struggle, burst into the room. I was standing opposite the door, and she rushed directly to me and clasped me with her arms" (3:276). The scene of the attempted rape occurs far offstage, "somewhere behind several doors, two or three rooms from the one we were in" (3:276). The reader can only guess at the nature of the scene based on the eloquent evidence of Nelli's torn dress and disheveled hair.

Arkhipov's desires are unambiguous, but Nelli's rush into Ivan's arms signals the beginning of a series of scenes between her and Ivan that have a strong erotic undercurrent, one that goes largely unacknowledged by Ivan himself. Ivan brings her home, unfastens the fancy dress in which she was sent to her planned deflowering, and gazes at her: "I looked at her pale little face, at her colorless lips, at her dark hair, pushed to one side but carefully combed and pomaded, at her whole toilette, at those pink ribbons that still survived here and there on her dress—and I decisively understood the whole revolting story" (3:276). Ivan fully understands the story of Arkhipov's designs on Nelli, but not the story of his own attraction to her. William Woodin Rowe, who was perhaps the first critic to identify the sexual undercurrent in the relationship between Ivan and Nelli, points out that in this scene, "Nellie is a shocking combination of pretty little girl and dishevelled victim . . . [her pink bows have] survived enough, it seems, to evoke the image of this victim's outrageously intended prettiness *without detracting from* (and perhaps intensifying by contrast) the ravaged results" (emphasis in original).[4]

Nelli continues to live with Ivan, resisting his plan to send her to live with Natasha's parents. Soon she has the opportunity to rescue her rescuer, as Ivan falls into a faint, exhausted by his efforts on behalf of Natasha (whose complex story will not be summarized here). With the help of the caretaker, Nelli gets the unconscious Ivan to his bed. Ivan vaguely recalls seeing "the dear image of the poor little girl flashing before me amid my oblivion, like a vision, like a little painting" (3:294). In the middle of the night, "I saw that Elena [Nelli] had laid her head on my pillow and was sleeping fitfully, with her pale little lips half open and her palm pressed to her warm little cheek" (3:294). A third vision of Nelli at his bedside again emphasizes her exotic beauty:

> I could not take my eyes off her childish little face, full even in sleep of a kind of unchildish sadness of expression and a sort of strange, sickly beauty; pale, with long eyelashes on her thin cheeks, framed by her pitch-black hair, which fell to the side, thick and heavy, in a carelessly tied knot. Her other hand lay on my pillow. I very quietly kissed this thin little hand, but the poor child did not wake up; only a kind of smile passed over her pale little lips. (3:294)

When Ivan recovers enough to talk to Nelli, she overwhelms him with her passionate entreaties that he let her stay with him, and that he love her:

All her feelings, restrained for so long, suddenly burst out all at once in an ir-
repressible rush, and I came to understand that strange stubbornness of the
heart that has *chastely* hidden itself for a time, and the more stubbornly and
severely it has hidden, the more powerful is the need to pour itself out, to express itself, and all of this until that inevitable outburst, when the whole being
suddenly, to the point of self-oblivion, gives itself up to that need for love,
gratitude, caresses, tears. (3:296–97; emphasis mine)

The word "chastely" is inserted here at a key moment, because the chastity
of Ivan's and Nelli's relationship is beginning to be subject to question in the
reader's mind.

Within the novel, the potential impropriety of Ivan's living arrangements with Nelli is alluded to at several points. The first to raise the issue is
Bubnova herself, when Nelli returns to her house after visiting Ivan: "Where
have you been? Where did you go? What protectors did you find for yourself?" (3:259). The word "protector" ("pokrovitel'") is often used to refer to
a man keeping a mistress, and the strangeness of a grown man living in a
small apartment with a thirteen-year-old girl is noted by several characters:
the doctor who treats the epileptic Nelli (3:277), Masloboev (3:279), and
Natasha's father Ikhmenev (3:289).[5] If Arkhipov is Ivan's unambiguously
pedophilic double, there are also other men who visit Nelli (often in Ivan's
absence) on whose behavior the shadow of improper relations is cast: Masloboev, who tempts her with candy (3:333); the doctor, to whom Nelli proposes marriage (3:373); and the man who turns out to be her biological
father, the evil Prince Valkovskii (3:339–40), who himself alludes to the
bizarre nature of Ivan's household arrangements: "That's a strange servant
girl you have" (3:340). Ivan's hesitant reply to the Prince reveals his own discomfort: "No . . . she's just . . . living with me for the time being" ("Net . . .
ona tak . . . zhivet u menia pokamest," 3:340).

Although we do not learn of Nelli's blood relationship to the Prince
until the end of the novel, her behavior at times betrays her kinship to the
man who so frankly discusses his lustful desires with Ivan Petrovich in the
restaurant scene in chapter 10 of part 3. Again and again it is Nelli who initiates physical contact with Ivan, beginning with her embrace of him at the
moment of her rescue from Arkhipov (3:296, 325, 370, 376). One of their
last embraces, as she lies mortally ill at the Ikhmenevs', is also one of the
most explicitly passionate:

Three days ago she caught me by the hand as I was passing by her little bed
and drew me to her. There was no one in the room. Her face was feverish
(she had gotten terribly thin), her eyes flashed with fire. She stretched toward
me convulsively and passionately [sudorozhno-strastno], and when I bent

over her, she firmly clasped my neck with her thin swarthy little arms and firmly kissed me, and then immediately asked for Natasha. (3:429)

The innocence of the final summons of Natasha does not efface the passion of this scene between Ivan and Nelli when "no one was in the room." The doctor's diagnosis of Nelli is that she has "an organic defect of the heart" ("organicheskii porok v serdtse," 3:371). Given that the word for "defect," "porok," also means "vice," we can read the diagnosis as a pun. Nelli has inherited a physical defect of the heart, but she may also have inherited from her father the "organic vice" of lustfulness, a vice that is prevented from developing by her early death.

Ivan very rarely acknowledges to himself that his relationship with Nelli is anything but purely innocent. At one point he restrains himself from kissing her, saying, "Somehow it was impossible to kiss her" ("Kak-to nel'zia bylo potselovat'," 3:324). At another point he says, "I myself do not know what it was in her that attracted me so. In my feelings there was something other than just pity" (3:255). He fails, however, to define for the reader or for himself what that "something other" is. One is left with the distinct impression that the true nature of Ivan's relationship with Nelli belongs to the category so precisely defined by her father, the Prince, of "not only that which one is afraid to tell and would not under any circumstances tell others, not only that which one is afraid to tell one's best friends, but even that which one is afraid sometimes to confess even to himself" (3:361). Despite the immediacy of the first-person narration, Ivan fails to "confess to himself," and by extension to the reader, an honest account of his intimacy with Nelli.

In Dostoevsky's next major novel, *Crime and Punishment* (*Prestuplenie i nakazanie*), the theme of the "insulted" female child recurs.[6] Although the narrative achieves a greater degree of frankness than does the story of Ivan and Nelli, the subject of pedophilia now appears in the form of minor subplots related to Svidrigailov rather than being an organic part of the story of the main hero Raskol'nikov. The shift from a first-person to an omniscient third-person narration increases the sense of distancing from this disturbing material. It is clear, however, that Dostoevsky is returning purposefully to the themes he raised vaguely in *The Insulted and Injured*, trying to find the appropriate artistic means for dealing with them, means that would provide the artistic "point of view" that avoids abuse of the audience.

The character of Bubnova, who attempted to sell Nelli to Arkhipov, reappears in *Crime and Punishment* in the form of a certain Mrs. Resslikh, "a foreigner and also a petty moneylender, who also dealt in other affairs"; Svidrigailov had had "very intimate and mysterious relations" with her (6:228). Resslikh had a distant relative, "a little girl of about fifteen or even fourteen," a deaf-mute whom Resslikh treated much as Bubnova treated Nelli, reproaching her for every piece of bread she ate and beating her inhumanly. This girl finally hanged herself in the attic, and "there later appeared a denunciation that the child had been . . . cruelly insulted [oskorblen] by Svidrigailov" (6:228). This story is offered second- or third-hand by the highly unreliable Luzhin, who himself admits that "it was all obscure, the denunciation was from another German woman, a notorious woman and not to be trusted" (6:228).

The image of the insulted young girl appears again late in the novel, in a more definite form, in a dream vision (or perhaps a memory) that visits Svidrigailov the night before he is to commit suicide. He sees a beautiful girl lying in her coffin, a girl who had drowned herself in shame: "She was only fourteen years old, but it was an already broken heart, and it had destroyed itself, insulted [oskorblennoe] by an offense that horrified and amazed this young, childish consciousness, flooding her angelically pure soul with unmerited shame" (6:391).[7] Following this vision (it is unclear whether he is awake or asleep), Svidrigailov has an even more disturbing encounter that turns out to be a dream but that at first seems to be an episode in his waking life happening before our eyes.

Svidrigailov goes out into the hallway of the fleabag hotel in which he is staying, and sees in a dark corner "some kind of strange object, something that seemed to be alive" (6:392). The "object" turns out to be a little girl no older than five. The eeriness of Ivan's first meeting with Nelli is echoed here; like Nelli, the child is all alone, wearing a ragged dress. Like Nelli, who upon her return to Bubnova's house is beaten mercilessly by her supposed mother-substitute, this child faces a beating if she returns to her unloving mother. In *The Insulted and Injured,* much is made of Ivan's teacup that Nelli deliberately smashes; she even goes begging on the street in order to replace it (3:384–86). The child whom Svidrigailov encounters is afraid she will be beaten because she too has broken a teacup. But unlike Nelli, whose age is vaguely defined and hovers between childhood and womanhood, this girl's status as a small child is emphasized even in her lisping speech, in which r's are replaced by l's (6:392).

Svidrigailov undresses the child and puts her to bed, just as Ivan does with Nelli after rescuing her from Arkhipov. Nelli's slyly humorous character often clashes strangely with her sickliness, as in the following passage: "The poor little girl had become very thin during these four days of illness: her eyes had become sunken, the fever had still not passed. All the more strangely was her face suited by her mischievous look and provocative flashing glances [shalovlivyi vid i zadornye blestiashchie vzgliady], which very much amazed the doctor" (3:372). The child rescued by Svidrigailov also seems to have a fever, and also has an inappropriately provocative look on her face: "It suddenly seemed to him that her long dark eyelashes were somehow trembling and winking, somehow lifting, and from under them there peeped out a cunning, sharp, somehow unchildishly winking little eye, as if the little girl were not sleeping but pretending" (6:393). Nelli's ambiguous provocation here breaks out into open sexual invitation, even as the girl's unambiguously infantile stage of development is again stressed: "But now she had completely stopped restraining herself; this was already laughter, open laughter; something brazen and challenging shone in that completely unchildish face; it was debauchery [razvrat], it was the face of a prostitute [kameliia], the brazen face of a French prostitute for sale . . . 'What! A five-year-old girl!' Svidrigailov whispered in real horror" (6:393). This terrifying vision turns out to be a dream, but not before the insulter Svidrigailov becomes the insulted: "There was something infinitely hideous and insulting [oskorbitel'noe] in that laughter, those eyes, in all that nastiness in the face of the child [or 'a child']" (6:393).

It is deliberately left unclear whether Svidrigailov ever "cruelly insulted" a girl child, but these horrifying dreams on the eve of his suicide would indicate that feelings of guilt are finding expression in some buried part of his mind. Ivan felt deep fear when he first encountered Nelli, but as the narrator he never connected that fear explicitly with the sexual attraction and discomfort that pervade his account. The omniscient third-person narrator of *Crime and Punishment*, privy to Svidrigailov's experiences but not identifying with him, is able to be more explicit about what is really going on between Svidrigailov and the child in the dream: her sexual provocation is much more explicit than Nelli's, and Svidrigailov's horror is more responsible than Ivan's—in other words, more explicitly linked to his own sense of guilt.

In his next major novel, *The Idiot* (*Idiot*), Dostoevsky maintains the distance of the third-person narrator, and here the man who preys on a young girl, Afanasii Ivanovich Totskii, is an even more peripheral character than Svidrigailov is in *Crime and Punishment*. Moreover, as the narration begins, his victim, Nastas'ia Filippovna Barashkova, whom he seduced when she was sixteen, is already a grown (25-year-old) woman. In *Crime and Punishment*, although we are distanced from the male subject by the third-person narration, there is a move toward greater explicitness about pedophilia and a greater sense of responsibility on the part of the man with pedophilic tendencies. In *The Idiot*, there is even more narrative distancing from the man's consciousness, and the man himself is much less inclined to assume any responsibility or sense of guilt. With *The Idiot* there is a step backward in the progression toward a more frank and intense engagement with the crime of pedophilia.

In Svidrigailov's dream, the five-year-old girl is said to have "litso kamelii," literally "the face of a camellia" (6:393). As Donald Rayfield has discussed, the use in Russian of the word "camellia" to refer to a high-class prostitute is derived from the novel *La dame aux camélias* (1848) by Alexandre Dumas fils, a novel that plays an important role in part 1 of *The Idiot*, as several critics have noted and as we will discuss below.[8]

When the hero Prince Lyov Nikolaevich Myshkin expresses his intention of attending Nastas'ia Filippovna's name-day party, his interlocutor mocks him for thrusting himself "into the charming company of camellias, generals, and moneylenders" (8:112). The story of how Nastas'ia Filippovna has become what several characters refer to as a "camellia" is an ugly one. The daughter of an ill-fated and impoverished nobleman whose estate borders that of the wealthy Afanasii Ivanovich Totskii, she is orphaned at the age of seven; her mother is killed in a fire that destroys the estate and the hopes of her father, who goes mad and dies a month later. Nastas'ia and her younger sister (who dies a bit later of whooping cough) are "magnanimously" taken in by Totskii and settled with the family of his steward. Just as the orphaned Nelli caught the eye of Arkhipov, Nastas'ia Filippovna at age twelve attracts the attention of Totskii, who had completely forgotten about her in the intervening years.[9] She is "a charming child . . . playful, sweet, clever, and promising exceptional beauty; in this regard Afanasii Ivanovich was an infallible expert" (8:35). Unlike the coarse Arkhipov, Totskii has the taste and elegance to wait a few years before deflowering Nastas'ia Filippovna. He arranges for the improvement of her education, and four years later he settles her in one of his distant estates in the village of Otradnoe ("Delightful"), where she is provided with "musical instruments, an elegant young lady's library, paintings, engravings, pencils, brushes, paints, an amazing [udivitel'-naia] Italian greyhound" (8:36). The conclusion to this lovely list is no less chilling for being fragmentary: ". . . an amazing Italian greyhound, and in two weeks Afanasii Ivanovich himself came to call . . . From that time he had a particular fondness for this estate of his out in the steppes, and would drop in every summer and stay for two or even three months, and thus passed a rather long time, about four years, peacefully and happily, tastefully and elegantly" (8:36). The ellipsis after "Afanasii Ivanovich himself came to call" is a telling omission, the first signal that this description, although narrated in the third person, is actually given from Totskii's vantage point. It is in the interest of his own self-image to be vague about what happened when he "came to call." The second signal that this description comes from Totskii's point of view is the idea that his sordid arrangement with Nastas'ia Filippovna is "peaceful and happy, tasteful and elegant." The narrator offers Nastas'ia Filippovna's contrasting perception of their relations only two paragraphs later. Nastas'ia Filippovna learns that Totskii plans to marry a rich young society lady. Instead of taking this news meekly, Nastas'ia Filippovna travels to St. Petersburg to announce to Totskii her intention of spoiling the match in any way she can. She explains to him that she is acting purely out of malice, and not because she cherishes any tender feelings for him. Her words, relayed by the narrator, clearly convey how the "elegant and tasteful" seduction was perceived by its female victim: "[She declared to him directly] that she had nothing in her heart for him except the deepest contempt, a contempt bordering on nausea, which had set in immediately after the first amazement [udivleniia]" (8:36–37).[10] Later at her party Nastas'ia Filippovna describes her relationship with Totskii in similarly ugly terms: "And this one [Totskii] would come: he'd stay for about two months a year, disgrace me, offend me, inflame me, debauch me, and leave [opozorit, razobidit, raspalit, razvratit, uedet]—a thousand times I wanted to throw myself into the pond, but I was too abject, I didn't have the courage" (8:144).[11] Nastas'ia Filippovna's list of verbs (disgrace, offend, inflame, debauch) are the plain-spoken counterpart to the wordless ellipsis that appears in the initial description of her deflowering.

William C. Brumfield describes Totskii as Dostoevsky's counterpart to the characters in *Thérèse philosophe* who attempt to rationalize libertine sexual conduct: "If one interprets libertinism solely in sexual terms, Totsky is Dostoevsky's *vrai libertin:* the inveterate sensualist not responsible for his conduct, and the rational egoist concerned with the preservation of *bienséance* and his own interests."[12] One could add that Totskii's behavior with Nastas'ia Filippovna mimics that of the respectable man in *Thérèse philosophe* who has Bois-Laurier abducted at the age of six and raised by a procuress until her age "would permit him to take her virginity."[13] This operation is attempted when Bois-Laurier reaches the age of fifteen, but thanks to her impenetrable hymen (not to mention the man's "old tool, rusty, wrinkled, and worn"), Bois-Laurier retains her physical virginity.[14] The "humor" of this scene in *Thérèse philosophe* is absent in *The Idiot;* Totskii's deflowering of Nastas'ia Filippovna is all too successful.

Another echo of *Thérèse philosophe* appears at Nastas'ia Filippovna's name-day party. The party occurs at a critical moment for Nastas'ia Filippovna; resolved once again to make a respectable society marriage, Totskii has arranged for Nastas'ia Filippovna to marry a somewhat reluctant young man, Gavrila Ardalionovich Ivolgin. At the party are gathered, among others, Totskii, General Epanchin (whose daughter Totskii plans to marry), Gavrila Ivolgin, and Prince Myshkin. One of the guests, the civil servant Ferdyshchenko, described earlier as "a very unseemly and obscene buffoon" ("ochen' neprilichnyi i sal'nyi shut," 8:39), proposes that the company play "a new *petit-jeu*" (8:120). Each guest is to tell an anecdote from his or her past: "what he himself in sincere honesty, considers the worst of all his bad acts over the course of his whole life" (8:120). This game promises to produce a great effect, according to Ferdyshchenko: "Just think, ladies and gentlemen . . . just think with what eyes we'll look at each other later, tomorrow for example, after these stories!" (8:121). The heroine of *Thérèse philosophe* also describes "de petits jeux" that she played with her friends at age nine and ten:

> We would often assemble, girls and boys of my age, in an attic or some secluded room. There we would play little games [Là nous jouïons à de petits jeux]: one of us was chosen schoolmaster; the slightest error was punished by the whip. The boys undid their pants, the girls tucked up their skirts and shifts; we looked at each other attentively; you would have seen five or six little asses by turns admired, caressed, and whipped.[15]

The girls kiss and caress the boys' penises, and "our little buttocks were kissed in their turn."[16] The nature of this "petit jeu" turns out to be not really so far in spirit from the verbal "petit jeu" proposed by the "obscene buffoon" Ferdyshchenko. It is unclear whether Dostoevsky was intentionally invoking Thérèse's childhood games in this scene in *The Idiot,* but as we have seen in the discussion of Prince Valkovskii in *The Insulted and Injured* (see chapter 1), the structure of exhibitionistic confession is clear. Freud's contention that "exhibitionists . . . exhibit their own genitals in order to obtain a reciprocal view of the genitals of the other person" is apposite to Ferdyshchenko's game. One is to reveal one's own bad acts in order to get a peek at the bad acts of others.

As the game unfolds at Nastas'ia Filippovna's party, the players use it not for sincere confession but for their own hidden purposes.[17] This is certainly true of Totskii, the player who is most important for the present discussion. Totskii's story has as its background Dumas's *La dame aux camélias.* He tells of how, twenty years before (i.e., two years before adopting the seven-year-old Nastas'ia Filippovna), he won the affections of a provincial society lady, the wife of a friend of his, by obtaining a bouquet of red camellias for her to take to a ball. The act is a "bad" one because in order to get the red camellias, Totskii acted perfidiously toward another of the lady's suitors: he found out where the young man was planning to get the red camellias, beat him there and bought them all himself. In his despair at losing the lady's affections, the young suitor subsequently went to war and was killed in the Crimea.

Nastas'ia Filippovna reacts quite violently to Totskii's story. Throughout its telling she picks at the lace border of her sleeve. As M. S. Al'tman points out, "This is not at all a lack of attention to the story, but rather a masking of her extreme agitation and . . . indignation, an attempt to restrain herself until the proper time."[18] Ultimately Nastas'ia Filippovna's restraint disappears, and she causes a public scandal that upsets all the reasonable plans of the man she scornfully calls "monsieur aux camélias" (8:137). Clearly Nastas'ia Filippovna has an abundance of reasons to be furious with Totskii, but there is something about the content of his story that seems to arouse particular emotion in her. As he concludes the anecdote, "They noticed that Nastas'ia Filippovna's eyes were flashing in a peculiar way and her lips were even trembling when Afanasii Ivanovich finished" (8:129–30). On the surface, it would seem that she is angered by hearing about one of Totskii's former lovers. But on a deeper level, the key to her anger lies, I believe, in the symbolism of the camellias.

Totskii's introduction to his story offers a characterization of Dumas's wildly popular novel and its social influence: "The charm of the story, the originality of the situation of the main character, that alluring world, analyzed in subtle detail, and finally, all those enchanting details scattered throughout the book (for example, about the circumstances for using bouquets of white and red camellias in turn), in a word, all these charming details, and all of that together, produced almost a shock. Camellias came into unusual fashion" (8:128). Totskii's friend the provincial lioness knows that all the other ladies will come to the ball with white camellias; she wants red, "to produce a certain special effect" (8:128). When Totskii speaks of the "originality of the situation of the main character" and her "alluring world," he is speaking of the life of a high-class prostitute as described by Dumas. The "enchanting detail" of "using bouquets of white and red camellias in turn" is what Rayfield calls a "crude code" used by Dumas's heroine Marguérite Gautier.[19] As most of Dostoevsky's readers and all of Totskii's listeners would have known thanks to the huge popularity of Dumas's novel, the white camellia signals the heroine's sexual availability; the red camellia is a sign that she is having her menstrual period. The following conversation from Dumas's novel between Marguérite and her lover illuminates the "enchanting detail" to which Totskii alludes. In the exchange quoted below, the first speaker is Marguérite's lover:

> "Well, I will be all that you wish."
> "We shall see."
> "When shall we see?"
> "Later on."
> "Why?"
> "Because," said Marguérite, releasing herself from my arms, and taking from a great bunch of red camellias a single camellia, she placed it in my buttonhole, "because one can not always carry out agreements the day they are signed."

"And when shall I see you again?" I said, clasping her in my arms.
"When this camellia changes colour."
"When will it change colour?"
"Tomorrow night between eleven and twelve. Are you satisfied?"
"Need you ask me?"[20]

Totskii, the man who considered it "tasteful and elegant" to keep an orphan sequestered for his own sexual pleasure, could well find the "crude code" of red and white camellias to be an "enchanting detail." Certainly it is strange that the society ladies in Totskii's anecdote were so anxious to emulate French prostitutes by carrying bouquets of white and red camellias. In contrast, Nastas'ia Filippovna, despite her "fallen" state, is clearly not flattered by the implied analogy between herself and Marguérite, or between herself and the provincial society lady.

In telling this story, Totskii is not really concerned with confessing his guilt about the unhappy lover who perished in the Crimea. He is sending a message to Nastas'ia Filippovna, one that focuses on the physical fact of menstruation—the sign of female sexual maturity. Totskii's message is: "I am not a pedophile; I waited until you were sexually mature before disgracing, offending, inflaming, and debauching you." Nastas'ia Filippovna rejects this message, and Totskii's implied request for absolution, with every fiber of her being.[21] Her wild rebellion, however, has no effect on Totskii. Far from feeling the mystical horror of Ivan Petrovich or Svidrigailov, he ends the party scene by congratulating himself for all the efforts he put into Nastas'ia Filippovna's education (8:149).

As we have seen, in dealing with the subject matter of pedophilia throughout the 1860s, Dostoevsky experiments with several variations in "point of view." In *The Insulted and Injured,* the immediacy of the first-person narration brings us very close to the potentially pedophilic subject, but his lack of self-awareness keeps guilt and responsibility at bay. In *Crime and Punishment,* there is a much more explicit acknowledgment of guilt and the nature of that guilt, but the third-person narration and the fact that the offender is a secondary character distance the reader from the immediacy of the crime. With *The Idiot,* the distancing is increased: not only is the victim a grown woman, not only was she technically an adult when the deflowering occurred, but her predator is a minor character who is kept at more than arm's length by the third-person narrator. Moreover, Totskii takes not the slightest responsibility for what he has done to Nastas'ia Filippovna. One could schematically summarize the three treatments as (1) no distance, no guilt; (2) distance, guilt; (3) distance, no guilt. With *The Devils (Besy),* in the chapter "At Tikhon's" ("U Tikhona"), Dostoevsky arrives at yet another configuration, one designed to have the maximum impact. The confessional text by the central hero Stavrogin that is embedded in the chapter brings us back to the immediacy of the first-person narration of *The Insulted and Injured.* But Stavrogin, unlike Ivan Petrovich, is attempting to take full responsibility for what happened between him and a little girl in a squalid apartment several years before. The combination "no distance, guilt" makes this text one of the most powerful Dostoevsky ever wrote and certainly the culmination of his search for the proper "point of view" with which to deal with pedophilia. That the search was an artistically continuous one is signaled by the strikingly large amount of textual material from *The Insulted and Injured,* specifically from the scenes between Ivan and Nelli, that is reworked in Stavrogin's text.

Dostoevsky planned for the chapter "At Tikhon's" to come near the center of *The Devils,* after chapter 8 of part 2. In this chapter, Nikolai Vsevolodovich Stavrogin, the mysterious hero whose actions and motivations remain enigmatic to all the people who surround him, visits the monk Tikhon and presents to him a text that he has had printed abroad and that he plans to circulate.[22] Stavrogin's text, in which he confesses to the rape of a child, is explicitly compared to the revolutionary pamphlets that are being circulated by Stavrogin's friend Pyotr Stepanovich Verkhovenskii: "The print was definitely foreign . . . It must have been printed secretly at some Russian printing press abroad, and at first glance the sheets looked very much like a proclamation" (11:12).[23] Dostoevsky draws a strong connection in *The Devils* between the secret literature of political radicalism and the secret literature of obscenity. The potentially salacious content of Stavrogin's confession makes it a candidate for inclusion in Tikhon's unorthodox library, which contains theatrical works "and maybe even something worse" (11:7).[24]

Other shadows are cast on Tikhon's image at the beginning of the chapter. He is said to have "some kind of weakness, maybe holy foolishness"; it is also rumored that he is "nearly insane, at the least a completely talentless creature, and without a doubt he drinks" (11:6). Despite all this, in the course of the chapter Tikhon proves to be a steadfastly Christian spiritual adviser with keen psychological insight into Stavrogin, a man he has just met for the first time. No doubt Tikhon's reasons for having "theatrical works and maybe even something worse" in his library are similar to the reason Dostoevsky gave his wife for reading French erotic novels: in order to "know everything" about the human personality. Similarly, despite the shadow cast on Stavrogin's privately printed, clandestine text, it is not a piece of titillating erotica but a sober attempt to speak in plain language about and take full responsibility for a very bad act, one that arouses pity and terror rather than lust. There is a long tradition of critical discussion of the nature of Stavrogin's confession and the degree to which he sincerely repents his act. That question is outside the scope of my discussion here, which is focused not on a global interpretation of Stavrogin's character but on the analysis of his confessional text as the culmination of Dostoevsky's quest to find an appropriate narrative form for representing the sexual abuse of a female child.[25]

The original version of "At Tikhon's" survives in the form of proofs for the December 1871 issue of the *Russian Herald;* the other major variant of the text is a partial copy made by Anna Grigor'evna Dostoevskaia from an unknown manuscript (12:237–38). The text of the Anna Grigor'evna Dostoevskaia copy seems to represent an attempt by Dostoevsky to revise the chapter in such a way as to make it acceptable to the editors of the *Russian Herald* and especially to the journal's publisher, M. N. Katkov. The following discussion is based on the earlier version of the text.

In bare outline, the story Stavrogin tells in Dostoevsky's original version of the chapter is as follows. While leading a life of idle debauchery in St. Petersburg, in addition to his main lodgings he rents a room from a lower middle-class family whose daughter Matryosha catches his attention. Alone with her one day, he initiates physical contact that culminates in something that is not described in the narrative but that is strongly implied to be sexual intercourse. Several days later, Stavrogin learns from the girl's mother that she is very ill, in delirium. He returns that evening at a time when he knows Matryosha will be alone. He sits in the apartment silently; Matryosha is in her mother's bed behind a screen. Finally Matryosha comes to the threshold of Stavrogin's room, shakes her head at him reprovingly, and threatens him with her "tiny fist" (11:18). She then runs out of the apartment. Stavrogin follows and watches her go into "a tiny storeroom like a chicken coop" next to the latrine (11:18), and then returns to his room. He coolly waits thirty-five minutes and then goes to the storeroom. He peeps in, and despite the darkness he is able to make out "what he needed to" ("chto bylo nado," 11:19). We soon learn that what he has seen is the hanged body of Matryosha.

If one moves step-by-step through Stavrogin's narrative, one is struck by the many points in it at which Dostoevsky revisits incidents and scenes from *The Insulted and Injured.* In general, the character of Stavrogin belongs to the taxonomic category of Prince Valkovskii, the unrepentant libertine. Indeed, the reason Stavrogin rents the room from Matryosha's mother is in order to carry on an affair with the maid of his lover, a society lady, an arrangement that recalls Valkovskii's ménage à trois with a lady and her French chambermaid (3:364). But most of the echoes of *The Insulted and Injured* that appear in Stavrogin's text relate not to Valkovskii but to Ivan Petrovich and his "innocent" relationship with Nelli.

Stavrogin's text vacillates about Matryosha's age. She is said at first to be "about fourteen," but "in appearance completely a child" (11:13). She is referred to several times as "rebenok" or "ditia" (both meaning "child"; 11:15, 16). Finally, several years after the sexual encounter, when Stavrogin is haunted by the image of Matryosha shaking her fist at him, he speaks of "the pitiful despair of the helpless ten-year-old being with her undeveloped reason" (11:22). The same sort of confusion reigns in *The Insulted and Injured*, where Nelli is referred to variously as eleven, eleven or twelve, twelve or thirteen, thirteen, fourteen, and fifteen (3:273, 333, 208, 273, 387, 273; her actual age appears to be thirteen). William Woodin Rowe has astutely summarized the literary technique involved in this deliberate ambiguity:

> As a child is victimized, its age abruptly becomes younger. But Dostoevsky typically derives persuasive effect from both halves of (strangely reconciled) contradiction. Despite the downward gradation of its age, a child victim remains old enough to think—to apprehend its plight. The Dostoevskian female pedophilia victim, for example, has almost invariably the sexual desirability of an older girl, the helplessness of a younger girl, and a near-woman's capacity for apprehending her victimization.[26]

The element here that is missing from Stavrogin's portrait of Matryosha is "sexual desirability." Completely absent from his descriptions of her are the exotic and romantic physical charms of Nelli (and of Svidrigailov's dead girl, and of Nastas'ia Filippovna). Stavrogin's unblinking honesty keeps him from implicitly claiming that "her beauty made me do it."

Matryosha lives in close quarters with Stavrogin, as Nelli does with Ivan, and like Nelli she is a kind of servant to him. Nelli offers to wash Ivan's linen and cook for him; at one point he catches her sweeping his floor, still wearing the fancy dress in which she was to be deflowered (3:285, 286, 283). Stavrogin tersely says of Matryosha, "This little girl acted as my servant and cleaned up for me behind the screen" (11:13). "Behind the screen" is where one's bed and one's chamber pot are located. This takes the intimacy of Nelli's washing Ivan's linen one step further.

Soon after Ivan first meets Nelli, he witnesses her savage beating at the hands of Mrs. Bubnova, who calls her foul names and reproaches her for nonexistent crimes (3:258–59). Stavrogin's interest in Matryosha begins when he witnesses her beating by her mother, who blames her for the disappearance of Stavrogin's penknife (11:13). In both cases, the child remains silent, refusing to cry out under the blows (3:259, 11:13). The major difference in the two scenes is in the behavior of the narrators. Ivan cuts a heroic figure, grabbing Bubnova by the arm and shouting, "What are you doing? How can you dare to treat a poor orphan in such a way?" (3:259). Not only does Stavrogin not intervene to save Matryosha, he fails to reveal that just before the beating began he found the knife in his bed: "It immediately came into my head that I should not announce it, so that she would be beaten" (11:14). Rather than taking part as a beneficent actor, Stavrogin sits back and enjoys the beating as a voyeuristic spectator.

The beating seems to be the impetus for the "meditated intention" ("zamyshlennoe namerenie," 11:15) that Stavrogin puts into practice three days later, when he arranges to be alone with Matryosha in the apartment. Stavrogin's description of what happens between him and Matryosha is worth quoting at length, because its terseness and compactness resist summary:

> I rose and began to steal up to her. They had a lot of geraniums in the windowsills, and the sun was shining terribly brightly. I sat quietly beside her on the floor. She shuddered and at first she became incredibly frightened and jumped up. I took her hand and quietly kissed it, I pressed her down again onto the bench and began to look into her eyes. The fact that I had kissed her hand suddenly made her laugh like a child, but only for one second, because she impetuously jumped up again, now in such fright that a convulsion passed over her face. She looked at me with horribly fixed eyes, and her lips started to tremble as if to begin crying, but nevertheless she didn't cry out. I again began to kiss her hands, and taking her onto my lap, I kissed her face and feet. When I kissed her feet, she jerked away and smiled as if in shame, but with a kind of crooked smile. Her whole face blazed with shame. I was whispering something to her. Finally something so strange occurred that I will never forget it, something that caused me amazement: the little girl clasped me around the neck and began to kiss me terribly [uzhasno] herself. Her face expressed complete rapture. I almost got up and left—this was so unpleasant to me in such a tiny child—out of pity. But I overcame my sudden feeling of fear and remained.
>
> When everything was over, she was embarrassed. I didn't try to reassure her and no longer caressed her. She looked at me, timidly smiling. Her face suddenly seemed stupid to me. (11:16)

Stavrogin's text in its entirety takes up only eleven pages of the Academy edition of Dostoevsky's complete works; this description occupies about half a page. In the same edition, the text of *The Insulted and Injured* is 442 pages long. But scattered throughout the earlier novel are movements and gestures by Ivan and Nelli that are precursors of the actions of Stavrogin and Matryosha in this scene.

The clearest way to see the textual parallels is by presenting them side by side:

The Insulted and Injured	"At Tikhon's"
She rushed straight toward me and clasped me with her arms.	The little girl clasped me around the neck with her arms.
Ona brosilas' priamo ko mne i obkhvatila menia rukami. (3:276)	Devochka obkhvatila menia rukami. (11:16)
She stretched toward me convulsively and passionately, and when I bent over her, she firmly clasped my neck with her swarthy, thin arms and firmly kissed me.	A convulsion passed over her face . . . the little girl clasped me around the neck with her arms and began to kiss me terribly herself.
Ona sudorozhno-strastno potianulas' ko mne, i kogda ia naklonilsia k nei, ona krepko obkhvatila moiu sheiu svoimi smuglymi khuden'kimi ruchkami i krepko potselovala menia. (3:429)	Sudoroga proshla po litsu . . . devochka obkhvatila menia za sheiu rukami i nachala vdrug uzhasno tselovat' sama. (11:16)
Her other hand lay on my pillow. I very quietly kissed that skinny little hand.	I took her hand and quietly kissed it.
Drugaia ruka ee lezhala na moei podushke. Ia tikho-tikho potseloval etu khuden'kuiu ruchku. (3:294)	Ia vzial ee ruku i tikho potseloval. (11:16)
I took her up in my arms, sat on the couch, put her on my lap and kissed her passionately. She blazed up.	I again began to kiss her hands, and taking her onto my lap, I kissed her face and feet . . . Her whole face blazed with shame.
Ia skhvatil ee na ruki, sel na divan, posadil k sebe na koleni i goriacho potseloval ee. Ona vspykhnula. (3:406)	Ia opiat' stal tselovat' ei ruki, vziav ee k sebe na koleni, tseloval ei litso i nogi . . . Vse litso vspykhnulo stydom. (11:16)

When scattered throughout the 442-page text of *The Insulted and Injured,* these gestures do not make much of an impact; they remain the impulsive physical tokens of an exalted and seemingly innocent friendship. But when concentrated into the half-page of Stavrogin's description, they add up to a scene of shocking sexual manipulation, if not rape. Vitalii Svintsov argues that since there is no obvious violence and Matryosha herself initiates the final stage of the encounter, one cannot speak of the incident as rape. Irina Rodnianskaia replies cogently, "Drawing a child emotionally into this act, arousing 'voluptuousness' [sladostrastie] in her, does not mitigate what has been committed, as Svintsov imagines, but makes it almost more horrible than brute violence."[27]

The link between Matryosha and Nelli is emphasized by Dostoevsky's use of the spatial detail of the threshold.[28] When Stavrogin returns to the scene of his crime and sits quietly in his room, Matryosha, who has been in delirium for three days but is now in her right mind, comes and stands on the threshhold ("na poroge") to his room. She shakes her head at him in reproach and threatens him with her tiny fist (11:18).[29] It is this image that pursues him years later: "I saw Matryosha, grown thin and with feverish eyes, exactly as she was then, when she stood on my threshold and, shaking her head at me, raised her itsy-bitsy little fist [kroshechnyi kulachonok] at me" (11:22). Nelli, who falls into delirium several times in the course of *The Insulted and Injured,* often appears on Ivan's threshold:

Suddenly there appeared some kind of strange creature on the threshold [na poroge]. (3:208)

She stopped once more on the threshold. (3:209)

We were talking on the threshold, by the open door. (3:324)

I had not had time to knock at the door of my apartment when I heard a moan, and the door hastily began to open, as if Nelli had not even gone to bed, but had stood guard the whole time on my very threshold. (3:369)

It was clear: she had had a fit while I was out, and it happened precisely at the time when she was standing by the very door. Waking up from the fit, she probably could not come to for a long time. At that moment reality merged with delirium, and she probably imagined something horrible, some kind of terrors. At the same time she vaguely realized that I must return and knock at the door, and therefore, lying down by the very threshold on the floor, she waited attentively for my return and got up at my first knock. (3:370)

What is missing from these threshold scenes with Nelli are the reproach and the threat in Matryosha's gestures toward Stavrogin: "She suddenly began shaking her head at me as people shake their heads in strong reproach [kogda ochen' ukoriaiut], and suddenly raised her tiny little fist at me and began to threaten me with it from where she stood" (11:18). In keeping with the much more diffuse narrative of *The Insulted and Injured,* Ivan feels this reproach and this threat from Nelli, but on two widely spaced occasions. When he asks Nelli to tell her whole painful story to the Ikhmenevs in the hope that it will reconcile them to their daughter Natasha, Nelli agrees, and then looks at him fixedly: "There was something resembling reproach [ukor] in that gaze, and I felt it in my heart" (3:407). In fact, the recounting of her story has a deleterious effect on Nelli's health. At the very end of her life, she makes a threatening gesture to Ivan, but one that is devoid of the seriously guilt-inducing weight of Matryosha's fist-shaking. Nelli tells Ivan that he should marry Natasha: "This, it seems, was her constant and long-standing idea. I smiled at her silently. Seeing my smile, she herself smiled, and with a mischievous look she threatened me with her thin little finger and immediately began to kiss me" (3:441).

Nelli's final scenes play out against the background of the setting sun, which creates a peaceful, picturesque backdrop for her quiet death (3:429–30, 441). Matryosha's death also happens at sunset, but it is a violent, self-inflicted death. It is the image of the setting sun that brings Matryosha's reproachful figure back to haunt Stavrogin years later. By the "bright slanting rays of the setting sun," in a hotel room in Germany, he sees a vision of the tiny red spider that he had seen "on the geranium leaf, when the slanting rays of the setting sun poured out in just the same way" (11:22) at the moment of Matryosha's suicide. As we look at the stories of Nelli and Matryosha, we see a pattern of parallel details which are transformed in such a way as to heighten the horror of Stavrogin's confession.

In returning to the textual material of *The Insulted and Injured,* in "At Tikhon's" Dostoevsky casts that material in a very different form and presents it from a very different point of view. As we have seen, the quasi-erotic gestures that were scattered innocuously throughout *The Insulted and Injured* are concentrated in Stavrogin's text into a powerfully distilled narrative of sexual abuse. The narrator's point of view has also changed, from the guiltless and unaware stance of Ivan Petrovich to the brutal honesty of Stavrogin.

In Dostoevsky's original version of "At Tikhon's," Stavrogin goes out of his way to stress the premeditated nature of what he does to Matryosha. Immediately after describing how he found his penknife but allowed Matryosha to be beaten anyway, Stavrogin offers a remarkable digression. First he describes the "incredible enjoyment" he receives from being in "a shameful, boundlessly humiliating, base, and above all ludicrous position" (11:14). Then he stresses that no matter how strong this feeling, he is always in control of it: "Even when [this feeling] reaches the point of the utmost fire, at the same time I could completely overcome it, even stop it at its highest point" (11:14). He even claims that he would be able to live his whole life "as a monk," despite his powerful sexual drive:

> After devoting myself, up to the age of sixteen, with extraordinary lack of moderation, to the vice to which Jean-Jacques Rousseau confessed, I ceased at the very minute I had set for myself, as soon as I turned sixteen. I am always master of myself when I take it into my head to be. So let it be known that I do not wish to claim lack of responsibility for my crimes by reason either of the environment or illness. (11:14)

The "vice to which Jean-Jacques Rousseau confessed" is masturbation.[30] Given the vicariously masturbatory pleasure Stavrogin seems to take in Matryosha's beating, this example he gives of his powers of self-control is both apt and ironic. Throughout his text, Stavrogin repeatedly reminds us of his conscious control. Just before approaching Matryosha, "I suddenly asked myself again: can I stop? and immediately answered myself that I could" (11:16). At the end of his text he even claims that he is in control of the haunting visions he has of Matryosha: "I know that I could make the little girl go away even now, if I chose to. I am completely in control of my will, as before" (11:22). He simply chooses not to rid himself of the vision that reminds him of his guilt.

After Matryosha's beating gives him the idea for his "premeditated intention," Stavrogin rehearses for his misdeed by gratuitously stealing a wallet containing the wages of a neighbor in his other lodgings, a poor civil servant with a family. The scene of the theft is linked to the later abuse of Matryosha in two ways. A striking feature of the scene in which Stavrogin abuses Matryosha, as well as the scene in which he waits for her suicide, is that he constantly checks his watch for the time, as if to emphasize his cold-bloodedness. When the civil servant actually catches Stavrogin stealing the wallet from his uniform left on a chair, Stavrogin puts him off by claiming that "while passing in the corridor I stepped in to see what time it was on the wall clock" (11:15). The other element linking the scenes is the word "timid" ("robkii"). Although the civil servant suspects Stavrogin of the theft, he fails to utter the accusation: "and he didn't dare tell anyone in the lodgings, so timid [robki] are these people" (11:15). Just before the incident of the theft, Stavrogin says that Matryosha "was very timid" ("byla ochen' robka," 11:15). When their sexual encounter is over, "She looked at me, timidly smiling" (11:16).

Besides emphasizing his mental control and the premeditation of his act, Stavrogin makes it clear that something physical occurred between him and Matryosha. The day after the incident he is overcome by fear: "Of course, I could deny it, but they could establish my guilt [menia mogli i ulichit']. I had visions of penal servitude" (11:17). The word Stavrogin uses, "ulichit'," derives from "ulika," "physical evidence."[31] Clearly, Stavrogin has done something to Matryosha that can be traced by investigators. Her suicide ends his fears: "No one found out that I had come in the evening. I didn't hear anything about the results of the medical examination" (11:20). The implication is that, since no one knew of Matryosha's connection to Stavrogin, the medical examiner did not look for evidence of sexual abuse.[32]

Tikhon recognizes that there is something remarkable about the degree of responsibility Stavrogin is taking for his act. Even acknowledging that such an act is at all unusual is in itself a kind of moral achievement:

> As for the crime itself, many sin in the same way, but they live with their conscience in peace and tranquillity, even considering it to be the inevitable peccadilloes of youth. There are even old men who sin in the same way, and even with a sense of consolation and playfulness. The world is filled with all these horrors. But you felt the whole depth of it, which very rarely happens to such an extent. (11:25)

Stavrogin's sarcastic reply, "Are you beginning to respect me after reading these pages?" calls forth Tikhon's final verdict on Stavrogin's act, one that is made on absolute, not relative grounds: "Of course there is and cannot be a greater and more terrible crime than your act with the maiden" (11:25; Tikhon uses an archaic, biblical-sounding term for "girl").

The version of "At Tikhon's" that survives in the copy made by Anna Grigor'evna Dostoevskaia apparently represents an attempt by Dostoevsky to placate Katkov and the *Russian Herald*, which had rejected the original version. In this later version, both the explicitness of the crime and Stavrogin's insistence on taking full responsibility for it are removed. Stavrogin's text is introduced with a digression by the novel's narrator that calls into doubt the document's authenticity and veracity, weighing the possibility that it might be "fake, that is, completely made-up and composed" (12:108). Stavrogin too says to Tikhon, "Maybe I just told a pack of lies, exaggerated in a fanatical moment" (12:116). Gone in the text itself are most of Stavrogin's assurances that he is in complete control of himself; gone is his boast about giving up masturbation, gone is the theft rehearsal. Gone also are references to "physical evidence" and "medical examination," and with good reason: even the central act of the chapter, Stavrogin's sexual abuse of Matryosha, is called into question. In this later version of "At Tikhon's," as Tikhon reaches the crucial moment in his reading of Stavrogin's narrative, the moment when Matryosha throws her arms around Stavrogin's neck, Tikhon asks Stavrogin for the next page of the text and Stavrogin withholds it from him. Stavrogin fills in the missing part of the narrative in an evasive fashion: "Calm down. I'm not to blame that the little girl was stupid and didn't understand correctly . . . Nothing happened. No-thing" (12:111). In the later version, Matryosha's age has also been altered from a vague fourteen to an unambiguous eleven, and a reference to her playing with dolls has been inserted (12:109). This revision downward of Matryosha's age, making her even more of an innocent child, is perhaps meant to reinforce Stavrogin's assertion to Tikhon that nothing happened, that the whole affair was a "psychological misunderstanding" (12:111).

The revisions in the later version of the chapter tend to soften Stavrogin's responsibility for the crime, and even to call into question the fact that a crime took place. Thus, after making the long artistic journey from the naively unaware narrative of Ivan Petrovich to the unblinkingly honest and responsible text by Stavrogin in the first version of "At Tikhon's," in this later version Dostoevsky takes a rather large step backward. In the later version of the chapter, when Tikhon asks Stavrogin to hand him the missing page of the text, Stavrogin replies, "That page . . . that page is subject to censorship for the time being" (12:110). Stavrogin's remark can be read as referring to Dostoevsky's own act of censoring himself in this revision of the chapter. Dostoevsky's attempt at self-censorship in the revised version of "At Tikhon's" failed to satisfy the *Russian Herald,* and the novel appeared without the chapter.[33]

Iu. Kariakin has discussed the ironic situation in which Dostoevsky found himself in 1872, eleven years after the "Egyptian Nights" debate: M. N. Katkov, the same man who in 1861 accused Pushkin of indecency, refused to publish "At Tikhon's," presumably for the same reason. Kariakin sees the rejection of "At Tikhon's" as Katkov's revenge for having been bested in the 1861 debate with Dostoevsky over "Egyptian Nights."[34] Whether or not such a motive lay behind Katkov's action, Dostoevsky himself must have been aware of the irony. In 1861 he had asserted that when presenting sexual material in literary art, "point of view is the main thing." Let us recall Dostoevsky's words, directed to Katkov, on that occasion:

> This *ultimate expression* [of passion], about which you speak so often, in your opinion may be corrupting, but in our view, it represents only a perversion of human nature that has reached such terrible dimensions and that is presented *from such a point of view* by the poet (and the point of view is the main thing) that it produces not an obscene but a shattering impression. (19:135; emphasis in original)[35]

It is clear that what Dostoevsky has in mind in the phrase "point of view" is not just a technical question of narrative vantage point, but also a problem of moral framing. From 1861 to 1871 Dostoevsky worked and reworked the potentially salacious subject matter of pedophilia until, in Stavrogin's confessional text, he had achieved the "point of view" that was fully honest and fully responsible, only to have the text rejected as obscene. The rejection clearly rankled with Dostoevsky even years later. In 1876 an article appeared in the *Russian Herald* that said, in a veiled but transparent reference to "At Tikhon's," that the *Russian Herald* had refused to publish "filth" and the depiction of "vice and debauchery."[36] Dostoevsky's notebooks contain his fragmentary reaction to this slander: "He proclaimed that the *Russian Herald* corrected my filth. I didn't answer. This didn't happen" (or "There was no such thing";"Etogo ne bylo").[37] "This didn't happen": In Dostoevsky's view, there was no "filth" in the chapter "At Tikhon's," but the work was censored all the same. The "point of view" that Dostoevsky had achieved by means of a long and painstaking artistic process did not save the text from being regarded as obscene in the eyes of his contemporaries, as represented by Katkov and the editors of the *Russian Herald*.

At a certain point in "At Tikhon's," Dostoevsky seems to anticipate what was going to happen to his text. As far as we know, he had had no trouble with Katkov and the editors of the *Russian Herald* in publishing a harrowingly explicit and bloody scene of the axe murder of two women in *Crime and Punishment*, yet the discreetly framed scene of Stavrogin's abuse of Matryosha was rejected.[38] In his conversation with Stavrogin, Tikhon offers an explanation for this phenomenon: "There are crimes that are truly ugly [nekrasivye]. In crimes, whatever they are, the more blood, the more horror—the more impressive they are, the more picturesque, so to speak; but there are crimes that are shameful, disgraceful, past all horror, so to speak, simply too inelegant" (11:27). Dostoevsky's attempt to find an artistic image for the crime of pedophilia, a crime that was "past all horror," was a failure, at least in the eyes of his contemporaries.

As V. N. Zakharov has discussed, Dostoevsky's problems with the *Russian Herald* in the 1870s gave rise to numerous rumors that Dostoevsky himself had molested a child.[39] This accusation cannot be definitely proven or disproven, although the preponderance of evidence lies on the side of Dostoevsky's defenders. But it is important to note, as A. S. Dolinin points out, that "the plot [siuzhet] of [Stavrogin's confession], which had so persistently haunted [Dostoevsky] and had been so fully elaborated by him, is never again reproduced by him."[40] If pedophilia were a personal obsession, one would expect it to persist in Dostoevsky's works. As a *literary* obsession, one that Dostoevsky had continued to work on for more than a decade, the theme of the man taking responsibility for an improper sexual relationship with a female child attained its fulfillment and most polished form in Stavrogin's confessional text, a text that never reached Dostoevsky's contemporary audience.[41] Even today, when the text is widely available, it is impossible to fully integrate it into the larger novel, due to the doubts about Dostoevsky's final intentions (12:246). As Kariakin says, rather melodramatically but in my opinion justly, "To this day we are paying for Katkov's crime against our culture, and we aren't aware of it, we deceive ourselves."[42] Katkov's censorship relegated Dostoevsky's unflinching depiction of the crime of pedophilia to the status of an underground text, despite the fact that on the attentive reader "it produces not an obscene but a shattering impression."

In his subsequent works, Dostoevsky continued to deal with the child's and adolescent's encounter with sexuality. The focus shifts, however, to the child's own point of view, particularly to the ways in which abandoned children and adolescents encounter sexuality without parental guidance. This is the subject of the following chapters.

Dostoevsky's Comely Boy: Homoerotic Desire and Aesthetic Strategies in *A Raw Youth*

THE CHAPTER "AT TIKHON'S," in which Dostoevsky confronted the sexual sin of pedophilia with the utmost frankness and responsibility, was censored from the text of *The Devils* and never appeared in print in Dostoevsky's lifetime. In his next novel, *A Raw Youth* (*Podrostok,* 1875; separate edition, 1876), he did not abandon the sexual theme, but treated it more subtly and less shockingly, as part of the moral and spiritual maturation of the narrator Arkadii Dolgorukii. In this chapter I will consider one aspect of Arkadii's sexual education, his encounter with the phenomenon of same-sex desire. Dostoevsky's approach here to the young person's early encounters with sex is different from that in novels like *The Insulted and Injured* or *The Devils.* We know very little about Nelli's or Matryosha's thoughts and feelings from their point of view. In *A Raw Youth,* the young person is the narrator, and we share with him his feelings of both unease and attraction as he encounters different forms of sexuality.

In his 1862 pseudo-autobiography *Notes from the House of the Dead* (*Zapiski iz mertvogo doma*), based on his experiences in a Siberian prison, Dostoevsky explains how prisoners deal with their sexual needs.[1] One method is to bribe guards to take the prisoner not to his work site but to a secluded hut for a tryst with a prostitute. But such expeditions, since they are expensive and risky, are extremely rare; as the narrator tells us, "lovers of the fair sex resort to other means, which are completely safe" (4:38). In what seems to be a digression but really isn't, the narrator goes on to describe the prisoner Sirotkin, whom he calls "khoroshen'kii mal'chik" ("pretty boy") twice in the space of one paragraph (4:38, 39). Sirotkin does not ply any of the prisoners' moneymaking trades, but he always seems to have sums of ready cash and new clothes, gifts from other prisoners. One can only conclude that Sirotkin represents that "other means" of satisfying sexual desire—male prostitution. Our narrator is curious about Sirotkin and his "comrades," and promises to describe them more extensively: "If circumstances permit, I will say something in more detail about this whole gang" (4:40).[2]

This promise is not kept in *House of the Dead,* but over ten years later in *A Raw Youth,* Dostoevsky created a character similar to Sirotkin and explored the phenomenon of homoerotic desire in much more detail than he was willing or able to do in 1862. The character Trishatov, also a "pretty boy" dependent on male admirers for nice clothes and pocket money, makes a brief but telling appearance in the novel and serves to elucidate the experimental and unorthodox aesthetics of this most challenging of Dostoevsky's works. Despite its substantial size and its appearance between the masterworks *The Devils* and *The Brothers Karamazov, A Raw Youth* has been largely ignored by readers and critics. No one assigns it to their undergraduates, few read it for pleasure, and almost no one includes a chapter on it in their studies of the major works of Dostoevsky. There are very good reasons for this neglect. The novel is extremely difficult to read and seemingly unrewarding. Unlike the *apparently* incompetent narrator of *The Devils,* in Arkadii it has a *truly* incompetent narrator, one who confuses us about times and dates, places wrong emphases, and introduces characters with portentous fanfare and never mentions them again. Jacques Catteau has aptly characterized the novel as "the most 'mad' and so the most neglected book in the canon." As he says, "It is a concentration of all those elements of the Dostoyevskian novel which are most irritating to the Euclidean mind."[3] When confronted by a work of seemingly chaotic form, readers try to find expedients that help them avoid dealing with that form. In the case of *A Raw Youth,* scholars have treated the novel as continuous with the voluminous notebooks and drafts for it, thus losing sight of what the artist finally included and excluded. We need to restore respect for the peculiar aesthetic form of *A Raw Youth,* difficult and obscure as it may be. In the process, I believe that this novel will help us better understand Dostoevsky's career as a whole.

The present chapter deals with one of the major keys to understanding *A Raw Youth,* Dostoevsky's treatment of homoerotic desire. His treatment of this theme is noteworthy in itself, and is discussed in the first part of this chapter. In the second part, I show how the same unconventional trajectories of desire that develop among the novel's characters are reflected on the metaliterary level, in the relations among narrator, implied author, and implied reader. Just as Dostoevsky transfers emotional energy in *A Raw Youth* from the conventional male-female relationship to the male-male relationship, he makes the most important metaliterary relationship not the conventional one between narrator and implied reader, but the one between narrator and implied author.

In the third and last part of *A Raw Youth,* the narrator Arkadii

Dolgorukii encounters Petia Trishatov, a mysterious but strangely appealing figure. Trishatov appears in only a few scenes but plays an important role both in the novel's plot and in its aesthetic system. Trishatov, a member of a gang of blackmailers headed by Arkadii's school chum and tormentor Lambert, is about twenty years old, but nineteen-year-old Arkadii almost always refers to him as "mal'chik" ("boy"): "the comely boy," "the strange boy," "my boy" (13:343, 406, 354). Unlike his companion Andreev, whose hands and clothes are filthy, Trishatov is beautifully dressed and impeccably groomed. Yet Lambert's mistress Alphonsine is repelled by him and refuses to let him touch her: "Ah, le petit vilain! . . . ne m'approchez pas, ne me salissez pas" ("Oh, you nasty little boy! . . . don't come near me, don't get me dirty," 13:346). Lambert tells Arkadii that Trishatov is a general's son, but "his family is ashamed of him, I got him out of being prosecuted, I saved him" (13:348). Indeed, Lambert appears to have a rather intimate relationship with Trishatov, buying him expensive presents like an elk-fur coat and a gold watch. The mystery of Trishatov is easily solved. Numerous hints in the text of *A Raw Youth,* plus the very fact that Lambert does not name Trishatov's crime, help us understand why Alphonsine shuns him and why he was to be prosecuted: for the crime covered by Article 995 of the criminal code, "muzhelozhstvo" ("men lying with men"), punishable by loss of civil rights and exile to Siberia.[4]

Before going any further, let me summarize briefly the plot of *A Raw Youth.* The novel is narrated by the eponymous "raw youth," Arkadii Makarovich Dolgorukii. Arkadii belongs to what his former tutor calls an "accidental family" ("sluchainoe semeistvo," 13:455). He is the illegitimate son of the nobleman Versilov and a peasant woman, Sof'ia, who is legally married to a saintly former serf, Makar Ivanovich Dolgorukii. Their family arrangements are highly unconventional. Versilov has two children from an earlier marriage whom he seldom sees. He lives with Arkadii's mother and sister Liza, but occasionally spends long periods away from them. Makar, who has become a pilgrim, continues to correspond with his wife and visits her once every three years. Arkadii has been raised in a boarding school and in another family in Moscow, but as the novel begins he is reunited with Versilov, Sof'ia, and Liza in St. Petersburg. There are not one but many plots in *A Raw Youth.* It is a psychological mystery novel, in which Arkadii seeks to solve the riddle of his complex and enigmatic biological father. It is a bildungsroman, in which the young man tries out several designs for living, including miserly accumulation of capital, the dissipated gambling life of a young aristocrat, and the holy quest for "blagoobrazie" ("blessed form") inspired by his legal father Makar.[5] It is also a penny-dreadful tale of intrigue, in which Arkadii, abetted by Lambert, plans to extort sexual favors from the beautiful Katerina Nikolaevna. As I will show, *A Raw Youth* is also an artistic experiment; Arkadii's sexual questioning and flirtation with homoerotic desire have their analogue in his unconventional, rebarbative narrative style.

Simon Karlinsky has claimed that Dostoevsky, "one of the most perceptive explorers of the human psyche that literature has known, does not seem to have been aware of the existence of gayness."[6] Karlinsky, an incisive and astute critic of Russian literature, the man who opened our eyes to the homoerotic dimension of Gogol's work, betrays an unaccountable blind spot here. It is inconceivable that Dostoevsky, to whom nothing human was alien, who was passionately interested in all the twists and turns of human desire, could have been unaware of the existence of same-sex desire. On the contrary, although homosexuality is not one of his major themes (and probably could not have been, considering the censorship), it does play an important role in many of his works, as Michael R. Katz has recently argued for *House of the Dead, Notes from Underground,* and *The Brothers Karamazov.*[7] Despite the evidence he adduces of homoerotic themes in Dostoevsky's work, Katz still agrees with Karlinsky's statement, believing that Dostoevsky was consciously unaware of homosexuality, but had an "intuitive knowledge" or "unconscious understanding" of it. In fact, there is both textual and extratextual evidence that Dostoevsky was quite consciously aware of the phenomenon of homosexuality.

What might Dostoevsky have known about homosexuality at the time of writing *A Raw Youth?* Leaving aside his earlier experience in a Siberian prison, there are two obvious sources of information and inspiration. One was his professional relationship with Prince Vladimir Petrovich Meshcherskii, whose homosexuality was well known in Russian society.[8] The other was the growing body of scientific and forensic research on homosexuality.

Meshcherskii, the archconservative owner of the journal *The Citizen* (*Grazhdanin*), of which Dostoevsky served as editor from January 1873 to April 1874, used his considerable influence with Tsar Alexander III (and later with Nicholas II) to promote the careers of his lovers, whom he called his "spiritual sons" ("dukhovnye synov'ia"). Count S. Iu. Witte, Meshcherskii's former protégé, even implied in a special appendix to his memoirs that Meshcherskii was the lover of Alexander III (and the procurer of a male lover for Nicholas II).[9]

The prevalence of homosexuality in Russian high aristocratic circles, as reflected in Meshcherskii's career, is also reflected, if only obliquely, in the text of *A Raw Youth,* most significantly in the hero's name. Arkadii is, as I mentioned, the illegitimate son of the nobleman Versilov and a peasant woman, but his legal father is the former serf Makar Dolgorukii. The Dolgorukii/Dolgorukov family was one of the most ancient Russian princely clans (the two versions of the name were interchangeable in the nineteenth century).[10] Arkadii suffers greatly from the bitter irony of bearing this glittering name without a right to the princely status it implies. Every time Arkadii introduces himself he is met by the question, *"Prince* Dolgorukii?" to which he must give the humiliating reply, "Net, *prosto* Dolgorukii" ("No, *just* Dolgorukii," 13:7; compare 13:266, 437). Arkadii says that "few people could be so furious at their own last name as I have been throughout my life" (13:7).

Arkadii's name, and his repudiation of it, have another, less obvious significance. One of the most famous bearers of the Dolgorukii/Dolgorukov name was Prince Pyotr Vladimirovich Dolgorukov, who in the nineteenth century was believed to have been the author of the anonymous letters that precipitated Pushkin's fatal duel.[11] The question of Dolgorukov's responsibility for circulating the "Order of the Cuckold" was raised in the Russian-language press several times in the decade preceding the writing of *A Raw Youth*. The anonymous letters and other documents relating to the duel were first published in Herzen's *Polar Star* (*Poliarnaia zvezda*) in 1861; the accusation of Dolgorukov first appeared in print in 1863; and the accusation was repeated in the journal *Russian Archive* (*Russkii arkhiv*) in 1872.[12] Although scholars have recently cast doubt on Dolgorukov's involvement, in the 1870s he was widely believed to have sent the letters and thus to have played a role in Pushkin's death. As Stella Abramovich has pointed out, Dolgorukov's homosexuality served as the psychological basis reinforcing suspicions of his guilt, since it seemed to unite him in a kind of conspiratorial union with Pushkin's killer Georges D'Anthès and his probable lover Baron Heeckeren.[13] Pushkin is a guiding literary spirit for Arkadii; works like *The Covetous Knight* and "The Queen of Spades" serve the young man as vital points of orientation in a disintegrating world. When he angrily denies that he is *"Prince* Dolgorukii," he is denying participation in a plot of homosexual aristocrats to destroy Pushkin. Although there is no indication in the text that Arkadii is aware of the connection, Dostoevsky and his audience would be, thanks to the discussions of the scandal in the Russian press in the 1860s and 1870s.

Thus in the 1870s the examples of Meshcherskii and Dolgorukov were available to bring the question of homosexual desire within Dostoevsky's ken. The larger society around him would also have been a valuable source of information, of course. Dan Healey has shown that it was in the 1870s that a modern homosexual subculture emerged in Russian cities, "against the backdrop of rapid urbanization and the accelerated introduction of market relationships."[14] It was also a time of growing scientific interest in the phenomenon of homosexuality. Dostoevsky was always interested in the opinions of scientists and medical experts on social issues (even if he at times disagreed with them). In the second half of the nineteenth century Russian science was forming a more detailed theoretical and clinical picture of homosexuality, under the influence of Western European researchers. For an understanding of the state of Russian scientific opinion in the 1870s, I have used two sources, one of which, V. O. Merzheevskii's 1872 adaptation and translation of Johann Ludwig Casper's handbook of forensic medicine, would have been available to Dostoevsky at the time of writing *A Raw Youth*. The other work, V. M. Tarnovskii's *Perversion of the Sexual Feeling* (*Izvrashchenie polovogo chuvstva*), was published only in 1885, but the theories it summarizes were no doubt in the discussion by the 1870s.[15] These works can serve as an appendix to our lexicon of the period, an aid in understanding the discourse about homosexuality that prevailed at the time Dostoevsky wrote *A Raw Youth*.

Casper-Merzheevskii offer case histories of homosexual behavior, two of which appear as episodes in *A Raw Youth* with all explicit reference to homosexuality suppressed. The first case serves to illustrate what Casper-Merzheevskii call "senile pederasty." (The term "pederasty" was used by nineteenth-century Russian writers to refer to all forms of homosexual behavior, from rape of children to anal intercourse between consenting adults.) A 65-year-old man advertised for young men, 16 to 20 years of age, to perform office work in his home. But instead of employing the young men as clerks, he engaged them in obscene conversation and then tried to rape them. As one of his victims related,

When I came there I was introduced to the old man, who began immediately to bombard me with the most indecent questions: had I begun having sex, how many times had I had sex, and so on. At first I was shocked by such questions and could not figure out what kind of person he was: was he insane or not? Finally I decided that such conversations about girls probably were his favorite hobby, and I agreed to work for him . . . But none of us ever got any clerical work to do, but just heard his constant talk about girls, which became quite vulgar; for example, he advised us to have sex with two- and three-year-old girls and insisted that it was quite possible to do so, especially if you had money.[16]

The old man's estates had been placed under trusteeship because of his inhuman treatment of his serfs, from whom he regularly demanded the droit du seigneur with their young daughters, in contravention of the laws and mores of his time; he had spent time in an insane asylum; and in the opinion of the author that was his proper place.[17] Tarnovskii also cites this case; he identifies the major sign of senile pederasty as "increasingly obscene conversations, primarily with very young people, youths, even boys. Such sick men especially like to corrupt boys with seductive pictures, books, and stories and thus accustom them first to onanism, and then gradually to passive pederasty."[18]

Arkadii Dolgorukii has a strikingly similar experience working as a clerk for the near-senile Prince Sokol'skii. Arkadii's aunt finds out that the Prince has a place for a young man to work for him in his home office. Arkadii soon learns that his work consists not of copying papers but of amusing the old man with conversations about women (13:24). The old Prince is particularly interested in hearing about Arkadii's early sexual experiences. At one point Arkadii angrily says, "You'd really love for me to go see some local Josephine and then come report to you about it" (13:27). ("Josephine" is Dostoevskian code for "prostitute"; in Dostoevsky's writings, prostitutes are often of German origin.) As Arkadii later complains, "It's humiliating to get a salary for telling scandalous stories" (13:29). The Prince has a sick habit of semi-adopting young girls and finding husbands for them. In the case of his protégées, his exercise of the droit du seigneur is only hinted, but his projected marriage to Arkadii's 22-year-old half sister brings his near-pedophilic tendencies to the fore. The plot of *A Raw Youth* hinges on the question of the old Prince's sanity. Arkadii plans to blackmail the Prince's beautiful daughter Katerina Nikolaevna with a letter she wrote to her lawyer inquiring about the possibility of having the Prince committed to an insane asylum (13:59). Thus the motifs of Casper-Merzheevskii's case history—senile dementia, obscene conversations with young men, sex with young girls, and involuntary institutionalization—are repeated in the novel; only anal rape is omitted.

The second case history relevant to *A Raw Youth* is Casper-Merzheevskii's discussion of the phenomenon of blackmail by gangs of youths. Casper-Merzheevskii write:

> [Blackmail (shantazh) consists of] the extortion of money, then the robbery and even the murder of those unfortunate men of property whose ill-starred passion attracts them to the members of that repulsive brotherhood of passive pederasts . . . Their main aim is to lure well-known and well-off people who are given to pederasty into a prepared trap, and then to force them to pay dearly for their shameful passion.[19]

Although Merzheevskii identifies Paris as the birthplace of this "particular trade," both he and Tarnovskii report that gangs of blackmailers have begun to appear in St. Petersburg.[20]

Arkadii's old friend Lambert, Arkadii tells us, "could be numbered among those loathsome gangs of petty scoundrels who associate with each other in order to engage in what is now called blackmail [shantazh] and for which definitions and punishments are now being sought in the criminal code" (13:322). The specific episodes of blackmail described in the text concern heterosexual scandals, but a loophole is left in Arkadii's description of Lambert's gang: among their activities are "samye griaznen'kie i netsenzurnye veshchi" ("the filthiest and most unprintable things," 13:322). The presence of Trishatov in Lambert's gang implies that one of those "filthy things" is the luring of well-to-do homosexual men into compromising situations for the purpose of blackmail.[21]

Another possible source for Dostoevsky's description of Lambert's blackmail gang is indicated in the memoirs of A. F. Koni, a St. Petersburg legal official who was an acquaintance and admirer of Dostoevsky. Koni describes his exposure of a gang of homosexual blackmailers in St. Petersburg in February 1875. He prefaces his 1912 recollection of this incident with an allusion to the emerging homosexual subculture of that time: "Already then, at the beginning of the 1870s in St. Petersburg, of course to a lesser degree than now, was spread that unnatural vice which recently, having found supposedly scientific defenders and apologists such as Professor Alletrino, has blossomed into a lush double-petaled poisonous flower in Berlin."[22] In the incident of February 1875, Koni's suspicions were aroused by the fact that in several official complaints of homosexual activity submitted to his office, the accusers were the same small group of men, who alternated in the roles of victim and witness. He surmised that they were blackmailers preying on provincial visitors "who wish to drink from the Petersburg cup of pleasures."[23] Koni describes the members of the gang in the following way:

> Seventeen-year-old Mikhailov . . . was wearing a brightly-colored silk shirt with a very low-cut neckline and belted with a silver cord, worn velveteen wide trousers, and boots with red tops; nineteen-year-old Mironov . . . was wearing an old frock coat that he had long grown out of, with the waist at his chest and sleeves ending a little below the elbows, and a velvet waistcoat that was too long for him.[24]

Mikhailov's effeminate outfit does not resemble Trishatov's impeccable clothing, but the description of Mironov is quite close to Dostoevsky's portrait of Trishatov's companion Andreev: "He was dressed very shabbily, in an old wadded greatcoat with a small, worn raccoon collar, which was too short for him—it was obviously a hand-me-down—and in nasty, almost peasant boots and with a terribly crumpled, discolored top hat on his head" (13:343).

The characters of Trishatov and Andreev, and the description of Lambert's blackmail gang, appear only in part 3 of *A Raw Youth*, which was published in *Notes of the Fatherland* (*Otechestvennye zapiski*) beginning in September 1875. According to the annotators of Dostoevsky's complete works, his serious work on part 3 began in April 1875 and continued through the summer (17:317). Given that Dostoevsky visited St. Petersburg in February 1875 (17:345), it is possible that he learned of the Mikhailov gang of homosexual blackmailers in time to incorporate them into the novel.

What I have said so far would seem to indicate that the images of homosexual behavior in *A Raw Youth* are not only heavily veiled but also strongly negative: conspiracy, rape, and blackmail belong to the typical stereotypes of the nineteenth century. But when we turn to Dostoevsky's depiction of Arkadii's own sexual development, we encounter a more complex, nuanced presentation. It is precisely Arkadii's lack of a "normal" heterosexual development that makes him such a compelling figure. Moreover, since the reader has developed an imaginative sympathy with Arkadii, when he expresses homoerotic feelings they become universal human feelings, not something alien and threatening.

One reason Dostoevsky can label his nineteen-year-old narrator a "podrostok" (literally, "adolescent") is that Arkadii is, at least physically, a virgin; he tells us that he learned about sex from his comrades at boarding school, but "only words, not the deed" (13:78). Part of the plot of *A Raw Youth* is the story of Arkadii's sometimes painful sexual education. In boarding school, a prime location for same-sex experimentation, Arkadii came under the influence of Lambert, a bigger, stronger, physically abusive classmate who used Arkadii "not just for taking off his boots" (13:27). It is clear that Arkadii has been verbally seduced by Lambert at a young age, as a memory of his childhood reveals. A conversation with Lambert about pistols and sabers takes a less innocent turn: "Lambert moved to his favorite conversation about a certain revolting subject [na izvestnuiu gadkuiu temu], and although I was secretly amazed at myself, I really liked to hear it" (13:273).[25]

One of Arkadii's confessions to the old Prince marks him as a textbook case of incipient homosexuality, according to the medical opinion of his time. A symptom of what Tarnovskii calls "congenital pederasty" is disgust at the sight of a naked woman: "For the congenital pederast all arousal disappears in the presence of women. The sight of an undressed young woman leaves him indifferent."[26] We learn early in the novel that Arkadii experiences a similar feeling; he amazes the old Prince by announcing, "When I was thirteen years old I saw female nakedness, the whole thing; since then I've been disgusted by it" (13:27). Not surprisingly, here again Lambert is involved. Arkadii tells of a day of dissipation spent with Lambert, during which Lambert accuses his own mother of sleeping with a priest, steals money from her, buys a canary and a rifle and blows the canary to bits, and finally brings Arkadii to a hotel and hires a prostitute: "That's when I saw all that . . . what I told you about" (13:27). When Lambert begins to beat the woman with a whip, Arkadii intervenes and Lambert stabs him with a fork. "Since then it's made me sick to think about nakedness; believe me, she was a beauty" (13:28).

With his usual frankness, Arkadii tells the reader of a much more recent experience that also has a homoerotic coloration. The incident took place a few months before the time of narration. Returning to Moscow on the train from the suburbs, Arkadii is strangely attracted to an unkempt young "former student" who spends the trip drinking vodka with lackeys and merchants. Arkadii quickly strikes up an acquaintance with the young man and they make a date to meet on Tverskoi Boulevard. Here they engage in a form of molestation that goes beyond normal male bonding to form a strong homoerotic connection between the two male participants. They choose an unaccompanied, respectable-looking woman and begin walking on either side of her. Their behavior is designed to torment her while denying her existence:

> With the utmost calm, as if we didn't notice her at all, we would begin to converse with each other in the most obscene way. We called things by their real names, with an air of utter serenity, as though it were quite proper, and we got into such subtleties, explaining various nasty and swinish activities [ob"iasniaia raznye skvernosti i svinstva], that the filthiest imagination of the filthiest debauchee couldn't have thought them up. (13:78)

It is not clear what is more important here: embarrassing the female victim or using her to heighten the excitement of the two men's sexual discourse. Soon Arkadii suggests an escalation in the game that graduates from words to deeds: "I told the student that Jean-Jacques Rousseau admits in his *Confessions* that when he was a youth he liked to hide behind a corner, expose the usually hidden parts of the body, and lie in wait for passing women in that state" (13:78). The student shows no interest in this new technique, and Arkadii soon breaks with him.

The episode with the student is a crude example of a particular sort of relationship that is typical for *A Raw Youth*. The configuration is a triangle consisting of two men and a woman, in which the most complex and emotionally charged relationship is between the two men; the woman serves merely as a pretext for intimate psychological games between the men. René Girard has of course explored in detail the phenomenon of triangular desire in his *Deceit, Desire, and the Novel,* which devotes sustained attention to Dostoevsky; Eve Kosofsky Sedgwick has emphasized the gender relations inherent in such triangles, examining among other things "the use of women as exchangeable, perhaps symbolic, property for the primary purpose of cementing the bonds of men with men."[27] To take as an example the classic triangle of Pechorin, Grushnitskii, and Princess Mary in Lermontov's *A Hero of Our Time,* a Girardian analysis would point out that Pechorin's desire for Mary is ignited by his knowledge that Grushnitskii desires her; his relationship with Grushnitskii the mediator is more intense than his conventional courtship of the Princess.[28] An analysis based on Sedgwick would go one step further to focus on the implicitly homoerotic bond that is thus formed between the two men in the erotic triangle. The most important such relationship in _A Raw Youth_ is among Arkadii, his father Versilov, and Katerina Nikolaevna, but other male characters like Lambert also intervene to siphon off emotional and sexual energy from the female object of Arkadii's desire. Such triangles are fairly common in nineteenth-century Russian literature, and Dostoevsky himself used them before _A Raw Youth_. But in no other Dostoevsky novel is the male-female connection as perfunctory, as vestigial, and as unconvincing as Arkadii's relationship with Katerina Nikolaevna. In fact, most of his meetings with her are not even narrated for us but merely summarized. By the end of _A Raw Youth_, Arkadii hints at a serious developing relationship with Katerina Nikolaevna (13:447–48).[29] The description of that relationship, however, much like Raskol'nikov's rather unconvincing Christian conversion, is deferred to "another story, a completely new story" (13:447). And just before this "happy" dénouement Arkadii has a tender and highly significant encounter with Trishatov.

The presentation of Trishatov's character is another instance of Dostoevsky's ambivalent attitude toward homosexuality in this novel. In some ways his portrayal of Trishatov adheres to the stereotypes of his time, and in other ways it departs from them strikingly. Alphonsine's disgust is what nineteenth-century Russian medical science considered to be the natural feminine reaction to a homosexual man. According to Tarnovskii, the homosexual "condemns himself to the greatest deprivation in life, not only to the deprivation of the love and attachment of women, but also to their complete loathing, contempt, and the arousal in them of a feeling of disgust."[30] But in his appearance Trishatov does not fit the stereotyped image promulgated by nineteenth-century Russian researchers. According to them, the typical homosexual man affects an excessively feminine appearance, with long ringlets, perfume, bracelets, cinched-in waist, and a hip-swinging walk.[31] Trishatov is "pretty" and "comely," but nothing in his dress, grooming, or walk is unmasculine. Dostoevsky excised an epithet that appears in the drafts, probably because it conformed too slavishly to the stereotyped image of the homosexual, who according to Tarnovskii is marked by "well-developed hips."[32] In Dostoevsky's notebooks the prototype of Trishatov is called "the fat-assed little prince" ("tolstozhopyi kniazek"); in the final text there is no such epithet, not even a euphemism.[33] Michel Foucault has discussed the way in which the nineteenth-century stereotypical portrait of the homosexual portrayed him as "a life form, and a morphology, with an indiscreet anatomy and possibly a mysterious physiology." Homosexuality was "written immodestly on his face and body because it was a secret that always gave itself away."[34] In the final text of _A Raw Youth_, Dostoevsky resists marking Trishatov with any "indiscreet" anatomical features, despite what the scientists of his time considered to be typical. Ultimately he seems to have relied on his personal experience, as reflected in the figure of Sirotkin, rather than on the stereotype. This is perhaps why Trishatov's homosexuality has escaped the notice of most Russian and Western scholars.[35]

Dostoevsky's presentation of Trishatov also eludes stereotype by enlisting the reader's sympathy for the character. When a homosexual couple appears in the officers' mess in Leo Tolstoy's 1874–77 novel *Anna Karenina*, Vronskii, the character through whom the scene is focalized, reacts with "a grimace of disgust" ("grimasa otvrashcheniia"); nothing in the text indicates that the narrator does not share that disgust.[36] But in *A Raw Youth*, the narrator Arkadii, with whom the reader feels an imaginative sympathy, is instantly attracted to Trishatov and treats him with an affectionate respect that wars with Trishatov's self-loathing. Arkadii's attraction to Trishatov inevitably communicates itself to the reader. And Alphonsine's disgust only enhances the reader's affinity for Trishatov, since she is perhaps the novel's most loathsome character. Her revulsion redounds to Trishatov's credit in our eyes.

When Arkadii meets Trishatov, the very linguistic texture of his narrative tells us that he is strongly attracted to the young man. He admires Trishatov's beauty repeatedly, and uses affectionate diminutives like "golosok," "lichiko," and "pal'chiki" (affectionate diminutives of "voice," "face," and "fingers") to describe him (13:343, 351).[37] Lambert takes Arkadii, Trishatov, and Trishatov's inseparable companion Andreev to a restaurant, where they meet a sinister figure referred to only as "riaboi" ("the pockmarked man"). Arkadii, despite his attraction to Trishatov, is uneasy about being seen in the "zagadochnaia kompaniia" ("enigmatic company") of Lambert's friends: "[The pockmarked man] could take me for one of the blackmailers accompanying Lambert"; "The thought that he would take me for one of Lambert's employees enraged me again" (13:349). But the evening soon develops into a tête-à-tête between Arkadii and Trishatov. Andreev causes a public scandal and Lambert drags him out of the restaurant. Arkadii says, "Trishatov started to run after them, but looked at me and stayed . . . He took his cup of coffee and moved from his place to sit next to me" (13:351). Arkadii is not at all averse to what amounts to an open flirtation. When Trishatov asks if Arkadii would receive him in his home, he replies, "O, prikhodite, ia vas dazhe liubliu" ("Oh, do come, I even like you a lot [or "love you"]," 13:352). After some personal conversation, Trishatov offers Arkadii two extraordinary literary fantasias, on Goethe's *Faust* and Dickens's *Old Curiosity Shop*, which I will discuss below. The climax of their encounter, when Trishatov's sad, champagne-enhanced memories get the better of him, is a moment of tenderness the likes of which we have not witnessed between Arkadii and Katerina Nikolaevna: "'Oh, Dolgorukii, you know, everyone has his memories!' And suddenly he lay his pretty little head on my shoulder and began to cry. I was very, very sorry for him." ("'Akh, Dolgorukii, znaete, u kazhdogo est' svoi vospominaniia!' I vdrug on sklonil svoiu khoroshen'kuiu golovku mne na plecho i—zaplakal. Mne stalo ochen', ochen' ego zhalko," 13:353.)

When Lambert turns his attention to Arkadii again he realizes that a dangerous intimacy has developed between him and Trishatov. He tries to discredit Trishatov in Arkadii's eyes by reminding Arkadii of Trishatov's untouchable status: "Trishatov was whispering to you about me: I saw—you were whispering to each other. You're a fool after that. Alphonsine is so disgusted when he comes near her . . . He's nasty. I'll tell you what kind of man he is" (13:356). Arkadii's response demonstrates that he is not repelled by Trishatov's "nastiness": "You said that already. All you can talk about is Alphonsine; you're terribly narrow" (13:356). At the end of the novel, even as Arkadii hints at a future relationship with Katerina Nikolaevna, he has not let go of Trishatov: "I long ago lost sight of Trishatov, no matter how I continue to try to track him down" (13:449).

Arkadii's experiments with nonstandard sexuality might seem at first to be yet another example of the novel's obsession with the disorder that threatens the Russian familial and social structure. Dostoevsky speaks in his notebooks of "decomposition" ("razlozhenie") as the "main visible idea of the novel" (16:17): "In everything is the idea of decomposition, because everyone is *separate* and there are no bonds remaining not only in the Russian family, but even simply among people" (16:16).[38] The novel explores all the forces of disorder at work in the modern world, with the disintegrative force of capitalism at the root of them all. As one might expect, Dostoevsky does seem to regard homosexuality as one of the forces of "decomposition" in the modern world, as the episodes of the old Prince, of Lambert, and of the molestation game suggest. Yet in *A Raw Youth,* homosexuality is not prosecuted with the same fury as adultery, capitalism, and child abandonment. The only clearly homosexual character, Trishatov, is treated with tact, sympathy, and an admirable effort to avoid stereotype. The moments of tender friendship and concern between Trishatov and Andreev or Trishatov and Arkadii stand out from the generally bleak landscape of human relationships in *A Raw Youth.* Homosexuality can lead to the creation of "accidental families" in the best sense, families based on elective affinities, not on blood. Thus homosexuality should not, in my view, be classed *only* with the forces of disorder in *A Raw Youth.*[39]

To move from the sociohistorical level to the aesthetic level, homoerotic desire also plays an important role in the narrative construction of the novel. What would today be called Arkadii's sexual "questioning" might fruitfully be regarded as analogous to his attempts to find a nonstandard literary discourse. On the first page of *A Raw Youth,* Arkadii vows to avoid all "literary beauties" (13:5); the measure of his success is the very low popularity of his narrative among critics and general readers. D. S. Likhachev has called the novel "a protest against literature and self-conscious literariness" ("protest protiv literatury i literaturshchiny").[40] Arkadii offers explicit support for the idea that his quest for literary originality is of the same order as the non-standard approach to sexuality we see in his expressed aversion to female sexuality (nudity) and his affinity for Trishatov. When he tries to explain what attracts him to the student in the train, he defines it as "an extremely vivid violation of generally accepted and officialized proprieties" ("slishkom iarkoe narushenie obshchepriniatykh i okazenivshikhsia prilichii," 13:78). Their molestation game is "something original, somehow exceeding the bounds of the usual official conventions" (13:78). These two phrases could be applied to Arkadii's narrative, which fails to obey most of the accepted, officialized conventions of sustaining reader interest, developing an intriguing plot, or achieving a pleasing formal symmetry.

Dostoevsky provides multiple possible motivations for the ineptitude of Arkadii's narrative. Most obviously, his chaotic narrative is motivated by his youth and impetuousness. Nathan Rosen argues that Dostoevsky re-creates and regenerates himself through "the marvelously bumptious, spluttering, gawky prose of Dolgoruky . . . The chaotic structure of *A Raw Youth* was the sacrifice that Dostoevsky willingly made so that he might create his new hero Dolgoruky."[41] Another factor is Arkadii's role as an aspiring blackmailer. The blackmailer has a story to tell—in Arkadii's case, the "document" revealing Katerina Nikolaevna's betrayal of her father, which he carries around sewed in his jacket—but the moment he tells his story he loses all his power over his victim. In his study *George Eliot and Blackmail,* Alexander Welsh draws a metaphorical connection that is relevant to Arkadii's peculiar narrative, which seems not really focused on communicating with the reader. In Welsh's view, the activity of the blackmailer is in a way contradictory to that of the writer:

> Though a detective is apparently allied with a novelist or storyteller in seeking to make known the original action, the blackmailer is opposed, threatening to reveal but also contriving to conceal secrets. Moreover, if storytelling is a pleasurable, social, and in some sense healthful activity, then blackmail, threatening to tell a story but at the same time not wishing to, is in some sense pathological.[42]

A third factor conditioning Arkadii's narrative is his complicated relationship to the Russian aristocracy. In the remarkable commentary on Arkadii's book by his former benefactor and tutor Nikolai Semyonovich, a commentary that ends *Dostoevsky's* book, pleasing aesthetic form is identified with the Russian hereditary nobility: "Only in this Russian cultural type is it possible to find at least the appearance of beautiful order and the beautiful impression which is so necessary in a novel for producing a refined effect on the reader" ("Lish' v odnom etom tipe kul'turnykh russkikh liudei vozmozhen khot' vid krasivogo poriadka i krasivogo vpechatleniia, stol' neobkhodimogo v romane dlia iziashchnogo vozdeistviia na chitatelia," 13:453). Although Arkadii spends much of his time with the old and young Princes Sokol'skii, he feels as much hostility to them as attraction, thanks to his own illegitimate status. As I discussed earlier, Arkadii smarts painfully under the irony of having inherited the brilliant Dolgorukii name from his legal father the serf, not his biological father the aristocrat. Arkadii's rejection of what he calls "literary beauties" is also a renunciation of his biological father's legacy of membership in the Russian nobility.

But the most important factor conditioning Arkadii's narrative, in my view, is his experimentation with nonstandard forms of desire, and here we must move beyond Arkadii's psychology to Dostoevsky's larger designs. Let us return to the triangular structure of relationships that marks the novel. In a triangle like that of Arkadii, Lambert, and Katerina Nikolaevna, if we look along the conventional male-female axis for narrative and psychological energy, we will be disappointed. The real action is between the two males. The same redirection of energy can be observed on the metaliterary level. Dostoevsky chooses an incompetent narrator because the true intensity here is not in the conventional relationship of narrator and implied reader, but of narrator and implied author. For the reader familiar with Dostoevsky's other texts, *A Raw Youth* is a compendium of Dostoevsky's lifelong obsessions, in which he revisits and rewrites key literary texts, his own included. This is a matter not just of returning to old *themes,* but of specific references to earlier Dostoevskian *texts.* The reader of *A Raw Youth* is not excluded from this process, but he will be frustrated unless he finds a way to tap into the vital narrator-implied author relationship.

Arkadii's conversation with Trishatov offers one example of what I am talking about: a scene in which a character's reference to a work of world literature turns out also to be a self-reference on the part of Dostoevsky. Left alone with Arkadii in the restaurant, Trishatov suddenly begins a discussion of art. First he outlines a fragment from an opera he would like to write based on Goethe's *Faust,* then he recalls a scene from a favorite work read in childhood, Dickens's *Old Curiosity Shop.* For the purposes of my argument, Trishatov's citation of *The Old Curiosity Shop* is more important than his reference to *Faust,* but a discussion of the latter is in order, since it illuminates both Trishatov's appealing character and Dostoevsky's complex technique of quotation.

Trishatov's plan for a Faust opera is worth quoting in its entirety:

Listen, do you like music? I really love it. I'll play you something when I come to see you. I play the piano very well and I studied it for a very long time. I studied it seriously. If I were to compose an opera, you know, I would take the plot from *Faust*.

I really love that theme. I'm always composing the scene in the cathedral, just in my head, I imagine it. A Gothic cathedral, the interior, choirs, hymns, Gretchen enters, and you know—medieval choirs, so that one can just hear the fifteenth century. Gretchen is in anguish, first it's a recitative, quiet but horrible, excruciating, and the choirs resound gloomily, sternly, impassively: "Dies irae, dies illa!" And suddenly—the voice of the Devil, the song of the Devil. He is invisible, it's just his song, along with the hymns, together with the hymns, it almost coincides with them, but at the same time it's something completely different—I have to do that somehow or other. The song is long, unwearying, it's a tenor, it has to be a tenor. It begins quietly, tenderly: "Do you remember, Gretchen, how you, still innocent, still a child, would come with your mama to this cathedral and would prattle the prayers from the old book?" But the song gets ever stronger, ever more passionate, ever more impetuous; the notes get higher: there are tears and an unceasing, hopeless anguish in them, and finally despair: "There is no forgiveness, Gretchen, there is no forgiveness for you here!" Gretchen wants to pray, but from her breast there burst only screams—you know, when you have convulsions from the tears in your breast—and the song of Satan still doesn't fall silent, still keeps piercing the soul ever deeper, like a razor's edge, it gets ever higher—and suddenly breaks off almost in a scream: "All is ended, you are damned!" Gretchen falls to her knees, clasps her hands before her—and now comes her prayer, something very short, half-recitative, but naive, without any ornamentation, something medieval in the highest degree, four lines, just four lines in all—Stradella has a few notes like that—and with the last note she faints! There's a commotion. They lift her, carry her—and now suddenly a thundering chorus. It is like a thunderclap of voices, an inspired, triumphant, overpowering chorus, something like our "Dori-no-si-ma chin-mi" ["That we may receive the King of all, Who is invisibly upborne by angelic hosts"]—so that everything is shaken to its foundations—and everything passes into an enraptured, rejoicing, universal exclamation: "Hosanna!" as if it were the cry of the whole universe, and they carry her, carry her, and that's when the curtain falls! No, you know, if I could, I would really do something! Only I can't do anything any more, but I just daydream all the time, daydream all the time; all my life has turned into nothing but a daydream, I even daydream at night. (13:352–53)[43]

Trishatov's scene is based mainly on one scene from Goethe, "Cathedral," and the ending of the final scene of part 1, "Dungeon," in which Mephistopheles' statement that Gretchen is damned is answered by a voice from above, "She is saved." Steven Paul Scher has explored in German literature what he calls "verbal music," which he defines as "any literary presentation . . . of existing or fictitious musical compositions."[44] Trishatov's description of his Faust opera employs several of the devices Scher has identified as characteristic of verbal music, including linguistic approximation of musical effects and devices (repetition, verbal crescendo leading to a climactic fortissimo, etc.); projection of music through technical vocabulary ("recitative," "ornamentation," etc.); creation of "musical" motion within a "musical landscape" (here the Gothic cathedral with its familiar and impressive acoustic qualities); and invocation of supernatural beings in order "to communicate the unearthly, metaphysical quality inherent in music" (here, the Devil himself is invoked, although in *Faust* he is called more ambiguously "Evil Spirit").[45]

Critics have had interestingly divergent reactions to Trishatov's *Faust*. A. Gozenpud, for example, gives it high marks but attributes the scene's success to the author, not the character: "Not a single composer who has treated the scene in the cathedral has such a wealth of musical images and such dramatic contrasts as Dostoevsky, from the austere sounds of the 'Dies irae' to the rejoicing 'Hosanna.'"[46] Horst-Jürgen Gerigk, on the other hand, attributes the scene to Trishatov but considers it a tasteless sentimentalization of Goethe.[47] In terms of artistic quality, both critics have a point. The scene is tasteless and sentimental, but "good taste" is not an important aesthetic category for Dostoevsky, and he is certainly not afraid of sentimentality. Moreover, the Gretchen tragedy itself is not a model of good taste, nor is it devoid of sentimentality. We can also agree with Gozenpud that Trishatov's conception is highly original in the context of the opera of its time. The fragmentary, allusive character of Trishatov's scene and its striking juxtaposition of contrasting elements, like the Latin "Dies irae" with the Orthodox hymn "Kheruvimskaia," make it seem more modernist than operas contemporary to *A Raw Youth*. Perhaps most original is Trishatov's insistence on a high tenor to sing the "song of the Devil." In the two major nineteenth-century Faust operas, those of Gounod (1859) and Boito (1868), and in Berlioz's dramatic legend *La damnation de Faust* (1846), Mephistopheles is sung by a bass.[48] Trishatov's innovative vocal casting, which works against cliché, was to be realized only in the twentieth century, in Ferruccio Busoni's *Doktor Faust* (1914–24). Arnold Schoenberg, in *Moses und Aron* (1931–32), and Benjamin Britten, in *The Turn of the Screw* (1954), also used mellifluous, melismatic tenors as the voices of seductive complicity with evil. It may be that Trishatov (as distinct from Dostoevsky) chooses to give the Devil a tenor voice as a way of increasing his effeminacy, thus projecting another, negative alter ego for himself in addition to the sympathetic figure of Gretchen.

One can understand not only the critics' disagreement over the quality of Trishatov's scene, which is both vulgarly over-the-top and compellingly dramatic and fresh, but also their confusion over just who is the primary author, Trishatov or Dostoevsky. On the one hand, Trishatov's *Faust* both illuminates his character and is a believable product of his psyche. On the other hand, it resonates with the plot of *A Raw Youth* in ways that could not have been contemplated by Trishatov.

To deal first with the Faust opera as a product of Trishatov's imagination: Trishatov reveals here that he has the mind of an artist, that he rises above the sordid circumstances of his life through the exercise of his fantasy. He is an artist manqué, though; the opera exists only as a daydream, and will probably never be realized.[49] The most telling words Trishatov speaks are, "If only I could, I would do something!" ("esli by ia mog, ia by chto-nibud' sdelal!" 13:353). Both Trishatov's latent power and his fatal weakness are embodied in his opera plan.

Trishatov's choice of subject is consistent with his character. He clearly identifies with Gretchen in her loss of innocence and fear of condemnation. Like Gretchen, Trishatov has succumbed to the temptations of the flesh and is ostracized by society; like hers, his sin is condemned by his religion. Goethe's scene in the cathedral includes a moment not quoted directly by Trishatov, but clearly relevant to his story. The Evil Spirit says to Gretchen,

Ihr Antlitz wenden
Verklärte von dir ab.
Die Hände dir zu reichen,
Schauert's den Reinen.[50]

The blessed ones avert their countenances from you. The pure ones shudder to give you their hands [translation mine].

Later, in the dungeon scene, Gretchen asks Faust, "How can it be that you do not shun me?" ("Wie kommt es, daß du dich vor mir nicht scheust?")[51] Alphonsine's rejection of physical contact with Trishatov is a parody of the shunning of Gretchen by the saints, and Gretchen's fear that Faust will shun her too is echoed in Trishatov's fear that Arkadii will not receive him in his house.[52] It is no wonder that Trishatov is obsessed with Gretchen's story of sin and ultimate salvation.

But Dostoevsky also has his reasons for evoking *Faust*, which go beyond anything the character Trishatov could be aware of. Gretchen has conceived an illegitimate child, which she eventually kills. Her brother Valentin fights a duel with Faust and Mephistopheles to defend the honor of his name, and dies cursing his sister as a whore. Arkadii finds himself in Valentin's situation, but rejects Valentin's response to it. Arkadii learns that his beloved sister Liza is pregnant by the young Prince Sokol'skii, who gives him the news himself:

> If someone had told me ahead of time and asked, "What would I do to him at that minute?"—I would probably have answered that I would tear him to pieces. But something completely different happened, and not by my will at all: I suddenly covered my face with both hands and began to sob bitterly. (13:236)

There is a cynical, despairing aspect to Arkadii's refusal to judge his sister: in a world of "accidental families," the idea of defending the honor of one's name has a hollow sound, as Arkadii thinks: "Why am I bothering? What's it to me? They're all like that or almost. What does it matter that it happened to Liza? What, am I supposed to save the 'honor of the family' or something?" (13:240). Still, the affection and respect with which Arkadii treats his sister contrast favorably with Valentin's violent condemnation of Gretchen. Finally, the evocation of Gretchen's neonaticide casts a somber light on the outcome of Liza's pregnancy: after the death of the child's father in prison awaiting trial for fraud, Liza sinks into a depression, "accidentally" falls down a staircase (the last three steps), and miscarries (13:450–51). Trishatov's evocation of the Gretchen tragedy in *Faust* helps to provide a serious underpinning to the sometimes weightless adventures of Arkadii and his family, which are narrated in an otherwise cursory way.

Yet another parallel between Goethe's *Faust* and *A Raw Youth* concerns Trishatov but is part of Dostoevsky's designs, not his. Homoerotic desire plays an important role at the end of part 2 of *Faust*. Faust has died, and Mephistopheles prepares to do battle with the envoys of heaven over Faust's soul. Suddenly Mephistopheles is overcome by lust for the angels:

> Hat mich ein Fremdes durch und durch gedrungen?
> Ich mag sie gerne sehn, die allerliebsten Jungen;
>
> . . .
>
> Die Wetterbuben, die ich hasse,
> Sie kommen mir doch gar zu lieblich vor!—
> Ihr schönen Kinder, laßt mich wissen:
> Seid ihr nicht auch von Luzifers Geschlecht?
> Ihr seid so hübsch, fürwahr ich möcht' euch küssen,
> Mir ist's als kämt ihr eben recht.
> Es ist mir so behaglich, so natürlich,
> Als hätt' ich euch schon tausendmal gesehn;
> So heimlich-kätzenhaft begierlich;

Mit jedem Blick aufs neue schöner schön.
O nähern euch, o gönnt mir *einen* Blick![53]

Has some strange spirit gone through and through me? I like the look of them, these darling boys . . . Those cunning youngsters attract me, though I hate them. You beautiful children, tell me, aren't you too descendants of Lucifer? You seem to suit me, you're so lovely, so kissable. It's all so easy, so natural, so strangely kittenishly lustful, as if I'd seen you lots of times before. And you're so enticing, you're getting prettier all the time. Oh, come nearer, oh, let me have *one* look![54]

Mephistopheles' desires are expressed graphically by the climax of the scene:

Auch könntet ihr anständig-nackter gehen,
Das lange Faltenhemd ist übersittlich—
Sie wenden sich—von hinten anzusehen!—
Die Racker sind doch gar zu appetitlich![55]

I'd like to see you not so fully dressed. It would become you better. Those long robes are prudish. Now the rascals are turning round. My, from behind aren't they appetizing?[56]

Distracted by his lust, Mephistopheles lets the angels get away with Faust's undeserving soul. In the final scene of part 2, the young angels celebrate their use of love against the powers of evil:

Statt gewohnter Höllenstrafen
Fühlten Liebesqual die Geister;
Selbst der alte Satansmeister
War von spitzer Pein durchdrungen.[57]

Instead of the usual punishments of Hell the spirits felt pangs of love; even the old master of devils was pierced by sharp agony [translation mine].

The angels' use of sexual wiles leads Mephistopheles to number them among the demons: "You call us the damned, but it's you who are the real witch-masters, seducing both sexes at once" ("Ihr scheltet uns verdammte Geister / Und seid die wahren Hexenmeister; / Denn ihr verführet Mann und Weib").[58]

At the end of *A Raw Youth* Trishatov plays a role parallel to that of the boy angels in *Faust:* using information obtained by means of his personal charms, he helps Arkadii to save the undeserving Versilov from committing murder and suicide. Lambert has stolen from Arkadii the document incriminating Katerina Nikolaevna and has joined forces with Versilov, who like his son hopes to force Katerina Nikolaevna into a sexual relationship. Trishatov comes to warn Arkadii of the plot, which he has learned about from his new protector, the acquaintance of Lambert's known only as "riaboi" ("the pockmarked man," 13:406). Trishatov's chain of ideas strongly hints at his relationship with his new master: "Consciously, by my own free will, I have agreed to every kind of nastiness and to such baseness that I'm ashamed even to utter it in your house. We're with the pockmarked man now" (13:406). Arkadii is glad to see Trishatov and tries to get him to sit down, but Trishatov refuses. Trishatov is in a ragged old coat because Lambert took his fur coat away, but he expects new clothes from another quarter: "You see, Dolgorukii, I'm acting bold to everyone and I'm going to go on a spree now. Soon they'll make me an even better fur coat, and I will ride in a carriage with trotters. But I will know secretly that after all I wouldn't sit down at your place because I condemned myself so, because I'm base before you" (13:406).

Trishatov condemns himself, but Dostoevsky grants him the opportunity to play an angelic role in the finale, like the captivating boy angels who save Faust's soul by seducing Mephistopheles. Arkadii is on his way to Lambert's apartment, where Alphonsine has falsely told him that the confrontation between Katerina Nikolaevna and Versilov is to take place. Arkadii speaks of Trishatov's intervention as a heavenly visitation: "But God preserved us all and saved us when everything was already hanging by a thread. We hadn't covered a quarter of the way when I suddenly heard a shout behind me: someone was calling me by name. I looked around—Trishatov was trying to overtake us in a cab" (13:441–42). Trishatov has been told by his new protector, the pockmarked man, that Katerina Nikolaevna is to meet Versilov and Lambert at the home of Arkadii's aunt, not at Lambert's as Alphonsine claimed. Thus Arkadii and Trishatov are able to stop Versilov at the last moment from committing the crimes of Shakespeare's Othello and Dostoevsky's Rogozhin, as he tries to kill Katerina Nikolaevna and then himself.

Now I would like to return to Trishatov's second literary excursus, which follows immediately after his speech about *Faust*. His second pseudo-quotation, from Dickens's *Old Curiosity Shop*, is, like *Faust*, important both for Trishatov's psychology and for Dostoevsky's larger designs. I will quote the passage in its entirety:

> "Oh, Dolgorukii, have you read *The Old Curiosity Shop* by Dickens?"
> "I have; what about it?"
> "Do you remember . . . Wait, I'll drink another glass—Do you remember

that one passage at the end, when that crazy old man and that charming thirteen-year-old girl, his granddaughter, after their fantastic flight and wanderings, have finally found shelter somewhere at the ends of England, near some medieval Gothic cathedral, and the little girl has found some kind of job, she shows the cathedral to visitors . . . And at one point the sun is going down, and that child is on the porch of the cathedral, all bathed in the last rays, she stands and looks at the sunset with quiet pensive contemplation in her childish soul, an amazed soul, as if faced with some enigma, because both one and the other are like an enigma, after all—the sun, as the idea of God, and the cathedral, as the idea of man . . . isn't that right? Oh, I don't know how to express it, but God loves those first ideas of children . . . And there, next to her, on the steps, that insane old man, the grandfather, looks at her with a fixed stare . . . You know, there's nothing so special in this little scene of Dickens, nothing at all, but you'll never forget it, and it remained all over Europe—why? That's real beauty! That's innocence! Eh! I don't know what's in it, but it's good. I used to read novels all the time in the gymnasium. You know, I have a sister in the country, only a year older than me . . . Oh, now everything's been sold and there's no village any more! We used to sit together on the veranda under our old linden trees, and read that novel, and the sun was also setting, and suddenly we would stop reading and tell each other that we too would be good, that we too would be beautiful—I was preparing for the university then and . . . Oh, Dolgorukii, you know, everyone has his memories!" (13:353)

The scene remembered by Trishatov is linked to the scene from *Faust* by the setting, a Gothic cathedral. But the theme of innocence, and Trishatov's identification with a female heroine, also link the two literary memories. In Gretchen, Trishatov has a model of a sinner repentant and forgiven; in Nell, the heroine of *The Old Curiosity Shop*, he tries to recapture his childhood self, when he and his sister could dream of a life of goodness. Sergei Durylin has claimed a deep significance for Trishatov's ability to connect the precious memory from literature with a memory from life: "Precisely this memory— the story of the slanting rays—casts on Trishatov that consummating reflection of sadness and pain, bearing witness to a profoundly injured existence, which makes his image noble and truthful."[59]

As with *Faust*, if we look at parts of *The Old Curiosity Shop* not quoted by Trishatov, we find connections to *A Raw Youth* that could not have been contemplated by the character. In the first part of *A Raw Youth*, Arkadii confides his cherished "idea": his plan to become a Rothschild. His inspiration is the typical newspaper story of the ragged beggar who upon his death is discovered to have amassed a fortune. Arkadii believes that self-deprivation and stubborn saving up of pennies is a "mathematically guaranteed" route to wealth (13:66–67). Later this obsession is replaced by gambling: "I flew to the roulette table as if my whole salvation, my whole way out, were concentrated in it" (13:265). Both of Arkadii's obsessions are reminiscent of Little Nell's grandfather in *The Old Curiosity Shop*. He lives in poverty and dresses in rags, but those around him suspect that he has a secret hoard of money. As the narrator says, "I could form no comprehension of his character, unless he were one of those miserable wretches who, having made gain the sole end and object of their lives, and having succeeded in amassing great riches, are constantly tortured by the dread of poverty, and beset by fears of loss and ruin."[60] Grandfather turns out to be genuinely poor; his mysterious hints at a prosperous future for Nell refer to his hopes of winning a fortune at cards, what Dickens calls "the old distorted faith."[61] Like Arkadii, Grandfather sees his "whole salvation" in gambling, and leaves Nell alone night after night as he foolishly tries to win her a fortune but instead ruins them both.

Trishatov's recollection of the scene from *The Old Curiosity Shop* resonates with *A Raw Youth* in yet another way: through its use of the sunset as a complex symbol of man's relation to God and the universe. The setting sun is a vitally important image for Dostoevsky, as Durylin and most recently Liza Knapp have shown, and in *A Raw Youth* it plays a major role.[62] The problem is that the setting sun plays a very minor role in *The Old Curiosity Shop*, and the scene closest to the one remembered or rather invented by Trishatov takes place in the morning. Not only is it morning, but Nell is in the church tower, not on the porch, and her grandfather is not present.[63] There are only two passages in *The Old Curiosity Shop* in which the sunset is described, and both precede unpleasant scenes of Grandfather's gambling obsession. The positive aura that Dostoevsky gives the setting sun is absent in *The Old Curiosity Shop*.

There *is* a novel which begins and ends with key sunset scenes and which, like *The Old Curiosity Shop,* has a thirteen-year-old heroine named Nelli who has a crazy, poverty-stricken grandfather; who is threatened by the pedophilic advances of a repulsive man; who regards beggary and homelessness as a kind of refuge and escape; and who dies as soon as she reaches a stable home. That novel is Dostoevsky's own *The Insulted and Injured* (1861).[64] The novel begins with the narrator's meditation on the sunset:

> I love the March sun in St. Petersburg, especially the sunset, of course, on a clear, frosty evening. The whole street suddenly gleams, bathed in bright light. All the houses seem to suddenly flash with light. Their gray, yellow, and dirty-green hues lose for a moment all their gloominess; it is as if one's soul grows clearer, as if you shudder or someone shoves you with their elbow. A new view, new ideas . . . It's amazing what a single ray of sun can do to the soul of a person! (3:169)

At the end of the novel little Nelli has her last conversation with the narrator while looking at the rays of the setting sun. So the pensive contemplation of the sunset that Trishatov remembers comes from Dostoevsky's own post-Siberian *hommage* to *The Old Curiosity Shop*, not from *The Old Curiosity Shop* itself.

This third, phantom text adds new elements to the intertextual relations evoked by Trishatov. Illegitimacy, loss of birthright, and "accidental families" do not play a role in *The Old Curiosity Shop;* Nell Trent has not been abandoned by her parents, they have died, and she has not been wrongly deprived of fortune and status. But Dostoevsky's Nelli is the biological daughter of the wealthy and evil Prince Valkovskii—possibly his legitimate daughter—and the life of misery and poverty she leads is caused by his malevolence and neglect. Nelli the unrecognized daughter of a Russian nobleman is closer kin to the characters in *A Raw Youth* than is Nell Trent the poor English girl. *The Insulted and Injured* also provides a secret link between Trishatov's two quotations. There is no reference to *Faust* in *The Old Curiosity Shop*, but in the opening scene of *The Insulted and Injured* we find the following passage. The narrator sees an old man (he turns out to be Nelli's grandfather) with a very old dog:

> This unfortunate dog also seemed to be about eighty years old; yes, it had to be. In the first place, it looked older than dogs ever get to be, and in the second place, why was it that the first time I saw it I immediately had the idea that this dog was not like all other dogs; that it was an unusual dog; that there had to be something fantastic and enchanted about it; that perhaps it was a kind of Mephistopheles in the guise of a dog and that its fate was connected by some mysterious, unknown means to the fate of its master. (3:171)

This of course alludes to the first appearance of Mephistopheles to Faust in the guise of a black poodle.[65] Thus through Trishatov's unwitting evocation of *The Insulted and Injured*, Dostoevsky the author intervenes in Trishatov's monologue to provide the unspoken link between *Faust* and *The Old Curiosity Shop*, the two apparently unrelated texts Trishatov quotes.

In *A Raw Youth* the true intensity in the relationship narrator-author-reader (or character-author-reader) is between narrator (or character) and implied author, not narrator and implied reader. The story of Trishatov offers an important example, not only of unconventional human desire, but of this metaliterary structure. When Trishatov quotes *The Old Curiosity Shop*, as we have seen, he is also unwittingly quoting Dostoevsky. We are not meant to think that Trishatov has read *The Insulted and Injured;* we sense that the implied author Dostoevsky is speaking through Trishatov to add a new, author-referential dimension to his quotation. This double type of quotation, in which a character (or the narrator) explicitly and consciously alludes to a literary work while implicitly and unconsciously alluding to an earlier work by *Dostoevsky,* is characteristic of *A Raw Youth.* If conventional male-female desire has its analogue in the conventional relationship between narrator and implied reader, unconventional same-sex desire has its metaliterary analogue in the relationship between narrator and implied author.

Trishatov's unwitting evocation of *The Insulted and Injured* is one example of this type of quotation, but there are more important ones, which there is not room to discuss here but which may ultimately provide a key to a more comprehensive interpretation of *A Raw Youth.* Most centrally, in each of the three parts of *A Raw Youth,* the narrator explicitly evokes a text by Pushkin while implicitly and unconsciously evoking a text by Dostoevsky. Part 1 is involved with Pushkin's *Covetous Knight* and Dostoevsky's *Crime and Punishment;* part 2, with Pushkin's "Queen of Spades" and Dostoevsky's *The Gambler;* and part 3, with Pushkin's *Table-Talk* aphorism "Othello was not jealous, he was trusting . . ." and Dostoevsky's *Idiot.*[66] One of the ways to find the aesthetic unity of *A Raw Youth* is to read it as a conversation with Dostoevsky's earlier literary self. Since Dostoevsky most often uses Arkadii to replay his melodramas and tragedies of the 1860s in a mode of farcical anticlimax, one could read the title *A Raw Youth* as referring to the younger Dostoevsky. Arkadii's narrative can then be read as a parody of Dostoevsky's own breathless narrative style.[67]

On the first page of *A Raw Youth,* Arkadii says, "I am just noting down events, avoiding everything superfluous with all my might, and especially avoiding literary beauties; a writer [literator] writes for thirty years and in the end doesn't know at all why he wrote for all those years [dlia chego on pisal stol'ko let]" (13:5). If we take extratextual evidence into account, we can read the implied author Dostoevsky as speaking along with Arkadii in the second part of this sentence. Those "thirty years" mark the span between Dostoevsky's literary debut in 1846 and the publication of *A Raw Youth* as a separate edition in 1876. In *A Raw Youth,* the callow, incompetent narrator is helping the writer to figure out "why he wrote for all those years."

Here Nathan Rosen's insight, that by writing *A Raw Youth* Dostoevsky was regenerating himself, can be of use. Lawrence Lipking has studied the life of the poet in terms of how the poet defines himself at crucial moments of his career, through particular types of works that Lipking labels "initiation," "harmonium," and "tombeau."[68] The "initiation," in which the poet refreshes and deepens his work by rereading his own earlier works, is apposite to Dostoevsky's task in writing *A Raw Youth.* (Although Lipking restricts himself to poets, I see no reason why the life of the novelist should not follow a similar path.) As Lipking writes, "A poet who wishes to grow must learn to read his own early work, to explore its secret life and hidden meanings."[69] The "initiation," despite its name, does not have to come near the beginning of a career; Lipking shows Yeats in his fifties, the stage of life at which Dostoevsky wrote *A Raw Youth*, creating such a work in *Per Amica Silentia Lunae:* "Time works against the aging poet; not many renew themselves. Is it possible that initiation happens only to the young? Will a new life dawn for the imagination simply because the imagination requires it?"[70] The test of the success of an initiation work, as Lipking sees it, is whether it fulfills its own prophecy of greater works to come: "Every work in the form must issue in a greater work, proving that its mastery of interpretation can be turned to account."[71] On this level if on no other, *A Raw Youth* can be considered a success. It does indeed contain a prophecy of greater works to come; Nikolai Semyonovich speaks of Arkadii's chaotic notes as material for a "future artistic work, for a future picture—of a disorderly but already past epoch" (13:455).[72] Nikolai Semyonovich is looking well beyond the immediate future, but in terms of Dostoevsky's own career the harvest sown by *A Raw Youth* is reaped much sooner, in his supreme achievement, *The Brothers Karamazov.*

In *A Raw Youth* Dostoevsky is interested in nonstandard, unconventional trajectories of desire. Throughout the novel Arkadii tries to convince us (and himself) that he is consumed by his desire for Katerina Nikolaevna, while his narration is in fact preoccupied with Lambert or with his father Versilov. On the metaliterary level, an analogous process takes place: the conventional connection between narrator and reader is subordinated to the interplay between narrator and implied author, an interplay of which the narrator is of course unaware. Arkadii, like the Underground Man, is extremely conscious of his potential reader, whom he constantly addresses as "chitatel'" ("reader"), anticipating the reader's responses and either apologizing for or boasting of the incoherence of his narrative. Arkadii flirts with the implied reader and tries to impress him—and Arkadii's misogynistic tirades seem to imply that he thinks of the reader as a "him" who might sympathize, not a "her" who would surely reject his arguments. But at the same time he denies the implied (and the real) reader what the reader actually needs—an engaging and minimally coherent narrative. The voice of Nikolai Semyonovich, which replaces Arkadii's voice to end the novel, acknowledges this when he speaks of the 450-page work as only notes for a future novel, "in spite of all their chaotic and accidental character" ("nesmotria na vsiu ikh khaotichnost' i sluchainost'," 13:455). In the final analysis Arkadii seems to lose his autonomy as the creator of this narrative project. The young Arkadii, breathless and seemingly incompetent as a writer, is the vehicle for the retrospective and prospective projects of the mature author Dostoevsky. Just as Arkadii appears ready to enter into a conventional male-female relationship with Katerina Nikolaevna at the end of the novel, Dostoevsky, as Nikolai Semyonovich's final critique would indicate, is ready to return to a more conventional mode of narration in his subsequent work. In *A Raw Youth*, to use Lipking's phrase, Dostoevsky "learned to read his own early work," thus making it possible to grow into the writer who wrote *The Brothers Karamazov*, in which the narrator-reader connection is reaffirmed with ferocious intensity.[73]

Different as it is from *A Raw Youth*, *The Brothers Karamazov* does not entirely abandon the concerns of that "failed" novel. Like Arkadii, Alyosha Karamazov is a young man who has not yet experienced sex as a physical act but who has to cope with it as an imaginative obsession and a spiritual and moral problem. The next chapter considers the ways in which Dostoevsky deals in his last two novels with the vulnerability of the virgin—not the female child, as in his earlier works, but the young man on the brink of maturity.

Chapter Four

The Sexuality of the Male Virgin in
A Raw Youth and *The Brothers Karamazov*

IVAN KARAMAZOV ASKS, "Who doesn't desire the death of his father?" thus seeming to anticipate Freud's Oedipal theory of human sexual development. But one must remember that Ivan speaks out of madness and error, and that the novel ends by emphasizing the love that exists between fathers and sons, not the hatred and rivalry. In pre-Freudian thought about sexuality, and in Dostoevsky's created world, there are no master narratives of human desire—there are only case studies. There are temperamental quirks, moral choices, and, especially in Dostoevsky, divine intervention. A close examination and reconstruction of the pre-Freudian, nineteenth-century European understanding of sexuality is central to a better understanding of Dostoevsky's artistic representation of human desire.[1] This chapter will deal with two of Dostoevsky's case studies, the sexual development of Arkadii Dolgorukii and Alyosha Karamazov.

As we saw in chapter 2, the corruption of female innocence is a major theme in Dostoevsky's novels, where the rape of female children is a haunting, obsessively recurring motif. But in his last two novels Dostoevsky was also concerned with depicting the way in which the virginity of young men is assaulted by the world. In *A Writer's Diary* for January 1876, Dostoevsky described Arkadii, the hero of his 1875 novel *A Raw Youth*, in terms that emphasize the themes of virginity and corruption:

> I took a soul that was sinless, but already befouled by the terrible possibility of depravity, by an early hatred caused by his insignificance and "accidental" birth, and by that breadth with which a still-chaste soul already consciously admits vice into his thoughts, already nurtures it in his heart, feasts his eyes upon it in his shamefaced, but already daring and passionate daydreams—all this being left exclusively on his own strength and his own powers of understanding, and also, it's true, on God. (22:8)

There are several ideas in this passage that are important both for Arkadii Dolgorukii and for the ostensible hero of *The Brothers Karamazov* (*Brat'ia Karamazovy*), Alyosha Karamazov, the course of whose sexual development, I will argue, is being unobtrusively narrated alongside the more lurid story of his father's murder. First is the idea that physical virginity does not coincide with moral virginity, that the sexually inexperienced person can yet have a rich and even debauched sexual life. The second, related idea is the power of dreams (mechty) to create such a life. Finally, there is the idea that God may play a role in helping the individual in his struggle with what Dostoevsky calls "depravity."

How does depravity—"razvrat"—enter the virginal soul? Through the ears. Arkadii has been educated in a typical Russian boarding school, where conversations "on a certain nasty subject" (13:273) are the norm. By the age of nineteen he knows about "various nasty and swinish things" that "the filthy imagination of the filthiest debauchee could not dream up" (13:78). "I of course acquired all this knowledge in elementary school, even before the gymnasium, but only the words, not the deed [lish' slova, a ne delo]" (13:78).[2]

The typical next step after hearing dirty stories is to develop them in fantasy, those "shamefaced but daring and passionate daydreams" of which Dostoevsky speaks in the *Diary of a Writer*. In *Emile,* Rousseau warns of the power of such images: "The memory of objects that have made an impression upon us, the ideas that we have acquired follow us in our retreat and people it in spite of ourselves with images more seductive than the objects themselves."[3] Such dreams are apt to lead to masturbation, which in turn leads to countless physical maladies: "It would be very dangerous if instinct taught your pupil to trick his senses and to find a substitute for the opportunity of satisfying them. Once he knows this dangerous supplement, he is lost. From then on he will always have an enervated body and heart. He will suffer until his death the sad effects of this habit, the most fatal to which a man can be subjected."[4] In the *Confessions,* Rousseau explains that it is precisely the dreamer of the Dostoevskian type who falls prey to this practice: "This vice, which shame and timidity find so convenient, has a particular attraction for lively imaginations. It allows them to dispose, so to speak, of the whole female sex at their will, and to make any beauty who tempts them serve their pleasure without the need of first obtaining her consent."[5] Dostoevsky was clearly aware of this passage. In preparatory notes toward the writing of *The Devils* (1871), the following phrase appears (probably in a speech destined for the lips of Pyotr Verkhovenskii): "Drunkenness, homosexuality, and masturbation like Rousseau are also useful. It all leads everything to the common level" ("Polezno tozhe p'ianstvo, muzhelozhestvo, rukobludstvo, kak Russo. Eto vse podvodit k srednemu urovniu," 11:272).

In his recent, definitive cultural history of masturbation, Thomas W.

Laqueur argues that masturbation becomes a "problem" in Western thought only in the early eighteenth century, and that the reasons for its problematic nature are intimately bound up with the very nature of the Enlightenment. The "three things [that] made solitary sex unnatural" are all issues that would have concerned Dostoevsky:

> First, it was motivated not by a real object of desire but by a phantasm; masturbation threatened to overwhelm the most protean and potentially creative of the mind's faculties—the imagination—and drive it over a cliff. Second, while all other sex was social, masturbation was private, or, when it was not done alone, it was social in all the wrong ways: wicked servants taught it to children; wicked older boys taught it to innocent young ones; girls and boys in schools taught it to each other away from adult supervision. Sex was naturally done *with* someone; solitary sex was not. And third, unlike other appetites, the urge to masturbate could be neither sated nor moderated.
>
> Done alone, driven only by the mind's own creations, it was a primal, irremediable, and seductively, even addictively, easy transgression.[6]

These three things represent the underside of the very values that the Enlightenment was involved in promoting. As Stephen Greenblatt puts it in his review of Laqueur: "[Eighteenth-century writers on the dangers of masturbation] had identified the shadow side of their own world: its interest in the private life of the individual, its cherishing of the imagination, its embrace of a seemingly limitless economy of production and consumption."[7] Given Dostoevsky's ambivalent attitude toward Enlightenment thought, it is no surprise that the "problem of masturbation" would have drawn his attention.

Rousseau's emphasis on the power of the imagination to provide sexual experiences that are as "real" as any physical sensations is echoed in an 1869 Russian sociological text, G. I. Arkhangel'skii's "Life in St. Petersburg according to Statistical Data."[8] Arkhangel'skii goes so far as to assert that virginity is impossible for men, if one defines it as a "lack of familiarity with sexual pleasure, with the pleasant shock to the organism that accompanies the *ejaculatio semenis*."[9] Even religious "fanatics" who have fled to forests and deserts in order to preserve their chastity are not safe: "Semen continues to be produced in the body, a reflex in the brain calls forth thoughts of a woman, a reflex of sight and hearing calls forth hallucinations, and the ascetic, who does not have the possibility of encountering a woman for hundreds of miles around, falls, seduced by a woman created by his imagination."[10] Clearly Dostoevsky could find multiple sources for the idea that virginity is a matter not just of body but of mind.

Arkadii is a quintessential dreamer who has concocted his own rich fantasy life, based on the idea of becoming a Rothschild. But he indicates that he has *not* succumbed to the temptation Rousseau warns against. According to the medical wisdom of the time, the masturbator could be recognized by his complexion, which is either excessively pale or jaundiced. Arkadii bears on his face the physical proof that he has abstained: "Yes, I daydreamed [mechtal] with all my might, to the point that I had no time to talk to people; from this they deduced that I was unsociable, and from my absent-mindedness they deduced even nastier things about me, but my rosy cheeks proved the opposite" (13:73).[11] Still, there is a sense that Arkadii's excessive devotion to his "mechty" has something masturbatory about it; he repeatedly speaks of "hiding under a blanket" when indulging in his fantasies (13:98, 164, 273).

One of the main objects of Arkadii's fantasy life, Katerina Nikolaevna, a seemingly unattainable, older society beauty, actually meets Arkadii for a tête-à-tête, mainly because he possesses a document that could lead to her being disinherited by her father. When Arkadii's father Versilov, who is also obsessed with Katerina Nikolaevna, learns of their meeting, he sends her an insulting letter accusing her, in so many words, of being a female version of the child abusers Svidrigailov and Stavrogin:

My Dear Lady,

Katerina Nikolaevna,

No matter how depraved [razvratny] you may be by your nature and art, I still thought that you would restrain your passions and at least not make an attempt on a child. But you were not embarrassed to do this . . . Do not corrupt [razvrashchaite] a young man for no reason. Spare him, he is still a minor, almost a boy, immature both mentally and physically; what use is he to you? (13:258)

Although Versilov's jealousy and incipient insanity have dictated this letter, there is a measure of truth to it. The reader has the queasy sense that Arkadii is easily taken advantage of by sexual predators like Katerina Nikolaevna and his schoolmate Lambert, even if their seduction remains a matter of words, not deeds.

Arkadii is the narrator of *A Raw Youth,* and the novel has no compelling plot to compete with the story of his sexual awakening. Although Alyosha Karamazov is introduced as the "hero" of *The Brothers Karamazov,* his own story is often eclipsed by the stories of his brothers, father, and spiritual mentor. But he like Arkadii is in the interesting and somewhat perilous situation of being a virgin, physically if not mentally. If we read books 1 through 7 of *The Brothers Karamazov* using *A Raw Youth* as a guide, the story of Alyosha's sexual development can be traced.

Like Arkadii, Alyosha has been subjected to "certain words and certain conversations about women" (14:19), foisted on him by his school classmates. But unlike Arkadii, who found to his own surprise that he "really liked to listen" (13:274), Alyosha cannot bear it: "[He] would tear himself away, get down and lie on the floor and cover his head, and all without saying a word to them, silently bearing the insult" (14:20). Although the narrator states that the boys' obscenities are a matter of "outer, not inner depravity" (14:19), Alyosha's violent reaction betrays his sense that there is real danger to his virginal soul in these words, these ideas. His very innocence is a magnet for the boys' "certain words." Schoolboys are one thing, but Alyosha's father and two older brothers have the same uncontrollable desire to tell dirty stories to a virgin. The most striking instance, of course, is when his father Fyodor's stories of his sexual torture of Alyosha's mother bring on an attack of hysteria. (Here, as in school where the boys call Alyosha "little girl" ["devchonka"], he takes on a female identity, suffering an attack of the exclusively feminine "shriekers'" illness.) Less obviously, the major conversations Alyosha has with his two brothers carry a tinge of verbal depravity. Dmitrii's "Confession of an Ardent Heart. In Anecdotes" begins as a set of sexual confessions that would not be out of place in a barracks. In the chapter titled "Rebellion," Ivan speaks of his collection of sadomasochistic stories in the coy diminutives of a pornographer: "You see, I am a fancier and collector of certain little facts [faktikov] and, if you can believe it, I write them down and collect from newspapers and stories, wherever I can get my hands on them, a certain kind of little anecdote [anekdotiki], and I already have a good collection" (14:218). (Given Dostoevsky's own artistic and journalistic practice, we can read this speech as a self-reference.) As Alyosha tries to preserve his spiritual virginity, the men nearest to him do their best to deprive him of it with their salacious words.

Like Arkadii, Alyosha has red cheeks (14:24), the telltale sign that he has not succumbed to the solitary vice of onanism. But there are also indications that his fantasy life has moved ahead of his physical experience. When Rakitin expatiates on the power of women's physical charms, Alyosha blurts out, "I understand that" (14:74). Rakitin replies:

"That means it's already a familiar subject to you, you've already thought about it, about sensual pleasure. Oh, you virgin! . . . The Devil knows what you've already thought about, the Devil knows what you already know about! A virgin, but you've already plumbed such depths." (14:74)

"Stalo byt', tebe uzh znakomaia tema, ob etom uzh dumal, o sladostrast'e-to. Akh ty, devstvennik! . . . Chert znaet o chem ty uzh ne dumal, chert znaet chto tebe uzh izvestno! Devstvennik, a uzh takuiu glubinu proshel."

Alyosha's constant blushing in the first part of the novel is a sign not only of his chastity but also of the potential impurity of his thoughts. As he says to Dmitrii, "I blushed not from what you said and not for what you did, but because I am the same as you . . . It's all the same ladder. I'm on the lowest rung, and you're up above, maybe on the thirteenth. . . . Whoever has stepped onto the lower rung will inevitably step onto the higher one too" (14:101).

Despite his inheritance of the powerfully sensual "Karamazov nature"—what the monk Father Paisii calls "the earthy Karamazov force, earthy, furious, and crude" (14:201)—Alyosha does not often display a strong sexual instinct. In the early chapters of the novel, his direct encounters with a potential erotic object, his betrothed Lise Khokhlakova, are affectionate but sexually tepid. The scene in which he becomes most obviously aroused is the scene at Katerina Ivanovna's, where he witnesses a moment of homoerotic passion, as Katerina kisses Grushenka repeatedly on her plump red lower lip: "Alyosha kept blushing and trembling with a slight, imperceptible tremble" (14:138). We are told later that he dreams of this scene the whole night (14:170). Although Alyosha is not eavesdropping in this scene—the women know he is there—his position as physically uninvolved but sensually aroused observer recalls that of the heroine-narrator of *Thérèse philosophe,* an eighteenth-century French erotic novel mentioned by Dostoevsky in *The Gambler.*[12] Many of the scenes in *Thérèse philosophe* involve Thérèse viewing and listening to the erotic encounters of others from a concealed spot or from the next room, and end with her relieving her inflamed feelings through masturbation. It is often remarked that the narrative machinery of *A Raw Youth* relies heavily on scenes in which Arkadii is conveniently secreted so as to overhear important conversations in the next room. It seems likely that, beyond serving as an expository convenience, these scenes allude to the archetypal scene of masturbatory arousal in *Thérèse philosophe.*

As with Arkadii, one of the objects of Alyosha's fantasies steps into his life and threatens to seduce him, in a reversal of the earlier Dostoevskian configuration of older man preying on girl child. In the early chapters of the novel, Alyosha hears from Rakitin, Dmitrii, and finally from Grushenka herself that she wants to "tear the cassock off his back" (14:74), "eat him up" (14:101), and "swallow him" (14:318).[13] At first he ignores these threats, but in his despair over the injustice of Father Zosima's posthumous disgrace when the "breath of corruption" issues prematurely from his corpse, Alyosha succumbs to Rakitin's temptations not only to eat salami and drink vodka, but also to lose his virginity to Grushenka. As the scene transpires, Alyosha ends up not physically tasting salami, vodka, or Grushenka, but something important does happen to him that changes his life and personality.

Liza Knapp has analyzed the scene of Alyosha's visit to Grushenka, showing how his encounter with her simple-hearted humanity transforms his despair and rebellion against the laws of nature into a new embrace of earthly existence.[14] As Alyosha says: "I came here in order to perish, and said, "So be it, so be it!"—and this because of my faint-heartedness, but she, after five years of torment, the first time someone came and said a sincere word to her—she forgave everything, forgot everything, and is weeping! . . . I just now, today, learned this lesson . . . She is higher in love than we are" (14:321). Alyosha returns to the monastery, where the smell of corruption from Zosima's corpse no longer disturbs him, thanks to his new acceptance and understanding of all things human. He has a dream-vision of the marriage at Cana, at which Father Zosima appears as a guest, and then Alyosha rushes outside and falls to the earth, kissing it and watering it with his tears.

This final scene is usually read as the initial stage in Alyosha's spiritual development, a development whose further stages promise to be narrated in the "second novel" of which Dostoevsky speaks in the author's foreword ("Ot avtora," 14:6). I would like to suggest an additional reading of the scene: as a culminating stage in Alyosha's sexual development, the stage at which he ceases to be a virgin susceptible to verbal and mental depravity.

The arc of our expectation from the moment Alyosha goes with Rakitin is for Alyosha to lose his virginity at the end of the episode. This expectation is supported at the end of the chapter "A Spring Onion," when it is mentioned that Rakitin "procured Alyosha for Grushenka" ("svodil Grushen'ku s Aleshei," 14:324). The expected consummation of the episode is missing, replaced by the emotional high point of Alyosha's dream and kissing of the earth. The expectation does, however, linger as a phantom presence, lending the dénouement an orgasmic quality. Dreams can, of course, be a space for sexual arousal. Arkadii's first orgasm is quite explicitly described as occurring during a dream in which Katerina Nikolaevna and Lambert appear: "I am seized by a new feeling, an inexpressible feeling that I never knew at all before, a feeling as powerful as the whole world . . . Oh, I no longer have the strength to walk away! Oh, how I like the fact that it's so shameless!" ("Menia okhvatyvaet novoe chuvstvo, nevyrazimoe, kotorogo ia eshche vovse ne znal nikogda, i sil'noe, kak ves' mir . . . O, ia uzhe ne v silakh uiti teper' ni za chto! O, kak mne nravitsia, chto eto tak besstydno!" 13:306). Against this background, the end of Alyosha's dream takes on a new coloration: "Something burned in Alyosha's heart, something suddenly filled it up to the point of pain, tears of ecstasy were torn from his soul . . . He stretched out his arms, gave a cry, and woke up" (14:327). Alyosha's dream is of the wedding at Cana; what traditionally follows a wedding is a sexual consummation. The language used to describe Alyosha's union with the earth has the potential for double entendre, thanks to the feminine gender of "zemlia" ("earth"):

He didn't know why he was embracing her, he didn't try to explain to himself why he had such an uncontrollable desire to kiss her, to kiss her all over, but

he kissed her weeping, sobbing, and watering her with his tears, and he fren-
ziedly swore to love her, to love her forever. (14:328)

On ne znal, dlia chego obnimal ee, on ne daval sebe otcheta, pochemu emu
tak neuderzhimo khotelos' tselovat' ee, tselovat' ee vsiu, no on tseloval ee
placha, rydaia i oblivaia svoimi slezami, i isstuplenno klialsia liubit' ee, liubit'
ee vo veki vekov.

This moment has the ritual significance of "making him a man," a
significance usually reserved for the loss of virginity: "He fell to the earth a
weak youth, and rose up a warrior firm for the rest of his life, and he recognized and felt this immediately at the very moment of his ecstasy. And
Alyosha never, never could forget that moment for the rest of his life" ("Pal
on na zemliu slabym iunoshei, a vstal tverdym na vsiu zhizn' boitsom i soz-
nal i pochuvstvoval eto vdrug, v tu zhe minutu svoego vostorga. I nikogda,
nikogda ne mog zabyt' Alesha vo vsiu zhizn' svoiu potom etoi minuty,"
14:328). Alyosha has been initiated into manhood not by Grushenka but by
God, through the mediation of Mother Earth. Alyosha is obeying Zosima's
pre-death injunction to "kiss the earth" and "water the earth with the tears
of your joy and love those tears" (14:292). It is precisely Alyosha's inheritance
of the "earthy Karamazov force" that renders him able to love the earth so
passionately, but in the way sanctified by Zosima. Alyosha's loss of virginity
is not physical orgasm but spiritual ecstasy, not a masturbatory fantasy but a
living connection to the holy.[15]

After this moment, Alyosha disappears from the narrative for two
books, as the story centers on Dmitrii. When he reappears, his demeanor has
changed dramatically from what it was in books 1 through 7: his constant
blushing and lowering of his eyes has ceased. He blushes only once, in response to Kolia Krasotkin's "declaration of love" (14:504). It is as if this conversation with a schoolboy who reads salacious books on the sly has re-
minded Alyosha of the impure thoughts of his own earlier life. But in general
Alyosha's blushing days are over—he has become a sober, self-possessed
man. Without physically losing his virginity, Alyosha has lost the virgin's terrible susceptibility to verbal and mental depravity. God has granted him a
kind of spiritual knowledge that has neutralized the power of masturbatory
fantasy. Peter Gay has written of the nineteenth-century view of masturbation as "a loss of mastery over the world and oneself."[16] Alyosha's moment of
spiritual awakening is also a moment in which he gains mastery over the self.
He has learned not to abuse the formidable sexual power of the Karamazovs
either in relation to himself or to others.

There are two other virgins in *The Brothers Karamazov*, Smerdiakov
and Lise Khokhlakova, whose fates are relevant to this discussion. Smerd-

iakov is Fyodor's servant and perhaps his illegitimate son, who murders Fyodor and ends by committing suicide. Smerdiakov's sexuality has attracted the attention of several scholars. The physical description of him upon his return from learning to be a cook in Moscow is suggestive: "He suddenly had aged unusually quickly, had developed wrinkles completely incommensurate with his age, had acquired a yellowish complexion, and had come to resemble a castrate" (14:115).[17] The narrator states that Smerdiakov despises both the male and the female sex (14:116). Gary Saul Morson refers to him as "both ageless and sexless."[18]

Has Smerdiakov always been sexless? A castrate is one who has been deprived of the sexuality he once had. Smerdiakov, after all, is probably a Karamazov—where is his Karamazovian sex drive? The answer may lie in a work that Laura Engelstein calls "the classic text on sexual abuse . . . most frequently cited by Russian educators": Samuel-Auguste-André-David Tissot's 1758 dissertation on masturbation, which was published in many editions in Russia in the nineteenth century.[19] Tissot, quoting one of his myriad sources, provides the following physical description of the chronic masturbator: "Young people . . . take on the appearance and the infirmities of old men; they become pale, effeminate, dull, lazy, cowardly, stupid, and even imbecile . . . Some succumb to seizures."[20] Smerdiakov's premature aging, yellow complexion, and loss of sexual appetite are all symptoms cited by Tissot.[21] Most telling of all, however, is his epilepsy (which worsens upon his return from Moscow). Tissot repeatedly adduces epilepsy as one of the major illnesses caused by masturbation.[22] This may explain why Fyodor Karamazov proposes to cure Smerdiakov's epilepsy by finding him a wife (14:116).

We can see a possible precursor for Smerdiakov in the character of Uriah Heep in Dickens's 1850 novel *David Copperfield*. Like Smerdiakov, Heep has a prematurely aged appearance: "I saw a cadaverous face appear at a small window on the ground floor . . . The low arched door then opened, and the face came out. It was quite as cadaverous as it had looked in the window . . . It belonged to a red-haired person—a youth of fifteen, as I take it now, but looking much older."[23] As Laqueur points out, "Charles Dickens's shift-eyed, pimply, sallow-complexioned, untrustworthy Uriah Heep is probably the most famous and easily recognized culprit [of masturbation] in Victorian fiction."[24] Dickens is more blatant than Dostoevsky, repeatedly emphasizing Heep's "long lank, skeleton hand": "Oh, what a clammy hand his was! as ghostly to the touch as to the sight! I rubbed mine afterwards, to warm it, and *to rub his off*. It was such an uncomfortable hand, that when I went to my room, it was still cold and wet upon my memory" (emphasis in original).[25] Dostoevsky's portrait of Smerdiakov is more subtle, but the family resemblance is clear.

Strangely enough, we can also read Smerdiakov's desire to learn French as yet another clue that he is a masturbator. Here our source is not Tissot or Dickens but Dostoevsky himself. In the *Writer's Diary* for July and August 1876, in the essays "Russian or French?" and "What Language Should a Future Father of Our Country Speak?" Dostoevsky offers a lengthy discussion of the fact that learning French too early has a stunting effect on the intellectual growth of Russian youth, who are thus deprived of their own language but will never be as creative in French as the most common Frenchman (23:79). Then he makes a strange and intriguing comparison:

> Every mother and every father, for example, knows about a certain horrible childish physical habit that in some unfortunate children begins already at the age of ten, and if not attended to, can transform them sometimes into idiots, into flaccid, decrepit old men while they are still youths. I will be so bold as to say straight out that the French nanny, that is, learning French from early childhood, from the first childish prattling, is the same thing in the moral sense as that horrible habit is in the physical sense. (23:83)

Morson has brilliantly analyzed the self-referentiality of Smerdiakov's discourse: "His self-destruction re-enacts the self-cancellation of language in paradox."[26] Smerdiakov refers to himself and kills himself; is it not likely, given his telltale physical symptoms, that he also has sex with himself?

There is one more virgin with a yellowish complexion in *The Brothers Karamazov:* Lise as she appears in the chapter "The Little Demon." Her "pale yellow face" (15:20, 24) is mentioned twice; she has been reading "nasty books" ("durnye knigi," 15:23) stolen from under her mother's bed pillows; she is racked by sadomasochistic fantasies of the torture of children; and she uses Alyosha as a messenger to carry notes "offering herself" to Ivan, who has clearly become the main object of her depraved mental life (15:38). As several critics have noted, Lise's sexual frustration is expressed through the texture of her language in this scene, the Russian version of which contains two highly significant puns. She says to Alyosha (I give the Russian first):

> "Ia khochu, chtoby menia kto-nibud' isterzal, zhenilsia na mne, a potom isterzal, obmanul, ushel i uekhal . . . A znaete, ia khochu zhat', *rozh zhat'*. Ia za vas vyidu, a *vy stanete muzhikom, nastoiashchim muzhikom, u nas zherebenochek*, khotite?" (15:21; emphases mine)

> "I want someone to torment me, marry me and then torment me, deceive me, and leave me . . . And you know, I want to reap, *to reap rye*. I will marry you, and *you will become a peasant, a real peasant, we'll have a little foal*, you want to?"

The phrases that are translated as "I want to reap rye" and "We'll have a little foal" are puns in Russian, which can be heard as also meaning, "I want to
give birth" and "We'll have a little baby." The word "peasant" also has the folk
meaning "husband" (and is in fact a diminutive of the word "husband").[27]
Although Lise has broken her engagement with Alyosha, she is still mentally
preoccupied with the sexual consummation of their projected relationship.

Alyosha expresses sympathy and solidarity with Lise, claiming to have
had the same recurring dream she has of demons encroaching on her bed.
But his failure to blush even once in this scene betrays the fact that he has
moved beyond the stage of masturbatory fantasy in which Lise is mired. In
the context of the pain that her evil fantasies are causing her, the following
words, quoted by Lise from the young Kalganov, have a tragic significance:
"He walks around daydreaming all the time. He says: Why live in reality, it's
better to daydream. You can dream up the jolliest things, but it's boring to
live" ("On vse khodit i mechtaet. On govorit: zachem vzapravdu zhit',
luchshe mechtat'. Namechtat' mozhno samoe veseloe, a zhit' skuka," 15:22).

Alyosha's "marriage at Cana," his spiritual consummation, has replaced
the planned marriage to Lise. As a result he has been liberated from the pernicious power of a virgin's dream life. The chapter "The Little Demon" implies that Alyosha's liberation has spelled Lise's doom, her fatal enslavement
to the spiritually dangerous world of fantasy.[28]

Freud reacted to the campaign against masturbation in the eighteenth
and nineteenth centuries by constituting the practice as a normal and ubiq-
uitous stage in the development of the infant, child, and adolescent. For
Dostoevsky, masturbation is not normal and inevitable, but a "horrible childish physical habit." It is the act of the individual who does not feel part of the
social—the dreamer, the outsider, the holy fool.[29] Such an individual may
succumb to his powerful fantasies and descend into hysterical madness, like
Lise, or commit suicide, like Smerdiakov. Or, with the help of God, he may,
like Alyosha, overcome the dangerous power of "daring and passionate daydreams," and end by mastering the self.

Chapter Five

The "Secret Vice" of Mariia Kroneberg:
A Writer's Diary

WHEN DEALING WITH issues of sexuality, Dostoevsky shows himself to be both a product of his nineteenth-century milieu who subscribes to many of the stereotypes and misconceptions of his day and an independent thinker capable of dispensing with stereotype when it is contradicted by his own empirical observations. We have seen how in *A Raw Youth* he creates a homosexual character who to some extent conforms to the stereotypical image of the "pederast" found in the contemporary medical literature, but who ultimately transcends that image, probably as a result of Dostoevsky's own direct experience with homosexuality during his prison years. In this chapter I will discuss another instance in which Dostoevsky sees human sexual behavior more clearly than most of his contemporaries, in his treatment of the Kroneberg child abuse case, published in the February 1876 issue of *A Writer's Diary* (*Dnevnik pisatelia*), a case that centers around the supposed sexual sins of a seven-year-old girl.

In his introduction to Kenneth Lantz's translation of *A Writer's Diary,* Gary Saul Morson points out that the first monthly issue of the *Diary* is devoted to the theme of children: "In the January 1876 issue, children are obviously a central focus. But instead of specific recommendations or programs, we are presented with a field of possibilities, an interaction of perspectives, and the beginnings of inconclusive dialogues."[1] One of those inconclusive dialogues is without doubt a dialogue on the question of childhood innocence. It begins in the third part of the second chapter of the January 1876 issue, with Dostoevsky's account of his visit to a colony for juvenile delinquents, and is continued in the second chapter of the February issue, with his response to the Kroneberg case.

Dostoevsky's visit to the juvenile colony in December 1875 was arranged by the legal official A. F. Koni (22:326). Early in his visit, Dostoevsky asks the director of the colony, Pavel Apollonovich Rovinskii, whether the young inmates, who range in age from ten to seventeen, are subject to "certain depraved childish habits" (izvestnye detskie porochnye privychki,

22:19). He is assured that this is impossible, because the boys are constantly observed. Dostoevsky notes, "But this seemed improbable to me." Some of the inmates had earlier been housed in the Lithuanian Castle prison in St. Petersburg along with adults:

> I had been in that prison three years before and had seen those boys. Later I learned with complete certainty that unusual debauchery reigned in the Castle, that those vagrants who entered the Castle and were not yet infected with this debauchery, and at first were repelled by it, later submitted to it willy-nilly, because of the mockery of their comrades at their chastity [tselo-mudriem]. (22:19–20)[2]

It is not clear whether Dostoevsky is referring here to homosexuality or masturbation (most likely the former), but a later reference is clearly to masturbation. Rovinskii tells Dostoevsky about a boy, earlier housed in the Lithuanian Castle, who was constantly getting in trouble, trying to escape, and ending up in solitary confinement. After a serious conversation with Rovinskii, the boy finally broke down:

> "He flung himself on me in tears, all shaken and transformed, began to repent, to reproach himself, began to tell me things that had happened to him before, things that he had hidden from everyone up to that time: he told me as a secret that he had long been given to a certain most shameful habit which he could not get rid of, and that it was tormenting him—in a word, it was a full confession. I spent about two hours with him," added P. A——ch. "We talked; I advised him about certain measures for overcoming his habit, etc., etc." (22:24)[3]

Dostoevsky says that Rovinskii firmly refused to elaborate on what he and the boy had talked about, but, Dostoevsky says, "You must agree, there is such a thing as a real skill at penetrating the sick soul of a deeply embittered young criminal who had never known the truth up to that time" (22:25). Dostoevsky's final word on this case is telling: "I admit, I would really like to find out the details of this conversation" (22:25).

Dostoevsky's curiosity is probably not simple prurience, but a continuation of his lifelong interest in the souls and personalities of children, who seem to him to be almost separate beings from adults. The title of this section of the *Diary* includes the phrase, "The Remaking of Depraved Souls into Chaste Ones" ("Peredelka porochnykh dush v neporochnye," 22:17). The phrase no doubt refers, among other things, to this tale of a fifteen-year-old boy who has submitted to a shameful sexual practice but who is still open to "the truth." In his account of the Kroneberg case, in which a similar "bad habit" played a vital role, Dostoevsky again upholds the principle that the "depraved soul" of a child is still capable of returning to chastity and innocence.

Dostoevsky's account of the Kroneberg trial of January 1876 was one of a number of journalistic responses which appeared that year, including essays by M. E. Saltykov-Shchedrin and P. D. Boborykin. According to one memoirist, Dostoevsky's response to the case bore a significance to his contemporaries that outweighed the importance of the case itself. Khristina Danilovna Alchevskaia records a conversation with Dostoevsky in spring 1876 in which she responds to a letter he had sent her. In that letter Dostoevsky explains the difficulty of the form he has chosen for *A Writer's Diary:*

> When I sit down to write, I have 10–15 topics (no fewer); but I am forced to put off writing about my favorite topics: they'll take up too much space, they'll require too much passion (the Kroneberg case, for example), they'll spoil the issue, it won't be variegated, there won't be enough different articles; and so you end up writing not what you wanted to write.[4]

Alchevskaia objects to this willful self-denial, calling Dostoevsky's account of the Kroneberg case the "chef d'oeuvre of your *Diary*":

> I know people who ascribe enormous significance to this article. They say: "Years will pass, the Kroneberg case will be forgotten, everything that was written and said on this case will be forgotten, all the phrase-filled feuilletons, all the cloying humanitarian speeches will be forgotten, and only *this* article will never lose its significance and will serve as a living rebuke to society, and the legal profession, and all of us." Yes, in my opinion, every work of a person into which he has put a particle of his own soul is immortal, and what if we were deprived of this article, because "it will take up too much space, it won't be variegated, there won't be enough different articles!"[5]

Dostoevsky apparently shared this view of the work's significance; in the working notebooks for the *Writer's Diary* of 1876, there are few subjects to which he devotes so many preparatory notes (24:66–187).

The facts of the Kroneberg case (possibly "Kronenberg," but I have used Dostoevsky's spelling) are as follows.[6] Stanislav Leopol'dovich Kroneberg (b. 1845) was a nobleman raised in Warsaw who was tried in 1876 for the torture (by beating) of his seven-year-old illegitimate daughter Mariia. The story behind the case emerges in the detailed account of the trial published in the newspaper *The Voice (Golos)* in January 1876. While studying for a law degree, Kroneberg had an affair with an older woman, a widow with children. Knowing that Kroneberg's strict father would not allow them to be married, the woman broke off the affair, but failed to tell Kroneberg that she was pregnant. In 1872, after serving with the French in the Franco-Prussian War and receiving the medal of the Legion of Honor, Kroneberg encountered his former lover, now remarried, and she told him that he had a daughter, whom she had given birth to secretly in Switzerland and had left in the care of peasants in Geneva. Kroneberg legally acknowledged the child as his daughter and moved her into the care of the de Combes, a Swiss pastor and his wife. In 1875, at the insistence of his lover Adelina Gesing, who longed to set up a proper household with him, he retrieved his now seven-year-old daughter Mariia and brought her to live with them in St. Petersburg. In the summer of 1875 the three moved to a dacha outside St. Petersburg, and on July 28 the mother of the caretaker of the dacha, Ul'iana Bibina, reported Kroneberg to the local police for severely beating his daughter several times, but particularly on July 25, when an especially prolonged and painful beating took place. A preliminary judicial investigation found that there were grounds to try Kroneberg for torture as defined in Statute 1489 of the Code of Punishment, and he was brought to trial before a jury on January 23, 1876. This was a criminal charge not specifically designed for domestic violence, and if convicted Kroneberg would have faced exile to a Siberian prison, as Dostoevsky points out in lamenting the impossibility of a just or satisfactory outcome to such a trial (22:51). Kroneberg's defense attorney, appointed by the court, was a brilliant jurist and former professor at St. Petersburg University, V. D. Spasovich (1829–1906), who succeeded in obtaining an acquittal for his client. The lurid details of the case, combined with the defense attorney's stunning success, gave rise to a wave of discussion and soul-searching in Russian public life, of which Dostoevsky's response is only the most salient example.

Gary Rosenshield has devoted two substantial articles to Dostoevsky's essay on the Kroneberg case, and in them he has achieved two major analytical tasks. First, he has discussed the case and Dostoevsky's response to it in the context of Dostoevsky's "moral-artistic critique" of trial by jury, a fairly recent innovation in the Russian judicial system. Dostoevsky's critique of the pitfalls of the jury trial, in which the defense lawyer becomes a prisoner of the institution and of his own talent, is part of a larger agenda, "the threat of Western rationalism, formalism, and legalism and the impersonal and bureaucratic institutions they engender."[7] Second, Rosenshield brilliantly analyzes the ways in which Dostoevsky compensates for the inadequate prosecution of the case by doing rhetorical battle directly with Spasovich. Spasovich had defended his client by focusing on the child's deficiencies that provoked the beating, thus "confiscating," according to Dostoevsky, her status as an innocent child (22:66). Rosenshield demonstrates the ways in which Dostoevsky restores the reader's natural sympathy and compassion for the child victim, making us hear again her repeated cries of "Papa, Papa!" as reported by Bibina and the cook Titova. These two peasant women who brought the charges against Kroneberg are the heroes of Dostoevsky's account. Rosenshield explains:

> In the Kroneberg article, Dostoevsky creates a work in imitation of the simple women of the people that can itself constitute a form of moral symbolic action. Moved by their action, Dostoevsky, the Russian intellectual, pays obeisance to their superior wisdom, attempting to instill in us the feelings that guided these women.[8]

In Rosenshield's view, Dostoevsky's ultimate aim is "to transform the Western legal record into moral narrative concerning Russian justice and truth."[9] Rosenshield's analysis focuses on the published version of Dostoevsky's essay on the Kroneberg case. My discussion will delve into the notes and drafts toward the essay, especially certain key elements of Dostoevsky's reaction to the case that he ultimately decided to suppress in his published essay.

Rosenshield highlights Spasovich's strategy of focusing on the little girl's supposed "vices and deficiencies" in an attempt to discredit her as a witness and to remove the jury's pity for her as a victim. Dostoevsky, who used Spasovich as a model for the defense attorney Fetiukovich in *The Brothers Karamazov,* makes this strategy of discrediting witnesses a central tool in the repertoire of Dmitrii's defender. Fetiukovich secretly believes that his client is guilty and thus has to deflect attention away from him and his crime, as does Spasovich with regard to Kroneberg.

To return to the question of Mariia Kroneberg's deficiencies, just what are they? The ones mentioned explicitly by Dostoevsky are lying and stealing, but he also alludes repeatedly to a "secret debauched vice" ("potaennyi razvratnyi porok," 22:66; also mentioned at 22:51, 57, 60, 62, 67, 68, 69, and 71). The "secret vice" is not specified by Dostoevsky, but it is specified—as "onanism"—in the account of the trial published in *The Voice,* the account on which Dostoevsky primarily relied. If we recall Dostoevsky's letter to Alchevskaia, we will realize that he restrained himself in writing about the Kroneberg case, so as not to have it dominate the *Diary,* in which he sought to maintain thematic variety. We must also remember that Dostoevsky would have assumed that most of his readers at the time had read the same newspaper accounts that he had. For these two reasons, the account of the Kroneberg case in *A Writer's Diary* may strike the modern reader as fragmentary and enigmatic. At least partly to save space and his own writing time, and also because he assumes his reader is familiar with the facts of the case, Dostoevsky employs a terse, telegraphic, allusive style. Thus a careful reading of the seemingly word-for-word transcript of the trial published in *The Voice* can enrich our understanding of Dostoevsky's response to the case and the central role accorded in it to Mariia Kroneberg's secret sexual vice. (A translation of the *Voice* account is provided in the appendix later in this volume.)

One has only to read the trial account in *The Voice* to realize that Dostoevsky's moral indignation about the treatment of Mariia Kroneberg is not at all excessive. As the prosecutor A. K. Kolokolov says in his summation, she belongs to the category of "unfortunate creatures who from the moment of their birth are subjected to all the adversities of a harsh life" (January 28). The trial is focused on the beatings she endured at age seven from her biological father, but it is clear that the child was abused beginning at a much earlier age, while she was in Switzerland. Kroneberg testifies that he had to use drastic measures in order to make an impression on the girl, because "when she was living in the village they punished her more severely, and therefore lighter punishments didn't have any effect on her" (January 26). Spasovich echoes this in his summation, saying, "the girl had gotten used to beatings at the de Combes'" (January 29). The deposition by Mrs. de Combe, which purports to explain many of the scars on the girl's face, sounds like the familiar abuser's litany of excuses: she fell out a window when she was two or three years old, she fell downstairs, she ran in the garden and fell face down and smashed her nose (January 27). Spasovich says, "When one looks attentively into the child's face, that face indeed is covered [ispisano] in all directions by thin scars" (January 29). Spasovich's point is that the scars are too faint to constitute the "disfigurement" mentioned by one of the medical witnesses, but his use of the word "ispisano" is more appropriate than he perhaps realizes. The word literally means "covered with writing," and Mariia's scars write a story that is all too clear and all too tragic.

The fairy-tale ending to that story, of the girl's discovery by her real father "on the street among peasant children," and his later adoption of her, is in fact only the beginning of an even sadder story (January 26). In St. Petersburg, Kroneberg beat the child in the face with his hand, causing welts, bruises, and nosebleeds. After moving to the dacha, he resorted to using a switch, first a "soft" one, then a bundle of thick rowanberry branches. The outraged servant Bibina tells of repeatedly hearing the child's screams and fearing that she would be beaten to death. Spasovich later casts doubt on Bibina's motives, implying that she had a grudge against Kroneberg because he deducted eighty kopecks from her wages to compensate for a lost chick (January 26). But during the preliminary investigation, it was Kroneberg's own lover Adelina Gesing who gave the most succinct and convincing account of chronic abuse:

The French national Adelina Gesing testified that as a father, Kroneberg subjected the girl to domestic correction; in the city he beat her on the hands and face, which caused the child to have bruises on her cheeks; at the dacha he beat Mariia two or three times, but he beat her lightly, although welts and stripes nevertheless appeared on the girl's body from this beating, and the witness would each time give the child sugar water to calm her down. Mr. Kroneberg usually beat his daughter in the evening, when she was already undressed for bed. (January 24)

At the trial, Gesing feebly attempts to claim that her testimony in the preliminary investigation was recorded incorrectly, but the detail of the "sugar water" rings too true to have been fabricated by her interrogator.

The climactic beating on July 25 with the switch made of rowanberry branches was the culmination of an attempt to terrorize Mariia into submission. Kroneberg gathered the branches in front of his daughter while out on a walk with her, bundled them into a switch, and hung it over her bed. During her testimony at the trial, Mariia indicates the switch lying on the table of material evidence, and says, "Papa said that this is a superior switch [prevoskhodnye rozgi]" (January 25). On July 25, when the child was caught trying to break into Gesing's trunk to steal some prunes, the "superior switch" was put to use. The results of the July 25 beating are described chillingly in the summary of the preliminary investigation:

On July 29, that is, on the fourth day after the last punishment with the switch, the girl was examined, and in the record of those proceedings it is noted that, when she was asked to undress, the girl did so with crying and fear, constantly looking around at her father and those present, and calmed down only when it was explained to her that she was not going to be beaten. Upon examination it turned out that the entire surface of her left buttock area and left thigh were a dark purple color, the right buttock area and right thigh were covered in places by bluish-purple spots and red stripes, up to seven inches in length. The same kind of stripes were scattered over the entire surface of the back and here and there on the lower surface of the stomach, and one near the left nipple, about one and a half inches in length. On the right arm were partly blending bluish-red spots and red stripes; the same was observed on the left arm, only to a lesser extent. (January 24)

An exchange between the prosecutor and an impartial female witness, who had been called in to be present at the examination, sums up the impact of this sight:

> *Prosecutor:* Did you not weep when the girl was undressed?
> *Witness:* I was so horrified that I began to feel ill.

Prosecutor: Why did this make such an impression on you?
Witness: The girl was all beaten up [vsia izbita]. (January 26)

The sadness of Mariia Kroneberg's story is intensified by the portrait of her attractive character that emerges from the testimony. She is described as "a very nice, pretty, and well-built little girl, who carries herself in an unconstrained manner" and who "answers the questions, posed through an interpreter [because she spoke only French], quickly and without shyness" (January 25). Several witnesses speak of her quick intelligence. Her friendship, across linguistic and class barriers, with the caretaker's mother Bibina and the cook Titova, although it enraged her father, strikes the modern reader of the trial as yet another point in her favor.[10] Her father says, "She has a very firm character" (January 26). One assumes that he does not mean this as a compliment.

It is true that some witnesses dispute the idea that Kroneberg was an abusive father, but all of them have a vested interest in pleasing him: Gesing is his live-in companion, and the rest are his paid employees. Mariia herself at first refuses to testify, and does so only after being instructed to by her father. She often answers, "I don't remember" or "I don't know," possibly in order to soften the effect of her testimony. Even Titova, who assisted Bibina in bringing charges against Kroneberg, seems unwilling to testify strongly and unambiguously against Kroneberg at the trial.

Spasovich's cause is helped by these witnesses, but even more by the testimony of the expert witnesses. Dostoevsky clearly was thinking of this aspect of the trial when he wrote one of the courtroom scenes in *The Brothers Karamazov*. At Dmitrii's trial, three expert medical witnesses give testimony regarding Dmitrii's mental fitness, based on the fact that he looked straight ahead while entering the courtroom. The elderly local Dr. Herzenstube claims that Dmitrii's mental abnormality is proved by his looking straight ahead rather than at the ladies, since he was an admirer of the fair sex and should have been worrying about their opinion of him. The visiting Moscow doctor agrees that Dmitrii is abnormal, but not because he was not looking to the left at the ladies, but because he was not looking to the right at his defense attorney, on whom his fate depended. The young local Dr. Varvinskii claims that Dmitrii is completely normal, and that it was quite appropriate for him to look straight ahead, at the presiding judge and members of the court, on whom his fate in fact depended (15:103–5).

The situation at the Kroneberg trial is only slightly less farcical. Five medical witnesses testify separately, basing their conclusions "on scientific data" (January 27). The first, a young doctor involved in his first forensic examination, considers that the beating was excessive, but claims that "we cannot draw a line between grave and light injuries . . . [because] there have been cases where people died from light injuries, and sometimes completely recovered from grave injuries" (January 27). (Spasovich later used this claim to his advantage in his summation.) The second expert makes the astounding statement that the injuries "could not produce any particular effect on the child's health, apart from the fact that the scars would remain her whole life" (January 27). The third expert finds that Mariia Kroneberg "belongs to the category of subjects in whom the irritation of the skin is more acute than in others." In this witness's opinion, "the punishment was not very harshly carried out [since her skin was not broken], because, taking into account the kind of instrument that was used in this case, blows inflicted with all one's strength could cut through thicker skin than a child's" (January 27). A fourth expert agrees with the first that the "the punishment inflicted on the girl . . . exceeded the bounds of corrective punishment" (January 27). The final expert expands on the contention of the third witness that Mariia's own physical makeup is responsible for the marks on her body: "Mariia Kroneberg belongs to the category of subjects on whose body the slightest touch produces bruises" (January 27).

Spasovich is quick to take advantage of the contradictory nature of the experts' testimony:

> The minutes of the examination must be analyzed separately, because they do not coincide with each other. If one lumps them together, as has been done in the indictment, then the result is something coherent, but if you analyze them separately, then it is evident that each of the investigating doctors pulled in a different direction, so that in their conclusions they diverged from each other to an immeasurable distance. (January 29)

Spasovich then enters into a detailed analysis and subdivision of the marks on the girl's body—what Dostoevsky calls "bukhgalteriia" ("bookkeeping," 22:63)—to prove that there really was only one beating, on July 25, and that it was not severe since the skin was not broken: "That it was only one punishment is confirmed by all the circumstances of the case. We cannot even speak of any preceding punishments" (January 29). Dostoevsky carefully studied Spasovich's "jesuitical" reasoning and provided a direct imitation of it in Fetiukovich's summation: "There is an overwhelming sum total of facts against the accused and at the same time not a single fact that will withstand critical analysis if you examine it individually, all by itself!" (15:153). There follow the famously ironic chapter headings characterizing Fetiukovich's speech: "There Was No Money. There Was No Robbery"; "And There Was No Murder Either" (15:156, 161).[11] Clearly these phrases are inspired by Spasovich's incredible claim that "there was only one punishment." Mariia's lifetime of abuse, including months of abuse at the hands of her father, is erased with one stroke.

Besides taking advantage of the contradictory nature of the witnesses' testimony, Spasovich resorts to the strategy of dwelling on Mariia Kroneberg's own deficiencies, as discussed earlier. The July 25 beating was precipitated by her attempt to steal some prunes (and perhaps some money, although this fact is never firmly established). She is also said to be disobedient and prone to lying. But several witnesses speak of a more mysterious defect, what Mrs. de Combe calls "evil propensities and habits" that she acquired from the peasants in Switzerland (which if true would make her no older than four at the time, since she was moved to the de Combes' in 1872; Mrs. de Combe's testimony, January 26). Her father testifies that "the little child had vices about which he did not wish to speak" (January 26). Gesing says, "In general, the girl doesn't obey, she's always dirty, and she has other deficiencies which I cannot explain [kotorye ia ob"iasnit' ne mogu]" (January 26). Both Spasovich and the prosecutor refer to this "vice" in similar circumlocutions (January 25, January 28). Only one witness describes the child's "secret vice" explicitly, without euphemisms: Nadezhda Prokof'evna Suslova (1843–1918).

Suslova's testimony provides one of the most riveting moments of the trial, and although brief, it apparently bore great significance for the prosecutor and defense attorney, as well as for the commentaries by Saltykov-Shchedrin and Dostoevsky himself. Before discussing it, however, we must provide some background on Nadezhda Suslova and her significance in Russian society and in Dostoevsky's personal life.

Suslova was the daughter of a former serf who served as manager of the estates of Count Sheremetev. Her father took pains to have his children educated, and Nadezhda pursued the study of medicine with iron determination. In order to attend lectures at the Medical-Surgical Academy in St. Petersburg, she was required to pass the final examination for the full (male) gymnasium course. She did so brilliantly (with the equivalent of a gold medal) at the age of eighteen.[12] While studying at the academy she worked with the famous physiologist I. M. Sechenov and contributed original research to his *Physiology of the Nervous System*.[13] In 1864, as an anti-nihilist measure, women were forbidden to attend lectures at the Medical-Surgical Academy. Suslova, overcoming great difficulties, moved to the University of Zurich, and after three years of single-minded work she defended her dissertation in 1867. Soon afterward she returned to Russia and obtained the right to practice as a doctor—the first woman doctor in Russia.[14]

Dostoevsky was personally acquainted with Nadezhda Suslova in the early 1860s, the time at which he began a passionate but painful affair with her sister, Apollinaria Prokof'evna Suslova (1840–1918).[15] Dostoevsky's relations with Apollinaria were at their most intense from 1862 to 1863, but they continued to correspond even after his second marriage in 1867 (most of their letters have been lost). The one letter from Dostoevsky to Nadezhda Suslova that survives is full of affection for her, although its primary subject is his thwarted love for Apollinaria: "At least don't you blame me. I value you highly, you are a rare creature among those I have met in my life, I do not want to lose your heart. I highly value your view of me and your memory of me" (letter of April 19, 1865; 28.2: 122). After hearing of Nadezhda's successful defense of her dissertation, Dostoevsky described her in a letter to his niece S. A. Ivanova as "a rare personality, noble, honorable, lofty!" (28.1: 252). It is likely that in 1876, when he read the transcript of the Kroneberg trial, Dostoevsky's attention was arrested by the testimony of his old acquaintance and the sister of his former lover.

Suslova enters the Kroneberg case not as one of the expert witnesses called in after the beating, but as Adelina Gesing's physician, who in attending her adult patient also had occasion to observe the child Mariia. A 1960 Soviet biography of Suslova characterizes the nature of her practice as that of a gynecologist for idle rich ladies with sexual complaints:

> Languid high-society lionesses and blindingly brilliant Pompadours who had been maimed and damaged during their service to Eros and Venus; hysterical noblemen's daughters long left unmarried, suffering from anemia, headaches, and a lack of suitors; immensely fat merchants' wives from the Volga and Siberia, complaining of barrenness—all of them made their way to her, vying with one another to ask for help, advice, radical, swift-acting remedies and medicines that didn't taste too disgusting, and also the preservation of secrecy . . . More than once, suppressing her compassionate nature, on the basis of medical ethics Nadezhda had to refuse aid to "victims of love" who demanded that she provide them with remedies that could preserve their honorable reputations and hide the consequences of their frivolous infatuations.[16]

According to this writer, Suslova used the proceeds from her rich patients to aid more virtuous poor women suffering from the effects not of "service to Venus" but of hard work.[17] The tendentiousness of the description aside, it is clear that a large part of Suslova's practice had to do with the sexual and reproductive problems of women.[18]

We have samples of Nadezhda Suslova's writing in two very different genres. Like her sister Apollinaria, Nadezhda dabbled in fiction writing, publishing three stories.[19] Her style is not wildly different from that of other women writing at the time; both sisters, like many of their contemporaries, were devotees of George Sand.[20] But Nadezhda devoted the vast majority of her efforts to science, first as a researcher and then as a physician, and it is safe to say that her normal daily discourse was the clear, precise, straightforward language of science. One of her few published scientific works is an 1870 review of a book on the care of infants and small children. It is a remarkable essay, in which Suslova's mastery of the scientific and diagnostic knowledge of her day, and of clinical issues, is clearly apparent. One passage from the review may give a taste of her style, which is quite unusual for a woman of the time. In pointing out errors made by the author of the work under review, Suslova dwells on the claim that pregnant women suffer from catarrhs of the stomach caused by the pressure of the enlarged uterus on the digestive organs:

> Mrs. Manasseina attributes to this catarrh the pregnant woman's whims of appetite, nausea, and vomiting; but such an explanation is not quite correct. Nausea, whims of appetite, and vomiting appear with particular acuteness at the very beginning of pregnancy, when there is no pressure from the uterus on the digestive organs, and therefore these phenomena have long been ascribed to a nervous origin and they are regarded as the consequences of that intensified nervous irritability that develops as a result of pregnancy . . . If these morbid phenomena were in fact only the result of pressure on the digestive organs, then they would always occur in cases of uterine tumors (e.g., fibroids), which does not occur in the majority of cases, and on the contrary, these same phenomena—nausea, vomiting, and lack of appetite—very often arise without any pressure on the digestive organs, in cases where there is a poor diet and irritation of the nervous system.[21]

It was this Suslova—the scientist, the speaker of hard truths in plain language, not the worshiper of the romantic outpourings of George Sand—who entered the courtroom to give testimony in the Kroneberg case.

At the Kroneberg trial, Suslova testifies that while giving Adelina Gesing medical treatment for an unspecified illness, she observed Mariia, who was "quick-witted" ("imela bol'shuiu soobrazitel'nost'") but "didn't know how to control her bodily functions [ne umela upravliat' svoimi estestvennymi nuzhdami]" (January 27). She continues:

> Besides this, the girl had bad habits which had a great effect on her health, namely: she engaged in onanism, and the girl had had this illness, in the witness's opinion, for several years already; the girl had herself later confessed to this illness [v etoi bolezni devochka vposledstvii sama soznalas']. (January 27)[22]

Dostoevsky mentions Suslova's testimony in his notes for the 1876 *Writer's Diary* (24:143), and in the rough draft of his article on the Kroneberg case he inserts the following phrase after the exclamation, "She has a vice, she has a secret nasty vice" (22:71): "You all say it, accusers, the expert Suslova" ("Govorite vy vse, obviniteli, ekspert Suslova"; 22:208, see also 22:159).

Dostoevsky was so interested in Suslova's testimony that he planned to develop it as an episode in his unrealized novel "Fathers and Sons," for which he took notes in March 1876: "The whole story of Kroneberg in an episode of the novel, and with Suslova, who testified about the little girl's vices" (17:7). Yet in his article on the Kroneberg case as published in *A Writer's Diary,* Dostoevsky does not mention Suslova and her explicit testimony, and he echoes the euphemistic language of "secret vices" used by the other actors in the trial.

Dostoevsky's decision not to refer directly to Suslova's testimony contrasts sharply with the approach adopted by Saltykov-Shchedrin, whose essay, published later than Dostoevsky's, is similar in its negative response to Spasovich's defense tactics. Saltykov-Shchedrin attacks Suslova's testimony head-on:

> Dr. Suslova testified that the little girl engaged in onanism and didn't know how to control her bodily functions. Yes, that is how the doctor testified, in those words, precisely and clearly, as if she was afraid to leave anything out. Others testified about the "vices" of Mariia Kroneberg evasively, as if not wishing to compromise the child, who even so had accused herself of thieving and lying in the most disgraceful way, but Dr. Suslova testified just as "it is necessary to testify of this before God and his Last Judgment." Where others stopped themselves at the thought that the girl still had a long life before her, Dr. Suslova, with what one might call a soldier's frankness, had no qualms about giving her a lifelong testimonial.[23]

Saltykov-Shchedrin mentions Suslova's testimony in the same mocking tone four more times in his essay.[24]

Of course, in expressing his outrage at the exposure of the little girl's sexual secret, Saltykov-Shchedrin intensified that exposure through his repeated attacks on Suslova. Dostoevsky chose a different route, omitting all mention of Suslova and her explicit diagnosis of onanism. He was perhaps partly guided by a lingering tenderness for his old acquaintance and an understanding of her professional position, but his main object was no doubt to preserve a zone of secrecy and obscurity around Mariia Kroneberg. Although most of his audience would probably have read about the trial in the newspaper, Suslova's testimony is brief and comes near the middle of a long sequence of witnesses, so it was not necessarily noticed by the casual reader (although it does come near the beginning of the fourth installment of the trial account as published in the newspaper *The Voice*).

In his notes and drafts toward the article on the Kroneberg case, Dostoevsky repeatedly cites an exchange between two characters in Gogol's 1842 play *The Gamblers* (*Igroki*):

"Yes, but a person belongs to society."
"He does, but not the whole person."[25]

"Tak, no chelovek prinadlezhit obshchestvu."
"Prinadlezhit, no ne ves'."

Although the Gogol reference did not make it into the published version of Dostoevsky's article, in the drafts he elucidates his interest in this bit of dialogue, trying to define areas, especially areas relating to the family, that "are hard to bring out in open court [glasnyi sud]" (24:135): "The family, by its very essence, is a matter that is half hidden, intimate, subjective. In the family is hidden that which in each person is intimate-personal, secret-personal [intimno-lichnogo, sekretno-lichnogo]" (22:252). Not all of Mariia Kroneberg belongs to society, not even in the essay in which Dostoevsky is trying to defend her.

The editors of Dostoevsky's complete works in 1981, under the puritanical strictures of Soviet scholarship, also fail to point explicitly to the vice of onanism about which Suslova testified. The notes to the article on the Kroneberg case say only, "The doctor N. P. Suslova, whom Dostoevsky knew personally, testified very frankly and mercilessly [besposhchadno] about the girl's vices" (22:348). At this point we should consider why Suslova was so "merciless." As we have seen, she was a person who had devoted her life to science, a realm in which euphemism and obscurity have very little place. As in the review of Manasseina, her language at the trial is indeed frank, straightforward, and devoid of euphemism. Whether it is "merciless" or not bears further consideration.

Suslova gave enormous importance to the raising of children. In the book review, she begins with a plea for the education of women, because in the patriarchal system children are brought up by the least educated and most limited members of society, that is, women:

> The poor mother, who has renounced everything on earth in favor of raising her children, as a result of her fundamental lack of education and consequently her utter incompetence for the task of upbringing, is tragically forced to harm her own children. And she does harm them and *must* harm them in all respects, because she usually does not even know the needs of the child's body and the conditions of a child's life—she does not even know how to feed her children.[26]

Among the issues that a well-informed mother of Suslova's day would have to know about was masturbation, which was considered an extremely dangerous and harmful practice, even a fatal one.

The key to Suslova's testimony is that, unlike the other actors in the trial, she uses the word "illness" ("bolezn'"), not "vice" ("porok"). Her "mercilessly frank" testimony may be conditioned by the fact that she regards Mariia as a suffering patient, not an evil sinner.[27] Still, her testimony does betray a certain ambivalence: she says that the little girl "confessed [soznalas'] to this illness." One does not "confess" to an illness such as the flu or tuberculosis, since confession implies culpability.[28] Suslova's seemingly dual attitude toward the "illness" of onanism as both malady and sin is reflected in the contemporary scientific and pedagogical literature.

To understand the seriousness with which the actors in the trial took Suslova's testimony, one has only to recall Tissot's laundry list of grave illnesses supposedly caused by masturbation (see chapter 4). According to Tissot, women are subject to additional problems beyond those caused in men. I quote from the 1845 Russian edition:

> Masturbation causes in women, besides the above-mentioned fits, severe hysteria combined with deep melancholia, incurable jaundice, spasms in the stomach, convulsions in the spine and lower back; the face becomes hideous, bleeding from the uterus arises with all its consequences; but most horrible of all is nymphomania [beshenstvo matki, literally "mania of the uterus"], which deprives a woman of all her good sense and drives her to extreme shamelessness.[29]

Tissot was of course highly influential, but another treatise on the causes and consequences of masturbation, V. Ditman's "The Secret Vice" ("Tainyi porok"), was published in a Russian pedagogical journal, *Pedagogicheskii sbornik (Pedagogical Digest)*, in 1871, much closer in time to the Kroneberg case.[30]

Besides the title, which is echoed in the phrase used to describe Mariia's onanism, this treatise includes several parallels to the Kroneberg case. The idea that a four-year-old child could be given to such a shameful practice is confirmed here; according to Ditman, "premature sexual arousal" can be caused by accident (the "insignificant arousals of the child's organism") and by the bad example of playmates or adults: "Often children who do not yet have any conception of the immorality and depravity of this practice, in the course of playing make the dangerous discovery of voluptuous sensations and give themselves up carelessly to the vice of masturbation [rukobludie]."[31] Even Mariia's tendency to pilfer sweets constitutes a clinical symptom, because according to Ditman, a taste for "sweets and treats" ("sladosti i lakomstva") is one of the warning signs parents should be alert for.[32] In his notes toward the Kroneberg article, Dostoevsky remarks that Mariia Kroneberg's rosy complexion complicates the picture of her subjection to masturbation, because according to Tissot and his heirs the masturbator is supposed to have a pale or jaundiced complexion. Dostoevsky says, "It's worth noting that the red cheeks and the vices contradict each other" (24:143).[33] Ditman even accounts for this seeming contradiction: "It sometimes happens that boys and youths who look healthy and plump and have red cheeks have irrevocably given themselves up to these secret enjoyments . . . One must know that the boy's external healthy appearance does not constitute *an absolute guarantee* that he is not subject to this vice."[34]

Ditman claims that his eighteenth-century predecessor Tissot exaggerates the evil effects of masturbation: "[Tissot] almost exclusively gives descriptions of the most horrible and extreme consequences of onanism."[35] Yet Ditman's own list is hardly a comforting one: wasting, slow growth, loss of appetite, sleep disturbances, nervous headaches, general convulsions of the whole body, epilepsy, convulsive rigidity, paralysis, weak urine stream, and bed-wetting. Among the psychic consequences are unnatural shyness and timidity, unsociableness, irritability, capriciousness, apathy, and weak memory.[36] The consequences of leaving the illness/vice untreated are as dire as anything promised by Tissot. Ditman writes: "The further development of morbid afflictions of psychic functions, of the reason, feelings, and will, leads little by little to their complete disorder in cases where onanism entirely takes possession of the unfortunates who have given themselves up to this vice, and *in the end follows death with all the signs of physical and psychic exhaustion* [istoshchenie]" (emphasis mine).[37] Faced with such awful consequences for allowing a child or adolescent to continue masturbating, it is no wonder that parents and educators took drastic measures against the practice. Thomas W. Laqueur describes an industry devoted to developing "a steady stream of appliances—erection alarms, penis cases, sleeping mitts, bed cradles to keep the sheets off the genitals, hobbles to keep girls from spreading their legs."[38] An 1884 French work on the disorders caused by masturbation, lesbianism, deflowering, and sodomy refers to a more drastic and disfiguring measure:

> It is indeed certain that when faced with a very serious case, when faced with acts the repetition of which produces a profound disturbance of the organism, which produces such mental disturbances that homicidal or suicidal madness can be the result, the doctor is authorized to destroy the organ which is considered to be the seat of sensual sensations, and to have recourse to its ablation, its excision either with the lancet or with thermo-cautery. This operation is a very simple one. But do not imagine, gentlemen, that it is free from dangers; serious injuries, even death, can result from it. Thus after some attempts to destroy the clitoris with the aid of thermo-cautery, there have been cases where abcesses or peritonitis developed.[39]

95

Against this background, the beatings to which Mariia Kroneberg were subjected appear in a new light.

Just because Kroneberg beat his daughter, there is no need to discount entirely the testimony, both his own and that of others, that speaks of his care and concern for her. Gesing testifies that he "loved his daughter very much" and punished her "with the goal of correcting his daughter and in her own interests" (January 26). Pastor de Combe claims that "Kroneberg wanted to give the little child a good education, in order to make her a woman useful to society, and not to let the child feel all the bitterness of her origins" (January 27). Although this statement is treated sarcastically by the prosecutor, it undoubtedly contains a grain of truth. Kroneberg was under no legal obligation to do anything for Mariia, yet he did take her into his home. He seems to have had the unrealistic expectation that after seven years of neglect she would instantly become "a woman useful to society." The fury of the beatings he inflicted on her cannot be justified. If, however, one takes into account the contemporary medical opinions on the fatal consequences of leaving the illness/vice of onanism untreated, one can at least begin to understand the desperation and fear that motivated him.

Dostoevsky seems to have understood this, and that is why in his published article he directs his anger mainly at Spasovich and not at Kroneberg.[40] A key passage in the notes toward the 1876 *Writer's Diary* demonstrates this clearly. Dostoevsky summarizes Spasovich's defense strategy in telegraphic phrases:

> To kill pity, and here she is. She's "sharp"—here are her cheeks—here are her vices—here the expert Suslova will testify as to her vices. But after all she's a child, not responsible . . . (It's worth noting that the red cheeks and the vices contradict each other, but on the whole the impression is made.) But that's not enough, as a deep psychologist, he has to produce revulsion, and pity will disappear, the secret vices
>
> Excuse me! Why, that's what they beat her for! That's what was tormenting her father. [Pomiluite, da ved' za eto-to i sekli! Eto-to i muchilo ottsa.]
>
> I agree, but after all, this shouldn't disturb Sp[asovi]ch, who knows better than anyone and anything that a seven-year-old girl is not responsible for all that. (24:143)

There is no punctuation after the words "secret vices," implying that Dostoevsky stopped in the middle of a line. Was he struck by the realization that Mariia's masturbation was the true provocation of the beatings? Dostoevsky's insight that it was onanism, not lying or stealing, that in fact precipitated the savage beating, is shared by the prosecutor. In his summation he complains that the defense has shifted the ground from under him. At the preliminary investigation, Mariia's "secret vice" was not mentioned:

[During the preliminary investigation] it was a question of the fact that the girl was constantly sleeping, that she was dirty, and that at the time of the punishment Kroneberg was in a nervous state. Here, however, to all this was added another circumstance which, because of its importance, has become *the main reason* for the severity of the punishment, namely that illness about which Dr. Suslova testified. (January 28; emphasis mine)

The prosecutor admits that this reason "is in fact a very important reason, it could make it necessary for any father to take more strict measures against the child" (January 28). Yet he dismisses this point because in the statute under which Kroneberg is charged, the "goal with which the torture is caused" is not to be taken into account in deciding guilt or innocence.

Strangely enough, Spasovich himself does not dwell on Mariia's onanism in his own summation. He mentions it only briefly, and emphasizes instead her lying and stealing. As Saltykov-Shchedrin notes, "One must do justice to Mr. Spasovich: he did not for a moment dwell on the soldierly-frank testimony of Dr. Suslova."[41] Why did Spasovich fail to elaborate on the one "deficiency" that was most likely to justify the actions of his client? The answer lies in the trial transcript, in an action by Spasovich that is not mentioned by Dostoevsky in his article on the Kroneberg case. At the very beginning of the trial, Spasovich moved to conduct the hearings in camera (literally "behind closed doors") because the case involved family matters, that which Dostoevsky himself called "the intimate-personal, the secret-personal." Spasovich explains:

> Kroneberg in his defense must recount the whole story of the child's origins, touching on her birth, the name of the girl's mother. Then several witnesses will tell about bad physical habits the girl has, which provoked the punishment and which are of such a nature that in the presence of the public one could hardly pose the questions to the witnesses that would elucidate these habits. (January 25)

The prosecutor objected to the motion, and it was denied on the grounds that the statute under which Kroneberg was being tried had no provision for holding sessions in camera. Thus in fact Spasovich did make an attempt to protect Mariia Kroneberg's privacy. He does not ask witnesses, not even Suslova, to elaborate on Mariia's "secret vice," and he does not emphasize it in his summation. He does, however, claim that Kroneberg was saving his daughter "from becoming a debauched [rasputnaia] woman" (January 29). The word "rasputnaia" has a clearly sexual connotation, and is not usually used in the context of theft, as Spasovich uses it here. The definition in the late nineteenth-century dictionary by Dal' makes this clear: "debauched, immoral, fleshly, bestial, giving oneself up to all the temptations of his sinful and beastly nature."[42] The dire fate Spasovich predicts for Mariia if she is not reformed is that she will end up stealing not prunes but banknotes. Yet he indicates with his use of the word "rasputnaia" that he is really thinking of nymphomania, the "mania of the uterus" that results from unchecked masturbation.

Although Dostoevsky must have noticed that Spasovich tried to protect Mariia's privacy by moving to hold the trial in camera, he still brought the full force of his anger to bear on the defense attorney.[43] In his notes it is clear that Dostoevsky held Spasovich responsible for shaming Mariia because as a sophisticated jurist he should have known better than the girl's father: "He had to . . . exhibit her secret vice (as if he weren't speaking of a seven-year-old girl and as if he didn't know that corporal punishment exacerbates this vice)" (24:141). Dostoevsky apparently does not entirely accept the prevailing views on the fatal consequences of masturbation, and expects that a man like Spasovich would also not be enslaved to the conventional wisdom. Dostoevsky seems to feel that Spasovich is cynically manipulating the feelings of the less sophisticated jury members.

As Rosenshield points out, Dostoevsky places himself in the position of the prosecutor, doing battle directly with Spasovich. Rosenshield elucidates Dostoevsky's clever technique of attacking Spasovich by means of one of his strongest points, his talent, a talent that in Dostoevsky's view is abused. We can see this strategy arising in the notes toward the 1876 *Writer's Diary:* "Talent. You speak not exactly against yourself, but you put yourself out and praise something you never thought about your whole life, or *you curse in another such vices [poroki] as in fact are in him himself from head to toe*" (24:142, emphasis mine; in Dostoevsky's somewhat chaotic notebook syntax, both the second and third person here refer to Spasovich). What does it mean for Dostoevsky to claim that Spasovich "curses in another such vices as in fact are in him himself from head to toe"? A clue can be found in an enigmatic phrase used both in the notes and in the published article to characterize Spasovich's talent. In the article Dostoevsky deplores the excessive "responsiveness" ("otzyvchivost'") of the person who allows his talent to control his actions and overrule his moral judgment: "In a conversation with me, Belinskii compared this excessive 'responsiveness' with, so to speak, '*bludodeistvie* of talent,' and despised it very much, assuming as its antithesis, of course, a certain firmness of soul, which could always control its responsiveness, even while in the most strongly poetic mood" (22:55). I have purposely left the word "bludodeistvie" untranslated because its proper translation is not easy to find. The word does not appear in modern dictionaries, and the definition offered in Dal"s dictionary is less than helpful: "*bludodei* and other compound words of this type are understandable without definition and are obscene." Since the word is not "understandable without definition" to a non-native speaker of the twenty-first century, I had recourse to an expert informant, Yuz Aleshkovsky, a contemporary writer with an outstanding command of the Russian language in all its varieties.[44] He at first indicated that "bludodeistvie talanta" refers to an unfruitful misuse of one's talents, a meaning that Dostoevsky clearly has in mind here. When I asked why then Dal' would call the word obscene, he replied, "Because it also means 'masturbation.'" Thus when Dostoevsky characterizes Spasovich's technique as "bludodeistvie talanta," he is metaphorically accusing him of masturbation. Here, then, is the heart of Dostoevsky's strategy in defending Mariia Kroneberg: to claim that the vice of which she is accused is in fact in her main accuser Spasovich "from head to toe."[45]

It is noteworthy that Dostoevsky adopts the phrase "bludodeistvie talanta" from Vissarion Belinskii (1811–48), the highly influential critic with whom Dostoevsky was very close in the 1840s. In 1992 V. Sazhin published a letter of 1837 from Belinskii to Mikhail Bakunin in which he confessed that he had been a dedicated onanist, beginning at age nineteen and ending only in 1835, that is, when he was twenty-four: "I was no longer a child but a student, I read Schiller and Byron, was delirious with Romanticism and was composing a drama."[46] In citing this letter, Laqueur claims that Belinskii confesses "that reading Byron and Schiller had driven him to masturbation when he first encountered them as a nineteen-year-old student."[47] I believe the force of Belinskii's statement is somewhat different: he is emphasizing the abjectness of his succumbing to masturbation when he was no longer an innocent child but a mature man capable of reading Byron and Schiller and of composing a play. Here he is in harmony with Dostoevsky, who absolves the innocent child for her "secret vice" but scorns the adult Spasovich for his metaphorical onanism. As we saw in chapter 4, Dostoevsky's heroes Arkadii Dolgorukii and Alyosha Karamazov are able to "grow out" of their masturbatory phase as they reach full adulthood. Spasovich has apparently not done so.[48]

According to Dostoevsky, as the antithesis to "bludodeistvie talanta" Belinskii identified "a certain firmness of soul." For Dostoevsky, the shame of masturbation lies not in a physical manipulation of the genitalia but in a weakness of the soul, the kind of weakness that only an adult can be held responsible for. In Mariia Kroneberg this weakness is a product of neglect and bad influences and is not her responsibility. On the other hand, in Dostoevsky's scheme of values Spasovich's metaphorical masturbation, his enslavement to his own talent that with cold calculation invades Mariia's sacred privacy, is a serious moral defect.

A few years after the Kroneberg case, in 1879, E. N. Opochinin recorded a conversation with Dostoevsky that illuminates his view of children as well as his fierce defense of Mariia Kroneberg's "intimate-personal" realm. Opochinin describes Dostoevsky watching a poor boy on the street admiring toys in a shop window. Dostoevsky remarks that it is impossible to guess what a child is thinking, and that "everything they write about children is nonsense and lies."[49] Dostoevsky claims that even if the boy were to tell you of his reveries, "even that wouldn't be the truth, for he would do it just for you—but that which is his own, truthful, genuine, he'll keep to himself." Opochinin asks, "Does that mean that children always lie?" Dostoevsky answers in frustration: "Oh, how can you not understand! . . . After all, even for grownups it's somehow shameful to open up one's soul, to share one's reveries, and not everyone can do it, but a child—a child is chaste [tselomudren] in the true sense of the word. He will not open his world to anyone. His truth only God alone hears."[50] It is in this sense that Mariia Kroneberg is absolutely chaste, no matter what her "secret vices." In his account of the Kroneberg case, Dostoevsky upholds the radical innocence of children, no matter what corrupting influences have touched them: "We must respect [children] and approach them with respect for their angelic visage (even if we do have something to teach them), for their innocence, even if they have some kind of depraved habit [dazhe i pri porochnoi kakoi-nibud' v nikh privychke]—for their lack of responsibility and their touching defenselessness" (22:69). The adult Spasovich weakly succumbs to his desire to display his talent and therefore transforms it into a form of masturbation—"bludodeistvie talanta." When in the course of doing so he violently forces open the chaste, private world of the child Mariia to the public, he becomes the true sinner in Dostoevsky's moral economy.

Like Arkadii Dolgorukii and Alyosha Karamazov, Mariia Kroneberg was an abandoned child, left to her own moral devices and prey to debauching influences that no parent was on hand to protect her from. In the next chapter we will return to the Kroneberg case for its illumination of Dostoevsky's conception of the family in its ideal state.

Chapter Six

The Missing Family

THE CHILDREN AND ADOLESCENTS in Dostoevsky's works who discover sexuality in some of its potentially harmful forms have one thing in common: they are deprived of a stable family with a mother and a father constantly on the scene to offer guidance. It may be that Dostoevsky originally borrowed the "poor orphan" theme from Dickens, but he indisputably made it his own over the twenty post-Siberia years of his career. In *The Insulted and Injured,* Nelli's somewhat inadequate familial caretakers, her mother and grandfather, have died, and the man who is probably her biological father, Prince Valkovskii, has no interest in adopting or acknowledging her (and would provide a very poor parental example if he did). She finds refuge first with Bubnova, who tries to prostitute her, and then with Ivan, in a relationship with dark sexual undercurrents. In *Crime and Punishment,* the five-year-old child in Svidrigailov's dream, like Nelli, is out alone at night, away from parental protection (she fears being beaten by her mother if she returns home). Nastas'ia Filippovna in *The Idiot* catches Totskii's eye after the death of both her parents, and has nowhere else to go but into genteel prostitution with her "benefactor." The child Matryosha in "At Tikhon's" does have living parents, but their emotional support is thin (as evidenced by her mother's unjust beatings), and they leave her alone in their apartment for long stretches, where she falls prey to the "gentleman lodger" Stavrogin.

Dostoevsky begins in these works by depicting the child's sexual victimization from the viewpoint of the victimizer. As he moves toward representing the adolescent's encounter with sexuality from within, he also moves from female to male young people, as if acknowledging that he is unable to master the female point of view, at least as far as the realm of sexuality is concerned.[1] In *A Raw Youth,* Arkadii's parents are alive but have never lived with him. He has acquired the habit of discovering the world on his own, making his own mistakes without guidance. He encounters the economic, spiritual, and sexual spheres of life in an experimental, blindly groping way; the last people he would turn to for advice are his mother and Versilov. In

The Brothers Karamazov, Alyosha's mother is dead, and his father is incapable of offering moral guidance, especially in the sexual sphere, even if he were interested in doing so.

In the real-life story of Mariia Kroneberg in *A Writer's Diary,* her "secret vice" of masturbation is instilled in her during her years as an abandoned illegitimate child in Switzerland. She is corrupted by strangers at an age when, as Dostoevsky says, "She did not yet have and could not have enough intellect to notice bad things in herself" (22:68). In sum, in Dostoevsky's world the child or adolescent who encounters sexuality without a supporting familial framework comes in contact with forms of sexuality that Dostoevsky saw as potentially damaging: pedophilia, homosexuality, and masturbation. There are few examples in Dostoevsky's fictional and non-fictional works of what an ideally functioning family, one that would foster healthy sexual development in its children, would look like. We can only try to form a picture of it by looking at Dostoevsky's journalistic statements, and by analyzing the negative image of the family offered in his works.

In the years of Dostoevsky's artistic maturity, the problem of the family had been framed most vividly by Ivan Turgenev in his 1861 novel *Fathers and Sons (Ottsy i deti,* literally *Fathers and Children,* but the novel's emphasis is firmly on sons, not daughters). Although this work is ostensibly about chaos and destruction, as embodied in the "nihilist" Bazarov, both the family structures depicted in the novel and the structure of the novel itself are remarkably harmonious and stable. Not only does Bazarov's callow friend Arkadii Kirsanov have a loving and devoted father and uncle, but Bazarov himself has salt-of-the-earth parents who worship the ground he walks on.[2] The novel is built on the classic structure of comedy: by the end, the disruptive character who calls the social order into question (Bazarov) has been neutralized (by typhus), and an idyllic family group, which has incorporated the peasant mistress and her illegitimate son as lady of the manor and young master, gathers to celebrate a new patriarchal order presided over by the just-married son Arkadii (whose "Arcadian" name sounds ironic at the beginning of the novel but ends by suiting the idyllic pastoral scene to a tee).[3]

Dostoevsky's creative efforts in the last years of his life were dominated by his desire to produce his own "Fathers and Sons." His last three novels, *The Devils, A Raw Youth,* and *The Brothers Karamazov,* can be seen as in part motivated by this quest to rewrite Turgenev. Dostoevsky's vision of the late nineteenth-century Russian family is the polar opposite of Turgenev's comedic idyll; as he writes in the drafts to *A Raw Youth* (1875), "In everything is the idea of decomposition, because everyone is separate and there are no bonds remaining not only in the Russian family, but even simply among people" (16:16).[4] This can be seen perhaps most vividly in the

1876 sketches to which Dostoevsky gave the heading "Fathers and Sons." In the space of less than two printed pages of the Academy edition of his works, Dostoevsky presents a grim kaleidoscope of family disintegration: a boy sits in a juvenile penal colony and dreams of being rescued by his relatives (whom he imagines as princes and counts); a man kills his wife in front of his nine-year-old son, who helps him hide the body under the floor; a father, who has learned after his wife's death that their son is not biologically his, abandons the boy on the street in the freezing cold; children run away from their father (17:6–7). There is also an allusion to the Kroneberg child abuse case (see chapter 5) and to homosexual seduction in a public bath. This unrealized "Fathers and Sons" was to depict a familial nihilism far beyond the imaginings of Turgenev.

We know from the essayistic portions of *A Writer's Diary* that Dostoevsky saw the depiction of the Russian family's dissolution as a civic duty. The comedic "happy ending" of Turgenev's *Fathers and Sons* was not an adequate response to what Dostoevsky saw as Russia's most pressing problem. In his view, only by first recognizing and describing the chaos could one even begin to dream of a new form of order. Dostoevsky writes in *A Writer's Diary* for January 1877:

> There are the features of some kind of new reality, completely different from the reality of the becalmed and long-ago firmly established Moscow landowning family of the mid-upper circles, whose *historian* for us was Count Lyov Tolstoy . . . And if even an artist of Shakespearean dimensions would not be able to search out a normative law and governing thread in this chaos in which for a long time, but especially now, our social life has abided, then who at least will illuminate even a part of that chaos, without even hoping to find the governing thread? . . . We indisputably have a decomposing life and consequently a decomposing family. But there must also be a newly forming life, based on new principles. Who will notice them, and who will indicate them? Who can even begin to define and express the laws both of that chaos and of the new creation? (25:35)

Throughout the *Writer's Diary* Dostoevsky repeatedly casts Russia's social dilemma in terms of "fathers and sons":

> The "accidental" quality of the contemporary Russian family, in my opinion, consists in the loss by contemporary fathers of any universal idea in relation to their families, universal for all fathers, binding them all together, an idea in which they themselves would believe and would teach their children to believe, would convey to them this faith in life. (25:178)

You are the fathers, they are your children, you are contemporary Russia, they are the future Russia: what will happen to Russia if Russian fathers evade their civic duty and begin to seek solitude or more precisely isolation, a lazy and cynical isolation from society, their nation, and their most important obligations to that society and nation? (25:192)[5]

Dostoevsky's last three novels are devoted to exploring the ways in which the fathers of Russia have failed in their obligations to the sons, and therefore to the nation's future. In the process Dostoevsky questions accepted definitions, both radical and conservative, of the family itself. Since the family is the proper social site for the sexual development of children, Dostoevsky's theory of the family is intertwined with his concerns about sexuality.

The decomposition of the Russian family is, in Dostoevsky's view, at least in part the result of the experimentation with new forms of family life carried out by radical intellectuals from Alexander Herzen to Nikolai Chernyshevskii and beyond. In both life and literature, these thinkers sought ways to disrupt the bourgeois patriarchal order, usually through the toleration of adultery. Irina Paperno, who has thoroughly analyzed the experiments of Herzen and Chernyshevskii, highlights the positive significance of the new family arrangements:

> In accordance with a cultural tradition that associated stability in marriage with the stability of society at large, Chernyshevsky proposed to make the rearrangement of family life into the basis for the rearrangement of society . . . But contrary to the opinion of Chernyshevsky's critics, the form of adultery advocated in [*What Is to Be Done?*] was not intended to undermine or destroy society. What appeared as a form of adultery . . . was for Chernyshevsky the foundation for emotional and social harmony and equilibrium.[6]

What seems to be lacking in the theories and practice of these intellectuals, and what Dostoevsky is to emphasize in his critical and literary responses, is any serious thinking through of what happens to the children produced by nontraditional sexual arrangements. In his highly influential 1845–46 novel *Who Is to Blame?* (*Kto vinovat?*), Herzen, himself illegitimate, depicted illegitimacy as one of the evil products of the stable patriarchal family. This is presented most pointedly in a scene in which the tyrannical landowner Negrov orders his valet to marry the peasant woman who has borne Negrov's daughter. In anticipation of the order, the valet says, "Whom can we oblige if not Your Excellency; you are our father, we are your children [vy nashi ottsy, my vashi deti]."[7] (The point is hammered home by a later reference to the story of Abraham, Hagar, Ishmael, and Sarah.)[8] In contrast, Dostoevsky is preoccupied with the illegitimate and abandoned children sired not by old-fashioned patriarchs but by intellectuals under the ideological influence of George Sand, Aleksandr Druzhinin, Herzen, and Chernyshevskii. Druzhinin's Sand-inspired 1847 novella "Polin'ka Saks," in which a civil servant nobly steps aside so that his wife can be united with her lover, thus earning her undying admiration and devotion, was of particular interest to Dostoevsky. Arkadii Dolgorukii, the narrator of *A Raw Youth*, clearly attributes his own illegitimate origins to the fact that his father, the nobleman Versilov, had read the novella just before visiting his estate, where he began an affair with a married serf woman, Arkadii's mother. Arkadii sarcastically refers to Druzhinin's story as a literary piece "that had a boundless civilizing influence on the generation that was then coming of age in Russia" (13:10).[9] In *The Devils*, the liberal Stepan Verkhovenskii is discovered by his radical son Pyotr reading Chernyshevskii's 1863 novel *What Is to Be Done?* (*Chto delat'?*), in which a ménage à trois on rational principles figures prominently. Stepan has claimed that the novel represents "our idea" (10:238). Almost immediately afterward, Pyotr reminds his father that Stepan had questioned Pyotr's parentage in conversations with Pyotr himself during his adolescence (10:238, 240).

In the *Writer's Diary*, Dostoevsky's most striking case in point of what happens to the children of radical experiments with the family is the suicide of Herzen's own daughter Liza. Liza was the product of Herzen's affair with Natal'ia Tuchkova-Ogaryova, the wife of his friend Nikolai Ogaryov.[10] She killed herself in Florence in December 1875 at the age of seventeen (almost six years after Herzen's death). Dostoevsky wrote about her suicide and especially her suicide note (which he embellished with a couple of telling details) in the *Writer's Diary* for October and December 1876. In the essays Dostoevsky does not mention her name but identifies her rather unmistakably for his readership by calling her "the daughter of a too-famous Russian emigré" (23:145). Liza's suicide appears to have been prompted by an unhappy love for an older married man, but Dostoevsky traces it—or rather the malicious tone of it as reflected in her suicide note—to her irregular upbringing and in particular to the role played in family relations by the radical theories of her extended clan: "I expressed the supposition that she died from anguish [toska] (a too early anguish) and the aimlessness of life—only as a result of her upbringing, *perverted by theory,* in her father's home, an upbringing with a mistaken conception of the higher significance and aims of life, with the intentional destruction in her soul of all faith in her own immortality" (24:54; emphasis mine). Earlier, in the *Writer's Diary* for March 1876, Dostoevsky had seen a glimmer of hope in the possibility that the children of the liberal and radical experimenters with the family would revolt against their parents not by means of suicide but by finding a new path:

What could the children of that time see in their fathers, what memories could they have preserved about them from their childhood and boyhood? Cynicism, desecration, merciless attacks on their children's first tender holy beliefs; and quite often the open debauchery of their fathers and mothers, with the assurance and the *teaching* that this is how it should be, that these are the true "sober" relationships . . . But since youth is pure, bright, and magnanimous, it may of course happen that some of these youths would not want to take after such fathers and would reject their "sober" instructions . . . And it is perhaps those very youths and adolescents who are now seeking new paths and who begin directly by repulsing that hateful cycle of ideas that they encountered in their childhood, in their pitiful natal nests. (22:102)

In his novels Dostoevsky presents a range of possibilities for the children of what he calls (in *A Raw Youth*) "accidental families," from suicide to the Christlike behavior of Alyosha Karamazov, itself a kind of radicalism in the opposite direction from that of Herzen.

Dostoevsky's last three novels focus on sons of the new, "decomposed" Russian family who encounter their fathers for the first time only after reaching maturity. In *The Devils* and *A Raw Youth*, the contribution of radical ideology to the family's disintegration is pronounced; by the time of *The Brothers Karamazov* one has a sense of a more pervasive and deeply rooted evil undermining the foundations of the Russian family and society. The hero of *The Devils*, Stepan Trofimovich Verkhovenskii, is a liberal of the Herzen generation who has seen his son Pyotr only once since his infancy. The child's mother died in Paris when he was five years old and he was sent to Russia, "where he was raised by some kind of distant aunts somewhere in the backwoods" (10:11). When the 27-year-old man appears in Mrs. Stavrogin's salon near the beginning of the novel, it takes his father several minutes to recognize him, even though his arrival has been expected (10:143–44). Arkadii Dolgorukii, the illegitimate hero-narrator of *A Raw Youth*, was raised "v chuzhikh liudiakh" ("by strangers," 13:14) almost from birth and comes to know his father and mother only at the age of nineteen. Arkadii has a vivid memory of meeting and "falling in love with" his father on one occasion as a child, after which he was packed off to a boarding school where he was mercilessly taunted about his parentage. His life since then has been given up to dreaming of his father Versilov: "I wanted all of Versilov, give me a father . . . that's what I demanded" (13:100). Fyodor Karamazov, of course, abandons not one but three (possibly four) sons after the deaths of their mothers, as perhaps most beautifully described by Diane Oenning Thompson in a chapter entitled "Forgetting." Thompson eloquently summarizes the failings of most of the adults in *The Brothers Kara-mazov:* "What should be remembered, children, neighbours, family, serfs who have legitimate claims on the attention of those responsible for their welfare, have been ignored, neglected, obliterated from memory . . . Forgetting, here in the form of social and parental neglect, functions as a critical index of morality, personal, familial, societal and national."[11] In *The Brothers Karamazov*, as in *The Devils* and *A Raw Youth*, the action proper of the novel begins as the sons make the acquaintance of the fathers who "missed" their childhood, boyhood, and youth.

In all three novels, fathers and sons separated physically have created mental images of each other—have "invented" ("vydumat'") each other. Stepan Verkhovenskii writes letters about his intimate affairs to a son in Paris who, far from being the sympathetic confidant Stepan imagines, turns out to be a vile intriguer who blurts out Stepan's indiscreet complaints and fears in the middle of Mrs. Stavrogin's crowded drawing room:

> "You wouldn't believe it, right next to the happiest lines he writes the most despairing ones. In the first place, he asks my forgiveness; just imagine, the man has only laid eyes on me twice in his life, and that was by accident, and all of a sudden now, when he's about to get married for the third time, he imagines that by doing so he's transgressing some kind of parental obligations and begs me at a distance of a thousand versts to forgive him and give him my permission!" (10:161)

The narrator tells us that Stepan's disappointment in his son is "a deep and *real* sorrow" (10:163). In *A Raw Youth*, Arkadii Dolgorukii similarly has to cope with a reality that fails to live up to the dream: "It turns out that this man is just my dream, a dream from my childhood. It's me who invented him this way, but in reality he turned out to be someone else, falling far short of my fantasy" (13:62). And Dmitrii Karamazov reveals his own fantasy at the meeting in Father Zosima's cell: "'I thought . . . I thought,' he said somehow quietly and with restraint, 'that I would come to my native town with the angel of my soul, my fiancée, in order to cherish him in his old age, but I see only a debauched sensualist and a base comedian!'" (14:68–69). In each case the fantasy is based on almost nothing, but it takes on reality as an obstacle to the already difficult process of a father's getting to know his adult son. The heavy load of the disappointment caused when the fantasy fails is added to the account of the father's failures against his son.

The orphaned children in these novels cope with their abandonment in two major ways: by finding surrogate fathers who provide the love and moral guidance their biological fathers have deprived them of, and by seeking closeness and solidarity with their siblings.[12] Arkadii's surrogate father is, ironically, his legal father, the peasant Makar Dolgorukii, who offers Arkadii a model of ascetic pilgrimage and the quest for "blagoobrazie" ("blessed form"), in stark contrast to the Herzenesque godless theorizing of Arkadii's biological father Versilov. An artistically more successful version of a similar relationship is embodied in Alyosha Karamazov's devotion to the elder Zosima. Dmitrii's connection to his serf "father" Grigorii is more elemental and earthy, based on the very mundane tasks Grigorii performed for the abandoned boy: "This old man—after all, he carried me in his arms, gentlemen, he bathed me in a trough when everyone had abandoned me, a three-year-old child, he was my own father [otets rodnoi]!" (14:414).[13]

God is of course the ultimate "surrogate father," but one who is also capable of abandonment, as dramatized most vividly in *The Brothers Karamazov*. It is not surprising that Ivan Karamazov is drawn to a medieval Orthodox tale about the Virgin's journey to hell in which it is said of some sinners in a burning lake that "God is already forgetting about them" (14:225). Versilov depicts a world without God as a world in which humans would discover a new brotherly love: "Orphaned people would immediately begin to press more closely and lovingly to each other; they would seize each other by the hand, understanding that now they alone were all in all for each other . . . They would become tender to each other and would not be ashamed of it as they are now, but would caress each other like children" (13:378–79). Arkadii and his sister Liza find, if only briefly, this kind of tenderness and consolation in each other in the midst of their "accidental family" (13:161–62). Throughout *The Brothers Karamazov* Alyosha strives to provide for his brothers the love and caring their father has denied them, and often succeeds.[14]

In contrast to Arkadii and the Karamazovs, Pyotr Verkhovenskii has neither surrogate father nor siblings, and this may account for the fact of his almost unalloyed evil. Instead of seeking a surrogate father, he sets himself up as a despotic father figure to his cell of five conspirators: "What is needed is a single magnificent, idol-like, despotic will, which rests on something that is not contingent and that has its own independent existence" (10:404). Instead of a true sibling, he has a parodic double in the form of Fed'ka the Convict, a serf whose life of crime is blamed on the fact that Stepan "lost him at cards," that is, sold him into the army in order to pay his gambling debts (10:181, 204). Stepan is confronted with his responsibility for Fed'ka in the middle of his appearance at the literary festival sponsored by the governor's wife. A provocateur in the audience interrupts Stepan's incoherent speech:

"Stepan Trofimovich! . . . Here in town and in the outskirts Fed'ka the Convict, an escaped prisoner, is now prowling around. He has been committing robberies and not long ago he committed a new murder. Allow me to pose the question: if fifteen years ago you had not given him up to conscription in order to pay your gambling debts, that is if you hadn't simply lost him at the card table, tell me, would he have ended up in a Siberian prison? Would he be cutting people's throats, as he is now, in the struggle for existence? What do you have to say, Mr. Aesthetician?" (10:373)

The question, parodic as it is, resonates as a question about Stepan's responsibility for his own abandoned son, who like Fed'ka is "prowling about the town," perpetrating atrocities and murder, including ultimately the murder of his "sibling" Fed'ka.

Responsibility is the key question when considering the Russian family, as the title of Herzen's novel *Who Is to Blame?* reminds us. In Dostoevsky's novels, Russian fathers do not prove to be very good at accepting responsibility for what has become of their sons. Stepan claims rather unconvincingly to have suffered throughout his absentee parenthood:

> "[Pyotr says] I gave him neither food nor drink, I sent him off from Berlin to —— Province, a babe in arms, in the mail, and so on and so forth, I'll admit it . . . 'You,' he says, 'gave me no drink and sent me off in the mail, and then you robbed me.' But, you unfortunate man, I cry to him, you know I suffered in my heart for you all my life, even if I did send you off in the mail!" (10:171)[15]

Versilov too refuses to accept full responsibility for his "accidental family," yawning openly in response to Arkadii's tales of his forlorn childhood (13:98, 101–2, 103, 110). And of course Fyodor Karamazov's sense of guilt over the abandonment of his sons is virtually nonexistent. At the meeting in the monk's cell he manages to shift the focus of blame to Dmitrii, the "parricide" (14:69). Fyodor's evocation of the ultimate crime of father-murder is subliminally bolstered by two of his references. He twice alludes to Schiller's 1782 play *The Robbers* (*Die Räuber*), which includes the speech: "The laws of God and Man are set at nought, the bond of nature is severed, the primal struggle is back, the son has killed his father."[16] In addition, Fyodor's repeated mention of the murder of von Sohn, whose name includes the German word for "son," increases the weight of the premonition that Dmitrii is to kill his father. In all three novels, the center of attention becomes the sins of the sons, not the fathers: Pyotr's incitement of riot, chaos, and murder; Arkadii's plan to blackmail an older woman into a sexual relationship; and, of course, the long-drawn-out scene of Dmitrii's trial for murder, in which the words "ottsa ubil" ("he killed his father") become an insistent refrain.

The speech at the trial by the defense attorney Fetiukovich poses the problem of the family in the starkest terms. Fetiukovich, a deconstructionist *avant la lettre*, calls into question the existence of all the elements of the alleged crime.[17] The centerpiece of his summation is his reduction of the terrifying taboo word "ottseubiistvo" ("parricide") to the status of "predras-sudok" (literally "prejudice," but with the connotation of "superstition"). Fetiukovich asserts that blood relation is not sufficient to make one worthy of the name of "father":

> Yes, it's a terrible thing to shed the blood of one's father—the blood of the one who conceived me, the blood of the one who loved me, the blood of the one who did not spare his own life for me, who ailed along with me in all my illnesses since my childhood, who suffered for my happiness all my life and who lived only through my joys and my success! Oh, to kill such a father—but it's impossible even to think of such a thing! . . . [But] my client grew up with only God's protection, in other words like a wild beast . . . We will prove . . . that the progress of recent years has reached even Russia in its development and we will say straight out: the one who conceives a child is not a father; a father is the one who both conceives and is worthy of the name of father. (15:168, 170)[18]

If Fyodor has not earned the title of "father," the logical conclusion is that Dmitrii's alleged murder of him is not parricide: "No, the murder of such a father cannot be called parricide. Such a murder can be accounted a parri-cide only through superstition [predrassudok]!" (15:172). Fyodor seems to have had a premonition of the defense attorney's argument when he says to Alyosha, "In today's fashionable world it's become the thing to consider fa-thers and mothers a superstition" (14:158).[19]

The use of the word "predrassudok" in relation to the family marks Fetiukovich as a person conversant with radical ideology, despite his con-stant references to the Gospel. In *The Devils*, the town radicals at a secret gathering begin a discussion of the "predrassudok" of the family:

> "We know, for example, that the superstition about God originated in thun-der and lightning," the female student suddenly burst in again, almost jump-ing at Stavrogin with her eyes. "It's very well established that primitive hu-manity, frightened of thunder and lightning, deified their unknown enemy, sensing their own weakness in relation to it. But where did the superstition about the family [predrassudok o semeistve] originate? Where could the fam-ily itself come from?"
>
> "I think that the answer to such a question would be indecent," Stavrogin answered. (10:306)

Stavrogin's answer points to a fact that Fetiukovich also stresses: the family originates in the act of sex. This fact is used by Fetiukovich to undermine the supposed holiness of family ties:

The sight of an unworthy father, especially as compared with other fathers, worthy ones, of the other children his age, inevitably suggests painful questions to the youth. His questions are answered pro forma: "He conceived you, and you are his blood, and therefore you must love him." The youth involuntarily falls to thinking: "But did he love me when he was conceiving me," he asks, becoming more and more amazed, "did he really conceive me for my sake: he didn't know me or even what sex I was at that moment, the moment of passion, perhaps inflamed by drink, and maybe he passed on to me his inclination to drunkenness—that's the extent of his benevolence . . . Why do I have to love him, just because he conceived me, and then failed to love me my whole life?" (15:171)[20]

The defense attorney's speech evokes two reactions in his audience. The sophisticated townspeople, including "fathers and mothers," applaud the idea that sons have a right to demand that their fathers explain why they should love them (15:171). As one of the onlookers says, "If I had been in the defense attorney's place I would have said straight out: he killed him, but he's not guilty, and the hell with you!" His interlocutor answers, "But that's just what he did, only he didn't say 'the hell with you'" (15:177). The other reaction, borne out in the guilty verdict by the "muzhichki" ("peasants") on the jury, is expressed by another member of the audience: "Yes, gentlemen, he's eloquent. But after all, we can't allow people to bash in their fathers' heads with steelyards. Otherwise where will we end up?" (15:177).

Is the family a sacred institution or is it a superstition? Does the name of "father" have to be earned by one's actions? Dostoevsky had tackled the same questions in the *Writer's Diary* for February 1876, and had come to conclusions that are superficially similar to those of Fetiukovich, even as he did rhetorical battle with an attorney, Vladimir Spasovich, who later served as a prototype for the sophistic defense attorney in *The Brothers Karamazov* (15:347). As discussed in chapter 5, the second part of the *Writer's Diary* for February 1876 deals with the Kroneberg case, in which a father was charged with the torture by beating of his seven-year-old illegitimate daughter. The child had been raised by Swiss peasants and then by a pastor in Geneva until the age of seven, when Kroneberg took her with him to Russia. Dostoevsky quotes the defense attorney's speech, which defends Kroneberg's rights as a father to punish his own child: "I think that to prosecute a father because he punished his child painfully but *justly* does a disservice to the family, a disservice to the state, because the state is only strong when it is founded on a strong family" (22:68; emphasis in original). Dostoevsky argues, however, that a father's rights must be earned, and that a father who missed his child's infancy, who doesn't really know his child, has a long way to go before he has any claim to sacred rights:

111

These creatures [children] only enter into our souls and become attached to our hearts when, after giving birth to them, we follow their development from childhood, without being separated from them, from their first smile, and then we continue to become close to them in soul every day, every hour over the course of our whole life. That is a family, that is something sacred [sviatynia]! After all, families are also *created*, not given ready-made . . . The family is created by the untiring labor of love [neustannym trudom liubvi]. (22:69–70; emphasis in original)[21]

Dostoevsky refuses to admit an a priori sacredness for the family: "We love the sacred thing that is the family when it is in fact sacred, and not just because the state is firmly founded on it" (22:72).[22]

    Why is it that in his essay on the Kroneberg case Dostoevsky seems to agree with Fetiukovich that a father has to earn his parental rights by "the untiring labor of love," while in *The Brothers Karamazov* that position is lampooned? The difference is one of context and purpose. Fetiukovich presumes that Dmitrii actually did kill his father, and is trying to help him evade responsibility by arguing that that father was not really a father at all. He is trying to get a guilty man off the hook. In the *Writer's Diary*, Dostoevsky is trying to put the father Kroneberg back on the hook. Kroneberg has no more right to be absolved because "the family is a sacred thing" than Dmitrii, had he actually killed his father, would have a right to be absolved because "families are created through the untiring labor of love." Dmitrii is no longer a child. Just because his father failed in his responsibilities to him, Dmitrii is not excused from the requirement to engage in "the labor of love," no matter how unworthy the object, from his own position as adult son.

    Dostoevsky offers an answer to the radical student's question, "Where does the family come from?" in the drafts to *The Brothers Karamazov*. Father Zosima was to have said, "God gave us relatives so that we could learn through them *how to love*. People who love humanity in general hate persons in particular" ("Bog dal rodnykh, chtob uchit'sia na nikh *liubvi*. Obshchecheloveki nenavidiat lits v chastnosti," 15:205). It is somewhat strange that this statement did not make it into the novel, linked as it is to Ivan's struggle with his inability to "love his neighbor," his repulsion from the sight of a "litso v chastnosti" ("person [literally, face] in particular"). The family situation presents this dilemma in its most concentrated form: in the family we are bound by nature to people whom it is our duty to love, but whose personalities, moral character, even physical appearance we may in fact dislike or hate. Thus, as Zosima in this draft indicates, loving our families can be excellent practice for loving all our fellow human beings. Such love is truly labor (trud), but it is also the only way to have any sort of claim to familial rights, as Dostoevsky points out in the *Writer's Diary* for July–

August 1877: "Only with love can we buy the hearts of our children, and not merely with our natural rights over them" (25:193).

The most beautiful family love in Dostoevsky's world is that which is given freely, not in exchange for good behavior. Arkadii Dolgorukii's mother in her Christian naivete expresses this idea with inadvertent humor in a dialogue with Arkadii. Arkadii says, "Family love is immoral, Mama, precisely because it is not earned. Love must be earned." His mother replies, "'Well, you'll earn it some day, but meanwhile we love you for no reason at all.' Everyone burst out laughing" (13:212). A similar idea is expressed in *The Brothers Karamazov* by Snegiryov and approved heartily by Alyosha:

> "Allow me to complete my introductions: my family, my two daughters and my son—my brood, sir. If I die, who's going to love them? And while I'm alive, who besides them is going to love nasty old me? This is a magnificent arrangement the Lord has set up for every person of my type, sir. For it is necessary that even a person of my type be loved by at least someone, sir."
> "Oh, that's so very true!" exclaimed Alyosha. (14:183)

"The family is created by the untiring labor of love," but before offering that love one cannot first demand proof of it from the other. The most meaningful examples of family love in Dostoevsky's last three novels are those in which nothing is offered in return: Arkadii's love for Versilov, Alyosha's love for Fyodor, and Stepan Verkhovenskii's love for his son Pyotr, which was lost in the face of the grown son's evil but recovered at the brink of death.[23] Pyotr has been absent from Stepan's thoughts during his final pilgrimage, but he surfaces, named by an affectionate diminutive, in Stepan's last words before lapsing into unconsciousness: "Long live the Great Idea! The eternal, boundless Idea! Every person, no matter who, has a need to bow before the Great Idea. Even the most foolish man has a need for something great. *Petrusha* . . . Oh, how I want to see them all again! They don't know, they don't know that even in them the very same Great Idea is contained!" (10:506; emphasis mine). Stepan's remembrance of "Petrusha," the son he lost through his failure to perform the untiring labor of love, is all the more poignant for having come far too late.

One aspect of the father-son relationships in Dostoevsky's last novels that I have not yet discussed relates to the role of women.[24] In both *A Raw Youth* and *The Brothers Karamazov*, a major component of the plot is a sexual rivalry between father and son. Both Arkadii and Versilov are obsessed with Katerina Nikolaevna Akhmakova; Dmitrii and Fyodor are locked in a fierce struggle over Grushenka. (In both cases the son "gets the girl" in the end, as the father has been neutralized by madness [Versilov] or murder [Fyodor].) Such relationships are often called "Oedipal," with the Freudian

113

sense of the term in mind.[25] It could be argued that Dostoevsky's version of the father-son rivalry is closer to the original myth of Oedipus (and its treatment in the tragedy by Sophocles) than to Freud's version. Freud's Oedipus theory arises in the context of the intact bourgeois family, where children are lodged close enough to their parents to observe "primal scenes," and mothers are on hand to notice childish masturbatory play and threaten castration. But Oedipus, like Arkadii and Dmitrii, is an abandoned child, left "on Cithaeron's slopes / in the twisting thickets" because of the prophecy that he is to kill his father and marry his mother.[26] In both *Oedipus the King* and Dostoevsky's novels, the father, encountered for the first time in adulthood, is perceived not as a father but as just another man. Although both Arkadii and Dmitrii express horror at the thought that they are competing sexually with their own fathers, one does not have the sense that the horror goes very deep (certainly not deep enough to stop the competition). The explanation for this surely lies in the fact that these sons have not known their fathers as fathers on an everyday basis, from childhood on. They meet their fathers on equal ground, man to man, as Oedipus met Laius at the crossroads.[27] For Freud the emotional weight and significance of the story lie in the fact that the son eliminates his father and has sex with his mother. But when read from the vantage point of Dostoevsky's preoccupations of the 1870s, it becomes a story of abandonment. It is Laius's abandonment of Oedipus that makes psychologically possible the realization of the prophecy he fears. Oedipus kills a father who is not really a father (and marries a mother who is not really a mother) in Fetiukovich's sense, and in the definition offered by Dostoevsky in the Kroneberg essay.

In his 1984 novel *The Unbearable Lightness of Being*, Milan Kundera returns to the Oedipus of Sophocles, ostentatiously omitting any mention of Freud. His hero Tomas offers a metaphorization of the Oedipus tragedy that has nothing to do with infantile sexuality and everything to do with guilt and responsibility, specifically the responsibility of those who led the countries of Central Europe into communism:

> Oedipus did not know he was sleeping with his own mother, yet when he realized what had happened, he did not feel innocent. Unable to stand the sight of the misfortunes he had wrought by "not knowing," he put out his eyes and wandered blind away from Thebes. When Tomas heard Communists shouting in defense of their inner purity, he said to himself, As a result of your "not knowing," this country has lost its freedom, lost it for centuries, perhaps, and you shout that you feel no guilt? How can you stand the sight of what you've done? How is it you aren't horrified? Have you no eyes to see? If you had eyes, you would have to put them out and wander away from Thebes![28]

This is the dimension of the story that is also closest to Dostoevsky—and even to Freud, if we look beyond the "scandalous" sexual content of his theory to its moral core. As the historian of psychoanalysis John E. Toews has recently written, "Recognizing ourselves in Oedipus is something of an ethical achievement, an assumption of guilt and responsibility in the creation of human suffering, including our own."[29]

The question "who is to blame?" fathers or children, emerges in an interesting way in the historical development of Freud's theory. Freud began with the "seduction theory," which posited that adult neuroses stemmed from actual sexual abuse by parents of their children. This theory "blamed the sufferings of the younger generation on the secret sexual perversions of their hypocritical elders, on those who held power over their fate and who had betrayed their trust. It traced the source of human suffering to the acts of the powerful and absolved the victims of complicity in their fate."[30] The development of the Oedipus theory shifted responsibility from parents to children: "After 1897 Freud's focus shifted to the agency of the child as a sexual subject, to the originating role of infantile psychosexual 'desire' in the formation of the human subject and its inner conflicts."[31] Frederick Crews offers a much less sympathetic description of this shift: "Psychoanalysis came into existence when Freud reinterpreted the very same clinical data to indicate that it must have been his patients themselves, when scarcely out of the cradle, who had predisposed themselves to neurosis by harboring and then repressing incestuous designs of their own."[32] Crews discusses the development in the 1980s of "recovered memory therapy," in which patients are guided to "remember" childhood sexual abuse by their parents (abuse which the patients had somehow completely repressed until therapy "recovered" the memory of it). Crews sees this development as another swing in the pendulum of blame from one generation to the other: "If early events are to be regarded as causes of later neurosis, it is easier to picture them as physical assaults on the child than as mere imaginings about penisectomy at the hand of a father who, the toddler supposedly reasons, must adopt that means of keeping him from realizing his goal of fornicating with his mother."[33]

The artistic complexity of Dostoevsky's world makes such extreme vacillations impossible, just as it makes impossible the explanation of all psychic disturbances by a single factor such as sexual abuse. In Dostoevsky's vision, guilt is not passed back and forth between fathers and sons. The defense attorney in *The Brothers Karamazov* tries to pin blame and responsibility on the fathers by selectively quoting the New Testament: "Ottsy, ne ogorchaite detei svoikh" ("Fathers, do not provoke your children," Colossians 3:21; 15:169 in Dostoevsky; see note, 15:601). He leaves out the two phrases that bracket this command in the Bible and that, when restored, are a microcosm of the Dostoevskian view of the family. The phrase quoted by Fetiukovich is preceded by a paraphrase of the fifth commandment: "Children, obey your parents in everything, for this is your acceptable duty in the Lord" (Colossians 3:20).[34] Children are responsible too, and their responsibility is mentioned first. Even more significant for Dostoevsky's universe is the phrase that follows the attorney's quotation: "Fathers, do not provoke your children, *or they may lose heart*" (Colossians 3:21; emphasis mine). The father's duty not to provoke his children is not for the purpose of avoiding being murdered by them, but of preserving their spiritual strength.

In the last analysis, what is most important for Dostoevsky is not one's generational position. Neither father nor son is categorically guilty or innocent. As a result, one cannot like Spasovich absolve Kroneberg by virtue of his being a father, or like Fetiukovich absolve Dmitrii by virtue of his being a son. The key moment is the individual's own acceptance of responsibility, as Dostoevsky illustrates vividly in the *Writer's Diary* for July–August 1877, in an imaginary speech by a presiding judge to a real-life couple who had abused their children:

> The main thing is that there is much to forgive on both sides. They [the children] must forgive you for the bitter, difficult impressions on their childish hearts, for the hardening of their spirits, for their vices. And you must forgive them for your egoism, your neglect of them, the perversion of your feelings for them, your cruelty, and the fact that you had to sit here and be tried because of them. I say this because you will not accuse yourselves for all this when you leave the court, but them, I'm sure of it! So as you begin the difficult labor of raising your children, ask yourselves: can you blame all these crimes and misdemeanors not on them but on yourselves? If you can, oh, then you will succeed in your labor! (25:191)

One must not be misled into thinking that this remarkable speech is directed only at the fathers; it could just as easily be directed at sons like Dmitrii, Arkadii, and Pyotr. The "untiring labor of love" that creates the family must be carried out by everyone.

Dostoevsky's definition of the family—the family that can truly be called a sacred thing—conforms neither to the conservative's blind worship of the name of "father" nor to the radical's attempt to "make the rearrangement of family life into the basis for the rearrangement of society."[35] For Dostoevsky, the traditional relationship of parent and child must be preserved, but must be based on the difficult, day-to-day labor of love, not merely on biological connection and the title of "father," a title which fathers like Stepan Verkhovenskii, Versilov, and Fyodor Karamazov assume only when it is convenient for them. If a conservative (or a liberal masquerading as a conservative, like Spasovich) claims to value the family because it is the foundation of the state, Dostoevsky, in both his artistic and journalistic works, values the family because it is at least potentially the foundation of the spiritually healthy individual. Like Freud he seeks the origins of spiritual disease in childhood, but he does not fall prey to determinism. The best proof of this is the three (or four) Karamazov brothers—all abandoned and abused, but each with his own spiritual and moral path.

The intact family based on mutual responsibility and forgiveness—the ideal family that Dostoevsky prescribed for Russia in his journalistic works and, by negative implication, in his novels—is largely absent from his artistic world. Instead, Dostoevsky's reader experiences with his child and adolescent characters a chaotic, hit-or-miss, unprotected process of education. In the sexual sphere this leads to encounters and experiments with forms of desire and sexual expression that were considered deviant by nineteenth-century Russian society and by Dostoevsky himself. According to E. N. Opochinin's memoirs, Dostoevsky said that "everyone is subject to [sexual] perversion to a certain extent, if not in deed then at least in his thoughts."[36] By following the orphaned child on his or her journey of discovery, Dostoevsky the artist was able to explore the intricacies and varieties of sexual desire, an indispensable component of the human. In doing so he worked constantly at crafting for himself the "point of view" that he had identified in Pushkin's treatment of sexual material. In the case of pedophilia, the reworking of textual material from *The Insulted and Injured* into Stavrogin's confession shows Dostoevsky moving from the psychologically insightful *description* of the thoughts of a man with sexual feelings for a young girl to a text that adds to such description a *moral position* that takes full responsibility for the horror of the situation. In *A Raw Youth,* homoerotic desire is portrayed as a phase that the hero Arkadii must grow out of and overcome, but in the process he finds within himself sympathy and understanding for the homosexual young man Trishatov. Through Alphonsine's behavior we see Trishatov shunned by society; through Arkadii's eyes we see him as a person of talent and compassion, even a guardian angel in the end. At the same time, the unconventional trajectory of desire provides the aesthetic model for Dostoevsky's experimental narrative.

For both Arkadii and Alyosha, the adolescent phase of masturbatory fantasy must also be overcome. In Arkadii's case, a conventional heterosexual relationship is promised as a solution; for Alyosha, spiritual ecstasy substitutes for physical loss of virginity and makes it possible for him to master his sensual nature in a way the other Karamazovs fail to do. Dostoevsky's moral position and "point of view" come strongly into play in his treatment of the Kroneberg case. Although in *The Brothers Karamazov* he was to acknowledge the supposed physical and moral dangers of masturbation through the characters of Lise Khokhlakova and Smerdiakov, in dealing with Mariia Kroneberg's "secret vice" he avoids the hysteria to which her father evidently succumbed. Dostoevsky redirects attention from the child's "shameful" physical habit, which leaves her untouched and innocent in spirit, toward the intellectual "bludodeistvie" of the attorney Spasovich.

Frederick Crews explains Freud's hostile posthumous psychoanalysis of Dostoevsky as the reaction of a jealous rival:

> Dostoevsky endowed some of his major characters with a high degree of conscious psychological reflection, thus anticipating some features of Freud's doctrine but suspending them, as Freud could not, in sophisticated fictive uncertainty and irony. Such a figure must have struck Freud above all as a rival who deserved the treatment he always reserved for his adversaries: reduction to a helpless example of his own pet notions about unconscious infantile compulsion.[37]

Unlike Freud, Dostoevsky was not seeking a scientific model for explaining human sexuality; he was using his powers as an artist to explore sexuality in all its variety. He not only suspended the subject of sexuality in "sophisticated fictive uncertainty and irony" but also placed it within a moral framework, the same framework in which he placed issues of love and hatred, ambition and crime, and the human quest for God.

Appendix: Newspaper Account of the Kroneberg Trial

From *The Voice* (*Golos*), January 24–29, 1876

January 24, 1876

Court Chronicle
Session of the First Department of the St. Petersburg District Court,
with the participation of a jury, held on January 23

The case of the banker Kronenberg [sic], accused of the torture of his
seven-year-old daughter

Judge Lopukhin presided; the prosecution was led by Prosecutor
Kolokolov; the defense was led by Defense Attorney Spasovich.

The substance of the case is the following [some preliminary technical information has been omitted]:

On July 28, 1875, the peasant woman Ul'iana Bibina, who was living at
the dacha of Mukhanov in Lesnoi Korpus [suburb of St. Petersburg, named for
the Forestry Institute located there], attested to the forest district police super-
intendent of the Petersburg suburban police that the nobleman Stanislav
Kronenberg, who was renting the Mukhanov dacha, would often and cruelly
beat his small daughter who was living with him, and on the last occasion had
flogged her horribly on July 25. Bibina's testimony was confirmed by an inquest,
and therefore on July 28 the case was transferred to a judicial investigator. A preliminary investigation revealed that Kronenberg had moved to the Mukhanov
dacha about the middle of June and lived there with his lover, the French national Adelina Gesing, and with his legitimized seven-year-old daughter Mariia.
The circumstances of this case, discovered by the preliminary investigation, are
as follows:

The peasant woman Bibina testified: On June 17, Kronenberg, the lady,
and the girl moved to the dacha of Mukhanov. Soon afterward, the witness began
to notice that the little girl's underwear and handkerchiefs were often bloodied,
her face beaten, and her nose bloody. Bibina could not ask the girl herself about

the reason for these phenomena, because the child did not speak Russian, but Kronenberg's cook explained to the witness that it was because the master beat the young lady so badly. Soon afterward, in the evenings, about 11:00, the witness began to hear the terrible screams and moans of the little girl, in which one could clearly hear the words: "Papa! Papa!" At first this wasn't repeated very often, but as time went on it happened more and more often. Judging by the little girl's screams, the witness believes that the beating continued for about a quarter of an hour, and sometimes even longer. Once, on an evening in July, Kronenberg again began to beat the little girl and this time beat her so long, and she screamed so terribly, that the witness became frightened and, fearing that the girl would be beaten to death, jumped out of bed, and just as she was in her nightgown, ran up to Kronenberg's window and began to shout for him to stop beating or she would send for the police; then the beating and the screams ceased. For about three days after this everything was quiet, but, after a certain interval of time, for three days straight Kronenberg tortured the girl so much that the witness decided to tell the police about everything. Before going to report to the police, Bibina and Kronenberg's cook examined the girl, and it turned out that the entire lower part of the child's body was a dark-blue and purple color and was furrowed with welts from the switch; on her arms there were also traces of the blows of the switch; both her cheeks were covered with dark-blue and purple spots. While being examined the girl cried bitterly and kept saying, "Papa, Papa!" At this time, Kronenberg's cook gave the witness a switch that she had found on the floor in the girl's room. The switch presented by the witness Bibina consisted of nine thick rowanberry branches bound together, with the ends broken off and dishevelled from use.

Kronenberg's maid, Agrafena Alekseevna Titova, confirmed Bibina's testimony in all its details, and added that while in the city Kronenberg treated the little girl rather well: sometimes it would happen that he would shout at her, and once, in the presence of the witness, he struck her on the face; but he didn't beat her with a switch and the girl was not beat up. But when they moved to the dacha, Kronenberg started to treat the girl cruelly: he beat her repeatedly on the face, so that she had dark-blue spots on both cheeks, and one cheek was beaten until it bled. About two weeks before, the girl's nose was so injured that up to that time (the time of the interrogation of the witness, July 29) she was suffering from nosebleed. Soon after they moved to the dacha, Kronenberg began to beat the girl with switches, an example of which was presented by the witness Bibina. The girl was beaten more than ten times in the course of three weeks at the dacha, and how many times she was beaten by hand, the witness didn't even know. In general the master and mistress treated the girl cruelly, although she was a submissive child, quiet and well-behaved. Now the girl always sits alone and doesn't talk to anyone. At this point Titova presented Kronenberg's shirt, which had splatters of blood on the cuff of the right sleeve; two bloody child's handkerchiefs, and a small woman's shift that was soiled with large drops of blood on the left sleeve and on the left side of the chest.

Kronenberg's manservant, Ivan Valevskii, testified that at the dacha he had heard screams and moans coming from the girl's room about four times. In them he could distinguish the words: "Papa! Papa!" Once he saw that one of the girl's wrists had been cut with a lash; another time he saw that the girl's face was beaten up, her cheek was bloody and had a dark-blue spot on it. The witness saw Kronenberg bring the switch home himself. The young lady was a quiet and well-mannered child.

The caretaker of the dacha, Efim Bibin, confirmed that his mother, Ul'iana Bibina, once threatened Kronenberg that she would send for the police if he didn't stop beating the girl, and that after that the child's screams stopped.

The French national Adelina Gesing testified that as a father, Kronenberg subjected the girl to domestic correction; in the city he beat her on the hands and face, which caused the child to have bruises on her cheeks; at the dacha he beat Mariia two or three times, but he beat her lightly, although welts and stripes nevertheless appeared on the girl's body from this beating, and the witness would each time give the child sugar water to calm her down. Mr. Kronenberg usually beat his daughter in the evening, when she was already undressed for bed. At the dacha as well, Kronenberg beat the girl several times in the face, so that she had bruises. The last time Mariia was beaten on July 25 on the following occasion: the witness came home and saw that someone had rummaged in her unlocked trunk. The girl said that she wanted to take some money from it. Gesing believed her, because Mariia had stolen things before, that is, once without asking, she had taken several prunes from the trunk. When he returned home in the evening, Kronenberg saw on the windowsill a new crochet hook belonging to the witness that had been broken. When he learned that Mariia had broken it and that she had gotten into the trunk, he called the maid, ordered her to hold the child by the arms, and beat the girl; he beat her hard and for a long time and was almost in an unconscious state. All the traces of the switch that had been found on Mariia's body were caused on this occasion, except for several dark-blue welts that had remained from previous beatings. This time Kronenberg beat the girl with the switch presented to the investigation by Bibina, because the other (thin) switch had been broken during the previous beating. However, in the opinion of the witness, Kronenberg had never treated the girl cruelly.

Kronenberg's daughter Mariia explained that when she behaved badly, her papa punished her several times in a row. The last time he had also punished her several days in a row. She didn't know how many times she had been beaten. When she was punished before, marks had also remained. Mamasha (Gesing) asked Papasha to break off a big twig from the switch down below, but Papasha said that it would give more force and the switch would not slip out of his hands. She didn't steal anything from Papasha and Mamasha.

On July 29, that is, on the fourth day after the last punishment with the switch, the girl was examined, and in the record of those proceedings it is noted that, when she was asked to undress, the girl did so with crying and fear, constantly looking around at her father and those present, and calmed down only when it was explained to her that she was not going to be beaten. Upon examination it turned out that the entire surface of her left buttock area and left thigh were a dark purple color, the right buttock area and right thigh were covered in places by bluish-purple spots and red stripes, up to seven inches in length. The same kind of stripes were scattered over the entire surface of the back and here and there on the lower surface of the stomach, and one near the left nipple, about one and a half inches in length. On the right arm were partly blending bluish-red spots and red stripes; the same was observed on the left arm, only to a lesser extent. In consequence of this, the doctor expressed the following opinion: all the injuries found upon examination were the result of beating with switches of the type introduced into evidence, and moreover the beating, judging by the type of injuries, had happened at various times. In any case, all these injuries must be classified as grave. The girl was again examined, seventeen days after the last punishment, and three expert doctors unanimously explained that in their opinion, the punishment of Mariia Kronenberg with a switch was very severe and done in a way that was out of the ordinary for the usual domestic corrective punishments, and if such punishments were to be repeated in the future, it would undoubtedly have an extremely injurious effect on the general state of health of the child.

The accused nobleman Stanislav Kronenberg did not admit that he was guilty in the torture of his daughter Mariia-Anna and explained that, being dissatisfied with her upbringing in Switzerland, in May 1875 he brought her to St. Petersburg. Here he began to notice that the girl had begun to lie and to deceive him, and as a result of this he began to punish her in various ways. In Petersburg he would beat her in the face to the point of bruising, but he never beat her so hard that her face bled. This happened several times. At the dacha, when he saw that his daughter was not reforming, he resorted to the switch. For this purpose he made a bundle of slender, flexible twigs, and he beat his daughter about three times, and did not see any blood on these occasions, and did not notice whether her body turned blue because he himself was in a nervous state. Whether he beat her for a long time or not, he could not ascertain. After the third time, the bundle broke, and wishing to scare the little girl, he made a new one out of thick branches, either the one that had been introduced into evidence or another one of about the same type. He hung this switch over the girl's bed, but on July 25, irritated by his daughter, he beat her with this bundle, beat her hard, and this time he beat her for a long time, beside himself, unconsciously, helter-skelter. Whether the switch broke during this last beating, he doesn't know, but he remembers that when he began to beat the girl, the switch was longer.

After considering the above evidence, the court decided that the infliction on a seven-year-old girl of such beatings in the face as Mariia Kronenberg suffered from her father, and such a punishment with the switch, the traces of which, at the time of the girl's examination, seventeen days later, gave the doctors grounds to conclude that this punishment exceeded the limits of usual domestic correction measures and that its repetition could have a harmful effect on the child's health, fit completely within the understanding of torture as provided in Statute 1489 of the Code of Punishment, even if these beatings and the punishment with the switch were used for correcting the girl. Therefore and taking into account the fact that Kronenberg tortured his own daughter, the court decides: the nobleman Stanislav Leopol'dovich Kronenberg, 29 years of age, should be brought to trial in the Petersburg District Court, with the participation of a jury, on the charge of the crimes stipulated in Statues 1489 and 1492 of the Code of Punishment.

January 25, 1876

After reading the indictment, the presiding judge addressed the accused with the following question: "You are accused of torturing your daughter Mariia by beating her on the cheeks to the point of bruising and cruelly whipping her in the summer of 1875. Do you confess your guilt?"

Kroneberg: I confess that I punished her, but I do not confess myself guilty of torturing her.

The defense attorney Spasovich made a declaration in which, following Statutes 2 and 620 of the criminal code, he asked that the inquest into the case be conducted in camera, since the case concerned family rights. Kroneberg was brought to trial under Statutes 1489 and 1492 of the Code of Punishment; the victim of the crime was his own daughter; in the court's decision it is stated that the punishment which it regards as torture and torment was carried out with the aim of correction, that is, during the exercise by a father of one of the functions of parental authority. Thus, the very charge points to the fact that we are dealing with an abuse of parental authority, that is, with a crime against family rights, provided for in the second chapter of the second section of the law code. These are the legal reasons why the defense petitions for sitting in camera. Moreover, Kroneberg in his defense must recount the whole story of the child's origins, touching on her birth, the name of the girl's mother. Then several witnesses will tell about bad physical habits the girl has, which provoked the punishment and which are of such a nature that in the presence of the public one could hardly pose the questions to the witnesses that would elucidate these habits.

The prosecutor, for his part, stated that he could not agree to the defense's petition, since Statute 620 of the criminal code, to which the defense attorney referred, does not indicate that cases of torture be investigated in camera. Kroneberg is charged according to Statute 1489 of the Code of Punishment covering torture: therefore the circumstance that this torture was inflicted by a father on his daughter is secondary and is significant only in defining the penalty. Thus one is not dealing here with the exceeding of parental authority, but with the infliction of torture, and therefore, the present case cannot fall under Statutes 2 and 620. The prosecutor further declared that, according to Statute 621 of the criminal code, sessions in camera can be permitted only in exceptional, exigent instances. As for the circumstances about which the defense wishes to make a statement during the inquest, nothing was known about them earlier, and at this time it is impossible to assume that these circumstances must definitively refute the entire indictment, and that Kroneberg must be charged not with torture but with some other sort of crime. Therefore the prosecutor proposed that no action be taken on the defense's petition.

The defense attorney Spasovich insisted that the inquest be held in camera.

The district court, bearing in mind that the crime of which Kroneberg was accused did not fall under Statutes 619 and 620 of the criminal code, to which the defense referred; and that on the basis of Statute 621 of the same code, sessions in camera are allowed only in the instances specified in Statute 620 of the criminal code, which is not operative here, decided to take no action on the defense's petition and to try the case in open session.

Then the court took up the examination of the witnesses.

The first witness was seven-year-old Mariia Kroneberg, who came into the courtroom accompanied by Mrs. Gesing, who then was taken away into the witness room. Mariia Kroneberg is a very nice, pretty, and well-built little girl who carries herself in an unconstrained manner; she speaks only French and answers the questions, posed through an interpreter, quickly and without shyness.

Presiding Judge: Mr. Interpreter, tell the witness that as the daughter of the accused, she may refuse to answer, and therefore she is asked whether she wishes to give evidence or not?

The witness answered that she did not wish to give evidence.

Defense attorney Spasovich asked permission for Kroneberg to say a few words to his daughter, who then might agree to give evidence.

Presiding Judge (to the accused): What do you wish to say?

Kroneberg: I want to tell my daughter to answer the questions, because they will be necessary for the prosecutor and my defense attorney.

Presiding Judge: You wish to ask her to give evidence?

Kroneberg: Yes, I do.

The interpreter conveyed everything to the witness, who answered, "Yes, I want to, because Papa wants me to." Then she explained that although her father beat her, he did it only a little bit [ochen' malo].

Presiding Judge: When were you beaten?

Witness Kroneberg: When we were living at the dacha.

Presiding Judge: You can't say anything more?

Witness: I can also talk about my vices.

Judge: Talk about whatever you wish.

Witness: I was dirty, then I stole things and I was punished.

Prosecutor: When you were living in Petersburg, were you punished with a switch or not?

Witness: No.

Prosecutor: And when you were living in Petersburg, were you often beaten on the face to the point of bruising?

Witness: I don't remember.

Prosecutor: Why did your nose bleed?

Witness: I stick my fingers in my nose.

Prosecutor: What were you punished for the last time?

Witness: I stole something from my papenka and intended to steal something from another gentleman.

Prosecutor: Were you beaten with this switch the last time, or not (he indicates the bundled switch, lying on the table of material evidence, about which one of the expert doctors stated that it was not a switch but "spitzrutens" [literally, "pointed twigs"])?

Witness: The last time I was beaten with that switch.

Prosecutor: And were you beaten for a long time?

Witness: I don't remember.

Prosecutor: Do you remember when you lived in Switzerland?

Witness: I lived with my godmother (Mrs. de Combe, who did not appear in court, and also her husband, a Protestant minister).

Prosecutor: Did they punish you there or not?

Witness: My godmother punished me with her hand.

Defense Attorney Spasovich: Did you study anything when you were with your godmother?

Witness: She taught me English, arithmetic, geography, and orthography.

Spasovich: When you came to Petersburg, did you continue to study with your father?

Witness: A few days after we arrived, I started to study again.

Spasovich: Both in the city and at the dacha?

Witness: At the dacha I had Mrs. de Troulle.

Spasovich: Did you play with anyone at the dacha? Were there girls and boys there?

Witness: Once I played with the caretaker's daughter.

Spasovich: Who took care of you at that time?

Witness: My mother and also my nanny (the witness calls Mrs. Gesing her mother).

Spasovich: Why did Papa get so angry and punish you the last time?

Witness: I wasn't a good girl.

Spasovich: Why weren't you a good girl, what did you do?

Witness: I stole money.

Spasovich: For yourself or for others?

Witness: I wanted to give it to the cook, and for myself I took sweets.

Spasovich: Where did you get all this?

Witness: The keys were on the chest of drawers; I opened it and started to eat sweets.

Spasovich: Do you love Papa and Mama?

Witness: Yes, I do.

Prosecutor: When you were beaten the last time, Mrs. Gesing asked Kroneberg to break off a twig at the end of the switch?

Witness: I don't remember.

Prosecutor: After you were punished, did you have to lie in bed, were you ill?

Witness: No, but I had bruises on the back of my body.

Prosecutor: You were also beaten on the breast, weren't you?

Witness: On my face, but not on my breast.

Prosecutor: And were you beaten on the stomach?

Witness: No.

Prosecutor: Why didn't you want to undress when they wanted to examine you the first time?

Witness: I don't remember.

Prosecutor: You said that you gave money to the servant. Did she really ask you to do that?

Witness: Yes, she did.

Defense Attorney Spasovich: Why didn't you tell Papa that the servant put you up to it, when he asked you about it?

Witness: I was afraid that they would put the cook in prison.

Presiding Judge: During recent times at the dacha, were you beaten often or not?

Witness: I don't remember.

Presiding Judge: Were you always beaten with this kind of switch?

Witness: A lot less often, and Papa said that this (she indicates the switch) is a superior switch.

Presiding Judge: Who brought this switch?

Witness: I don't know.

Presiding Judge: Were you beaten the last time in the morning or the evening?

Witness: In the evening, when Papa returned from the city.

Presiding Judge: In what room did he beat you?

Witness: In my room, which is next to Papa's room.

Presiding Judge: So did he take you into that room, or were you there already?

Witness: He ordered me to go and undress.

Presiding Judge: Did he bring the switch with him, or was it already there?

Witness: Papa had made it earlier.

Presiding Judge: Where was the switch?

Witness: It was hung on the wall over my bed.

Presiding Judge: Why was it hung there?

Witness: So I would be afraid, so I wouldn't behave badly, and Papa said he would punish me with it.

Presiding Judge: The next day did you show anyone you had been beaten?

Witness: I didn't want to show it, but I showed Mama.

Presiding Judge: And besides her no one examined you?

Witness: The cook saw me the same day. I agreed to show her my back part.

Presiding Judge: Where were you when you showed her?

Witness: I don't remember.

Prosecutor: Did your mother ever punish you?

Witness: No, never.

Prosecutor: On July 25, before your father came home, did your mother make you stand on your knees?

Witness: Yes, before Papa came home she made me stand on my knees for two hours.

Prosecutor: Why?

Witness: Because I had planned to steal from my mother, but didn't succeed in doing it.

Prosecutor: Who told your father that you had broken your mother's crochet hook?

Witness: Mama told him.

Witness Bibina testified that she saw Kroneberg beat his little daughter, who often had swollen cheeks, and that all this lasted about a month; that the little girl was all covered with bruises. The last time he beat the little thing so badly "that I couldn't stand it and I jumped out of bed and went to the window," says Bibina, "and I see, my God, what is he doing! I'll go right away to the police station and make a statement. At first I thought it would stop, but he beat her again, and then again, and once he beat the girl for more than a quarter of an hour. The last time he beat her, I got dressed, ran out to the high road, and I thought the girl was going to die. Earlier I wanted to leave them, but they wouldn't give me my passport; now I thought, what if something happens: the master has my passport; it's just terrible. I went out onto the road and I met our bailiff, who asked, 'What's going on?' And I answered that the master was beating the little babe painfully; he said I should go to the police station, but I didn't go because it was late, and I went in the morning. When I got up in the morning, I took the young lady, lifted her little dress, and saw that her whole body was covered by purple spots, it was just a pity. The cook brought me the switch they had beaten her with; I took it, brought it to the police station, and made a statement about everything. I asked the young lady who had beaten her, and she said it was Papa."

Prosecutor: Did the girl scream for a long time?

Witness: Yes, for a long time.

Prosecutor: Did you see her being beaten?

Witness: I only heard it.

Prosecutor: Did anyone else hear the screams besides you?

Witness: The cook heard.

Prosecutor: The girl had bruises on her cheeks?

Witness: They never disappeared from her cheeks. All her handkerchiefs were bloody.

Prosecutor: Were there scars on her arms?

Witness: I don't rightly know.

Prosecutor: You looked at her back, but not her breast?

Witness: I only looked from behind.

Prosecutor: Why didn't you tell the bailiff anything?

Witness: I said: my Lord, the master has been beating the girl for three days. He said: go to the police station and make a statement.

Prosecutor: Didn't the maid tell you that the little girl was taking things from the trunk?

Witness: She never said anything about that.

Prosecutor: The accused didn't make a complaint about you to the bailiff Nikol'skii?

Witness: I don't know whether he did or not.

Prosecutor: Was the girl constantly with this lady (Gesing)?

Witness: Yes.

Prosecutor: Was she allowed to go for walks, to play?

Witness: Yes, she would run around the garden.

The defense declined to ask any questions.

January 26, 1876

The witness Titova asked for questions to be posed to her.

Prosecutor: Did Kroneberg and Gesing treat the girl well here in Petersburg, before moving to the dacha?

Appendix

Witness: They treated her well. They punished her once, but not cruelly.
Prosecutor: What sort of punishment was it?
Witness: I saw marks on her body.
Prosecutor: From a switch?
Witness: No, just from hands.
Prosecutor: Were there bruises on the girl's face?
Witness: Not in Petersburg, but at the dacha there were.
Prosecutor: Are you sure you remember that when you lived in Petersburg, there were no bruises on her face?
Witness: I can't say, but at the dacha I remember very well that there were.
Prosecutor: Did they beat the girl on the cheeks in your presence?
Witness: One time.
Prosecutor: And were there bruises left after that blow?
Witness: There were no bruises, but after they punished her with the switch, there were.
Prosecutor: And before that there were no bruises on her face?
Witness: I can't remember.
Prosecutor: The last time, did they punish her in your presence?
Witness: Yes, but only a little bit, he hit her three or four times, but not cruelly. Then I went to Petersburg and returned the next morning.
Prosecutor: When you saw the girl, were the same marks visible as on the day before, or were there more?
Witness: The day before I didn't see, but in the morning the caretaker's mother and I looked at the girl, and she had been very cruelly punished.
Prosecutor: Was she a quiet girl or a naughty one?
Witness: I can't say; I only heard her scream a lot.
Prosecutor: Loud screams?
Witness: Yes.
Prosecutor: Did you hear the caretaker's mother say that she wanted to report to the police?
Witness: I didn't hear that, but she came to me and started to cry.
Prosecutor: So they punished the girl about eight or nine times?
Witness: I can't say for sure; about eight times.
Prosecutor: When you came to work for Kroneberg, did you see on the little one's face any scars, or any marks on the bridge of her nose, on her left temple, on her forehead?
Witness: I can't remember.
Prosecutor: Gesing also punished the girl?
Witness: No. She might pull her ear, but she never punished her with a switch; she treated her affectionately, but sometimes . . . not so well [kak pridetsia].

129

Prosecutor: Did you ever see the girl steal?

Witness: Once I saw her steal some prunes.

Prosecutor: So did they punish her for that or not?

Witness: No. When they punished her the last time, I thought it was because of the prunes, but I was told that she had stolen money.

Prosecutor: Did the girl give money to the cook or the caretaker's mother?

Witness: I never saw her do that.

Prosecutor: You don't speak French?

Witness: No.

Prosecutor: And does the cook speak French?

Witness: I *am* the cook.

Defense Attorney Spasovich: When they began to punish the girl, they called you in order to hold her?

Witness: Yes.

Spasovich: Did you hear them punish her nine times or did you see it yourself?

Witness: I saw it only once.

Spasovich: Did you give the judicial investigator the linen that is lying here?

Witness: Yes.

Spasovich: Did you produce the evidence yourself or did you give it to Bibina?

Witness: I was told to produce it at the police station, so I took it there.

Spasovich: When you returned from the city the day after the punishment, did you see the girl playing with dolls in the garden?

Witness: I can't remember.

Spasovich: What was the incident between the caretaker and the master?

Witness: I only know that one of the chicks disappeared and that Kroneberg deducted the price of the chick from Bibina's wages, and she said, "Well, the Lord be with him, God will repay him for this."

Spasovich: Did you notice earlier that the girl had an abscess in her nose?

Witness: No.

Prosecutor: Did the father and Gesing treat the girl affectionately or cruelly?

Witness: I can't say. When it was just Gesing, it was good, but sometimes it wasn't so good, because it was none of my affair, and Kroneberg treated the girl quite severely.

Prosecutor: Did he beat her on the cheeks?

Witness: One time I saw that, but I never saw it again.

Prosecutor: You said earlier that the girl's cheek was beaten until it bled.

Witness: Not her cheek, but her nose. That was when we were moving to the dacha.

Prosecutor: What caused this, a blow or something else?

Witness: A blow.

Prosecutor: That means you don't deny that Kroneberg beat the girl on the cheeks?

Witness: Yes.

Prosecutor: Where was the switch kept?

Witness: Over the young lady's bed.

Prosecutor: You say that you swept the room. Did you often have occasion to sweep up remnants of a switch in the girl's room?

Witness: I can't remember.

Prosecutor: Do you recognize this switch (he indicates the switch lying on the table)?

Witness: Yes, that's the same switch.

Presiding Judge: Was Kroneberg cruel to his daughter?

Witness: Yes.

Presiding Judge: How do you conclude this?

Witness: When he would come home, he wouldn't greet her and always scowled at her.

Presiding Judge: Didn't he play with her?

Witness: At the dacha he didn't play with her.

Presiding Judge: The switch hung over the bed constantly?

Witness: Constantly.

Presiding Judge: Why was it hung there?

Witness: I can't say; the girl pointed it out to me once.

Presiding Judge: You say that in your presence Kroneberg struck the girl with the switch about three or four times?

Witness: Yes.

Presiding Judge: Why did you conclude that he was beating her cruelly?

Witness: In my presence he hit her very hard with the switch about three or four times.

Presiding Judge: And the day before he didn't beat her?

Witness: Not in my presence.

Presiding Judge: And the day before that did he beat her?

Witness: Yes.

Presiding Judge: Did you hold her that time or not?

Witness: I only held her one time.

Presiding Judge: Did he beat her with this very switch or not (he indicates the bundle)?

Witness: With that one.

Presiding Judge: A week before the last time, do you remember that he beat the girl badly?

Witness: He beat her constantly.

Presiding Judge: Did you see the girl the day after she was beaten the last time?

Witness: Yes. She came into the kitchen and said, "Papa, Papa"; I undid her little underdrawers and looked.

Kroneberg: I broke off the twigs for the switch that is lying here when I was on a walk with my daughter, and she brought them home herself.
Presiding Judge: What kind of switch did you use to beat her before?
Kroneberg: Then I took a soft switch that I had made, because I have to punish her.
Presiding Judge: Did you beat her with this very switch that is lying here?
Kroneberg: It's hard for me to remember. I took the big bundle of branches and gave it to her to carry home; she brought it home, and in her presence I bound it together and said, "If you are a bad girl, I'll beat you with this switch."
Presiding Judge: Could you please tell us the details?
Kroneberg: I punished her with a switch because all other means of punishment were unsuccessful. I made a soft switch and it was hanging on the wall for a rather long time, over the course of four weeks. I beat her with the switch three times very lightly, so that it wasn't painful.

He explained further that, dissatisfied with the behavior of his daughter, once while out on a walk with her at Poklonnaia Gora, he broke off a very big bundle of branches, "with the view of correcting my daughter"; he gave it to the little child, forced her to carry it home, and hung it over her little bed in her little room. "I must report," the accused said, "with regard to the severe punishment that Titova witnessed and said that I gave her three blows, in fact I gave her more than four blows."

Presiding Judge: Why did you increase the punishment?
Kroneberg: Here are all the circumstances I was in (long pause). When I was still a student in Warsaw in the faculty of law, I had relations with a certain lady who was a great deal older than I was. These relations later broke off.

He explained further that he spent time abroad in German universities, where he finished his education. During the last Franco-Prussian War, he fought in the ranks of the French army and participated in many battles against the enemy. When he returned home, he found out that he had a child who was living in Switzerland. He set off to look for her and found his little daughter on the street among peasant children. He took the child with him, acknowledged her as his daughter, and gave her to the wife of the Protestant minister de Combe to be raised, where the girl lived for two and a half years; he constantly received information about her and kept up a correspondence. The wife of de Combe informed him that when his daughter was living among the peasant children, she had acquired such evil propensities and habits that it was very hard to educate her. When in the summer of 1874 he returned from abroad with the unmarried lady Gesing to Petersburg, he was compelled to stay here for a long time in order to complete certain business enterprises. Being completely alone, he accepted Mrs. Gesing's proposal that she leave her family and live with him. This woman, according to Kroneberg, very much liked to engage in homemaking. In the spring of 1875 Gesing became ill, and they went to Paris to consult with doctors there. Since he was living with Gesing as man and wife, it was not a secret to her that he had a daughter; Gesing expressed the desire to take the child, to which he at first did not agree, because of family circumstances, so that his family would not find out that he had an illegitimate daughter. Finally he took the girl and brought her to Petersburg, where he became convinced that she had evil propensities. Later he noticed that the little child had vices about which he did not wish to speak; moreover, it became clear that the girl was a persistent liar, and she had been raised in Switzerland not in the way the accused would have wished. He also noticed certain not very good habits of cleanliness and neatness in the child, so that one couldn't even sit down to eat with her. In order to break her of these habits, he began to take various measures. "I had to punish her," Kroneberg said, "and I began the punishment by making her stand on her knees or leave the table. But none of this was successful, and it's quite understandable, because when she was living in the village they punished her more severely, and therefore lighter punishments didn't have any effect on her. Moreover, she has a very firm character. At the dacha I punished her in precisely the same manner, and came to the conclusion that I had to punish her a little more severely." He explained further that at the dacha he encountered various unpleasantnesses. "In general I saw," the accused said, "that the more severely I treated my daughter, the better she became. She would go to see the caretaker and his wife [*sic*], which I really didn't like, so that this led to a fight between my daughter and me. Of course this was very offensive to me. I had recourse to the switch when the previous punishments were no longer having any success. I punished her with the switch three times, with the soft switch. The last time I punished her on Monday. On Tuesday or Wednesday we went for a walk, and I took a switch, brought it home, and hung it on the wall, and on Friday I punished her." Further, the accused began to tell the story of the chicks, one of which was very attached to Mrs. Gesing and his daughter; that the caretaker, wishing to spite the accused (for what reason, Kroneberg didn't explain), arranged that one of the four chicks disappeared. Kroneberg deducted 80 kopecks from the wages of the caretaker's wife [*sic*], who did laundry for him by the day; this greatly annoyed both the caretaker and his wife [*sic*]. Further, the accused declared that the girl screamed constantly, and very loudly, and then he said, "I am a father; I have the right to punish and I must do so. On Friday I beat my daughter severely . . . I couldn't bear for my daughter to enter into a compact with other people (greatly agitated), my daughter, whom I took to be with me, whom I take care of. I completely admit that I punished her with this switch, but there was no blood; I did not make any marks on her body. Now you understand why I had to increase the punishment, and the last time I gave her a good beating, so that she would remember it. This lesson had its consequences, and although this investigation has shaken my parental authority, the lesson did correct the girl, who has already become an excellent little girl. She no longer makes a mess in her room and now it is pleasant to eat with her."

Presiding Judge: You have the right not to answer these questions, but if you wish, please tell me: do you remember your own childhood?

Kroneberg: Yes.

Presiding Judge: What measures were used against you then? Did you have brothers and sisters?

Kroneberg: I have two brothers and two sisters.

Presiding Judge: Were you ever punished the way you punished your daughter?

Kroneberg: No.

Presiding Judge: Were you ever hit in the face with anything other than a switch?

Kroneberg: No, I don't remember that I was.

Presiding Judge: And were your brothers or sisters?

Kroneberg: I don't remember.

Presiding Judge: You positively deny that you beat your child in the face to the point of bleeding?

Kroneberg: Yes, positively.

Presiding Judge: You don't deny that your daughter had bruises on her face?

Kroneberg: I didn't intend to do that; but it has been said here that I hit her several times, but it is true that I hit her once. I must speak of a certain circumstance, namely, the girl has a little pimple in her nose that often bleeds, and moreover, she sticks her fingers in her nose. I could show you many of the girl's bloody handkerchiefs, stained with blood from her nose. This pimple may be examined by the doctors.

Witness Valevskii, in essence, testified that when he was Kroneberg's servant, he only saw that the girl was crying; that he heard from others that the girl was punished three or four times, and finally, the day after the last punishment with the switch he saw the girl, who was "so-so, neither happy nor sad."

The witness Gesing was brought into the courtroom, and was examined with the aid of a French interpreter.

Prosecutor: How did Kroneberg treat his daughter in Petersburg: affectionately or cruelly?

Witness: He was never strict with her, although she often deserved punishment.

Prosecutor: Did he beat her on the cheeks with his hand while you were still in Petersburg?

Witness: Yes.

Prosecutor: Were there bruises on her face from these blows?

Witness: Never.

Prosecutor: When you moved to the dacha, was Kroneberg's treatment of his daughter just as affectionate, or did it change?

Witness: He always treated her well, and I noticed that Kroneberg loved his daughter very much and always caressed her.

Prosecutor: How many times did he punish his daughter?

Witness: Twice with a very small switch, which didn't have any effect, and the third time the switch was a bit bigger.

Prosecutor: Were there any marks on her body from the first two punishments?

Witness: No. In general the girl doesn't obey, she's always dirty, and she has other deficiencies which I cannot explain [kotorye ia ob"iasnit' ne mogu].

Prosecutor: Did Kroneberg do this with the aim of correction?

Witness: With the goal of correcting his daughter and in her own interests.

Prosecutor: Why did he punish his daughter the last time?

Witness: For theft.

Prosecutor: What did she steal?

Witness: She stole sugar, coffee, and oranges out of my trunk, and she wanted to steal money out of a portfolio in order to give it to Agrafena (the cook), who had asked for it; the girl broke a crochet hook, but she didn't succeed in taking the money.

Prosecutor: Why do you assume that she wanted to steal money, and from whom did you hear this?

Witness: The girl herself told me this.

Prosecutor: Didn't she say that she was asked to give money to Agrafena?

Witness: She was very friendly with the caretaker and Agrafena.

Prosecutor: Did you punish the girl for breaking the hook?

Witness: I made her stand on her knees until she told the truth.

Prosecutor: And did she stand on her knees for a long time?

Witness: About ten minutes or a quarter of an hour. But I said she would have to stand there for two hours.

Prosecutor: Did you see marks on the girl's body after the last punishment?

Witness: Yes, there were marks.

The defense declined to ask any questions of the witness.

The prosecutor, as proof of the contradiction between the witness's testimony and the testimony she gave the judicial investigator, asked that the latter be read out, in which, among other things, it is said, "In the city Kroneberg sometimes beat the girl with his hand on the arms and face, from which there remained blue marks on her cheeks, but I didn't see any blood."

This passage was translated for the witness, who answered, "Since I don't understand Russian, I don't know why the investigator wrote down such testimony."

Defense Attorney Spasovich: Did the investigator question you himself or through an interpreter?

Witness: Himself.

Spasovich: Did he read what was written before you signed it, or not?

Witness: He read it himself in Russian.

Presiding Judge: Did the investigator translate the testimony to you word for word, or did he just make you sign it?

Witness: He translated it; but I didn't give any testimony about bruises.

The witness Balashova stated that she had been called to be a witness during the examination of the girl, who at first would not undress because she was terribly afraid of her father. There were many bruises on her body.

Prosecutor: What kind of marks were there?

Witness: Blue and black.

Prosecutor: Were there marks on the back, on the breast, on the stomach?

Witness: Everywhere.

The defense declined to examine the witness.

Presiding Judge: Do you have children?

Witness: Yes.

Presiding Judge: Have you ever had occasion to punish them with a switch?

Witness: Never.

Presiding Judge: Have you ever seen people who had been flogged?

Witness: Of course I have.

Prosecutor: Did you not weep when the girl was undressed?

Witness: I was so horrified that I began to feel ill.

Prosecutor: Why did this make such an impression on you?

Witness: The girl was all beaten up.

The witness Mikhailova, who had also been a witness at the examination of the girl, testified that the little child's body, especially the back, was all black and "horribly cut up."

The witness de Lorne explained that she was giving lessons to the girl at the time that Kroneberg lived at the dacha; she came three times a week. Kroneberg and Gesing treated the girl "very attentively, with care."

Defense Attorney Spasovich: On July 26, were you at Kroneberg's dacha?
Witness (through an interpreter): Yes.
Spasovich: Did the girl have lessons that day?
Witness: Yes.
Spasovich: Had she prepared her lessons?
Witness: Yes.
Spasovich: Did you notice any blue marks on the face and arms of the girl?
Witness: No.

January 27, 1876

Upon further questioning by both sides, de Lorne testified that it was very hard to deal with the girl, that although she was quick on the uptake, she was absent-minded. As for the girl's behavior, the witness stated that she could not form an opinion, and finally, that Kroneberg very often caressed his daughter and played with her.

The witness Linn, also a Frenchman, explained through an interpreter that he didn't know anything about the case except that Kroneberg came to him several times with his daughter in order to have her teeth pulled.

Defense Attorney Spasovich: Did Kroneberg and the girl come to see you on July 24?
Witness: I think they came on that day.
Spasovich: Why did they come and what did they do?
Witness: Kroneberg came with his daughter in order for me to pull two of her teeth.
Prosecutor: Did you notice any scars on the girl's face?
Witness: I didn't see anything.
Presiding Judge: Are you a dentist?
Witness: Yes.
Presiding Judge: Why do you remember so positively that this happened on July 24, on Thursday?
Witness: Because several days later I was interrogated by the judicial investigator and at that time I remembered well the day that Kroneberg had visited me.

Doctor Suslova testified that she had given medical treatment to Mrs. Gesing in the spring of the previous year, when she was ill; that she had observed Kroneberg's daughter, who was very quick-witted, but who had one deficiency, namely, that she didn't know how to control her bodily functions. Besides this, the girl had bad habits which had a great effect on her health, namely: she engaged in onanism, and the girl had had this illness, in the witness's opinion, for several years already; the girl had herself later confessed to this illness [v etoi bolezni devochka vposledstvii sama soznalas'].

Foreman of the jury: Did you notice any other signs of illness in her?

Suslova: The girl was completely healthy.

The witness De Troulle, the little girl's governess, stated that the girl was disobedient, had little fear of her parents, and that the witness had difficulty making her obey. The little girl was constantly going to see the caretaker, despite the prohibitions of her parents and of the witness.

Defense Attorney Spasovich: Did the girl speak to you about Geneva and the life she led there?

Witness: Yes, she said that [the interpreter's words were inaudible], then she said that if her father would punish her severely, then she could get better.

In conclusion the witness stated that she continues to give the girl lessons to this day.

Witness Kovalevskii, Kroneberg's servant, asserted that the father loved his daughter a great deal.

The bailiff of the dacha, Nikol'skii, among other things, stated that Kroneberg had had unpleasantnesses with the caretaker, about whom he had complained to the witness, and that these unpleasantnesses were over water. It wasn't clear on what terms Kroneberg's dacha had been rented, that is, with water or without. At first they brought water from an inn, but then, when the owner of that establishment refused to provide water, the caretaker began to carry water to Kroneberg from a well at the dacha. Kroneberg began to demand that he bring the previous water, but the caretaker said that they were asking two rubles for that water. Kroneberg complained to Nikol'skii about the caretaker, saying that he didn't obey and didn't listen to him. As for the story with the chicks, the witness testified that he knew that one of Kroneberg's little chicks had disappeared, for which he deducted a working day from the wages of the caretaker's mother. The mother of the caretaker told him that she had never undertaken to guard Kroneberg's chicks and that she didn't know why he had deducted from her wages. From the tone of this woman's story the witness could not conclude that she wanted to take revenge on Kroneberg at all costs because he had deducted from her wages on account of the chick.

Lunch break.

After the break, the court began reading the testimony of witnesses who did not appear, as well as various documents.

From the testimony of the wife of the pastor, A. de Combe, it was learned that she had known Kroneberg for three years. Kroneberg's relations with his daughter were most noble and tender; he did everything a tender father could do for the child. As for marks on the girl's face, she had the following scars on her forehead and the bridge of the nose; they were caused by her falling out a window when she was two or three years old. The mark on her cheek came from falling down stairs. Another mark happened when the child was still with her wet nurse; while walking in the garden of Doctor Faucon, the child ran to meet an acquaintance and fell face down on the ground and smashed her nose; when the nose began to heal, a scab appeared on it, and later a little bump. There is also a little pimple in the girl's nose, which she would pick open, and that is why she often bled. The child had various deficiencies, the most important of which was lying. Various measures were taken for rooting out these deficiencies, but all efforts were in vain. Kroneberg would not give up trying to raise the moral character of his child; he asked that the girl be given lessons at home by people whose morals had been tested.

The testimony of Pastor E. de Combe said essentially the same things, and among other things the witness said that Kroneberg wanted to give the little child a good education, in order to make her a woman useful to society, and not to let the child feel all the bitterness of her origins. The witness noted that the girl lied, and her tendency to this vice continued despite persuasions and even punishments, as Kroneberg had been informed. Once, while walking in a park, the girl fell down a hill nose first and received an injury.

Then the minutes of the examination of Kroneberg's daughter Mariia were read, after which the expert doctors, who had been in the courtroom the whole time, were invited to offer their conclusions regarding the injuries caused to the girl by her father. The experts each gave their conclusions separately; they recounted in detail the phenomena that had been observed on the child, and each of them drew his conclusions, based, according to their statements, on scientific data.

Doctor Lansberg stated that as a young doctor, this was the first time he had had occasion to conduct an examination, and for his part, he attested that he could not regard the kind of punishment that was inflicted on the girl as domestic corrective punishment, and that if such punishment continued it would have a very harmful effect on the child's health. From the marks that remained on the little child's body, one could conclude that during the punishment the child twisted and turned from one side to the other and the person punishing her didn't pay any attention and just beat her wherever he could. The division between grave and light injuries is strictly speaking a legal term, and "we cannot" draw a line between grave and light injuries, Lansberg said. As for the classification of the injuries inflicted, there have been cases where people died from light injuries, and sometimes completely recovered from grave injuries. In medical terms, an injury can be considered grave if the skin is disfigured.

Defense Attorney Spasovich: You found only spots and stripes on the body, but you did not find any lacerations of the skin?

Lansberg: I didn't find any.

In conclusion, the expert stated that in his opinion the injuries could be considered grave with regard to punishment, but not with regard to the blows inflicted.

Doctor Cherbishevich stated among other things that the injuries had in all probability been inflicted at various times, so that they could not produce any particular effect on the child's health, apart from the fact that the scars would remain her whole life.

Spasovich: Do you still maintain the opinion that the girl was disfigured?

Cherbishevich: I believe that the scars on her face constitute a certain disfigurement, especially for a girl.

The expert further stated that, in his opinion, the scar on the child's temple was of recent origin. As for the scar on her nose, if the girl had knocked her nose, it would not produce a wound on top of the nose, and in any case the scar would be uneven, that is, it would be wider in one place and narrower in another and would have an irregular form; but in the present case the scar is perfectly linear. On the child's cheek a scar is also visible and, in the expert's opinion, these two scars were produced simultaneously from a blow with several twigs, for example, with a switch. In any case, they are of earlier origin.

Spasovich: That is, they were produced over the course of several years?

Cherbishevich: Maybe over several years, and maybe over three weeks.

Expert Florinskii expressed the opinion that Mariia Kroneberg belongs to the category of subjects in whom the irritation of the skin is more acute than in others. In his opinion, the punishment was not very harshly carried out, because, taking into account the kind of instrument that was used in this case, blows inflicted with all one's strength could cut through thicker skin than a child's. As for the spots on the face, which the expert had carefully examined, with the exception of one of them, they are of earlier origin and, in the expert's opinion, were produced by a switch. In general, Mr. Florinskii does not consider the beatings to be grave; but nevertheless, if they were to continue, they would have a major effect on the child's health.

According to the statement by Doctor Gorskii, the punishment inflicted on the girl cannot be considered a corrective measure, because it exceeded the bounds of corrective punishments.

Finally, the last expert, Doctor Korzhenevskii, expressed the opinion that it is impossible to judge the punishment on the basis of the blows, since one must know the force of the blow, that Mariia Kroneberg belongs to the category of subjects on whose body the slightest touch produces bruises, that in the given case the injuries were to the topmost layer of the skin, and finally, that the next day after the child was examined, no signs of abnormality were discovered.

Then excerpts from three letters from Kroneberg to de Combe and vice versa were read, after which the material evidence was presented to the jury: the bundled switch and various linen of Mariia Kroneberg. The inquest was ended and, after a short break, the court began the concluding arguments.

January 28, 1876

Prosecutor A. K. Kolokolov: Gentlemen judges and jury members. In criminal court practice one often encounters cases during the investigation of which questions arise one after another, which arouse the interest of society in the highest degree. From the very beginning of such cases people talk about them a great deal: some condemn the accused, others express sympathy for him; but if the accused is brought to the dock, the interest grows, and everyone impatiently awaits the court's verdict, a verdict that alone can resolve the doubts that have arisen. The present trial belongs to this category, despite its simplicity, despite the fact that the defendant himself does not dispute the facts of which he is accused. The father has been brought to trial before you because in punishing his daughter, he caused her torture. Thus the case concerns the relations between parents and children, it is a question of the rights of parental authority, a question that is indeed important; it is a question that cannot help but interest each of us, because the action takes place in a family, where a particular kind of authority exists, an authority we must all respect, an authority protected by the law: parental authority. Gentlemen of the jury, as we decide this case in its essence, in comparison to similar cases, it is even more necessary than in all other cases to renounce these side issues, to dwell only on the circumstances uncovered by the judicial investigation, to study them coolly, attentively, and impartially, since only such an attitude to the case will guarantee the fairness of the verdict that justice demands of you. That is why I, gentlemen of the jury, consider it my duty to ask you, first of all, to dismiss any idea that bringing a father to trial for the torture of his child can shake parental authority, that such a trial runs counter to the rights we as parents are granted by the law. Each of us knows very well that parental authority, according to our legislation, is a very broad authority, extending to children of both sexes and of all ages. Parents, by virtue of this authority, can take domestic corrective measures against their children. If these measures are unsuccessful, the law grants parents the right to petition the court with the demand that more severe measures be taken. Further, it is not permitted to accept complaints brought by children against their parents in cases of personal insults and offenses. Children who permit themselves to disobey their parents or act in any abusive way are strictly punished. Parental authority, as you see, is supported by firm principles and is strictly protected by the law. And it cannot be otherwise; a society in which parental authority was not respected, in which it was not protected in an appropriate manner, would give poor promise for the future. No one denies the right of parents to punish their children. To correct our children is not only our right but our duty. What is a family? It is a primary school, in which future actors in the fatherland and the state are educated. That is why the state demands of us that we direct all our attention to the moral upbringing of our children and that we try through domestic education to raise the level of their morals, furthering the aims of the state. Whether you choose one or another measure for correcting your children—this is no one else's business and in this case parents are unlimited in their actions. Parental authority is limited in only one way: the state demands that in relation to the persons of their children, parents not allow themselves to take actions that are prosecuted by the criminal law. If signs of such violations of the law exist in the parents' actions, the case must be investigated in the established way. In bringing Kroneberg to trial, the court perceived in his actions signs that corresponded to the action covered in Statute No. 1489 of the Code of Punishment. Thus parental authority cannot be shaken in the slightest by this trial, as Kroneberg stated here. That authority remains just as firm as before, and we, gentlemen of the jury, can move completely calmly to the investigation of the question—did the actions of the defendant Kroneberg include those illegal actions that are ascribed to him in the indictment?

The judicial investigation presents us with sufficient material in order to retrace the life of Mariia Kroneberg, to study the environment in which she grew up and which surrounds her at the present time. I must say frankly that from this study I personally carried away a painful impression. There are in the world, gentlemen, unfortunate creatures who from the moment of their birth are subjected to all the adversities of a harsh life. Without at all disparaging the virtues of the defendant Kroneberg, I find that Mariia Kroneberg belongs precisely to this category of unfortunate creatures. She was born in 1868 as the result of the illegitimate union between Kroneberg and a woman unknown to us. Her mother was forced to leave her child in the care of strangers. Thus Mariia Kroneberg was born and immediately left an orphan. It's true, Kroneberg adopted her and took measures for her care, but we know that, no matter what environment the little girl grew up in, it could not resemble one in which children grow surrounded by their parents' affection. The girl was given to be raised by a wet nurse, a very good woman, as the witnesses de Combe, brought into the investigation from Switzerland, testify. I suppose that this wet nurse may be a good woman, but from the testimony of the same witnesses I conclude that the supervision and care of the child by the wet nurse were far from what one would desire to see. The witnesses told us that when the child was two or three years old, when she therefore required particular looking after, she flew out a window, fell down a staircase. Kroneberg himself attests that when he arrived in Switzerland he found his child in the most neglected state, among peasant children, in a word, the child was in a situation that Kroneberg himself admitted it was necessary to change. The girl was given over to Pastor de Combe and his wife. Unfortunately, these persons did not tell us in detail how the girl lived with them; they speak only of how Kroneberg himself treated her. By the way, if they had attested that the girl grew up in a good environment, that she was given particular attention, this could hardly be reliable testimony, since Kroneberg explained that he didn't like the education and treatment of the child by de Combe, and he decided to take his daughter to Petersburg. In general, I consider it necessary to dwell on the testimony of the de Combe couple. For me their testimony has great significance, namely, they say that Kroneberg was concerned to raise the moral level of his child; according to Pastor de Combe, Kroneberg, wishing to make his daughter into not a brilliant woman but a useful one, did everything to force the child to forget the bitterness of her origins and existence. Thus here is the program of pedagogical activity that Kroneberg spoke about, probably orally, about which he may even have written. Let us see now to what extent he followed this program when he brought the girl to Petersburg. With the financial means at Kroneberg's disposal, it would seem that he would be extremely fastidious in his choice of people into whose care he would give his daughter. And so? Kroneberg, as you know, constantly occupied with business, leaves his daughter in the care of Mrs. Gesing, who has replaced the girl's mother as Kroneberg's companion. Even assuming that Mrs. Gesing truly possesses all the qualities of a good educator, even in this case the choice could not be called completely correct. Can we really not assume that Mariia Kroneberg serves Gesing as a living proof that there exists in the world another woman who, as the mother of the girl, has more rights to Kroneberg than she, Gesing? I do not want to say by this that Gesing as a result would really allow herself to do something; but I think that on the basis of this consideration, Kroneberg was not especially cautious in his choice. Kroneberg was not always at home and didn't know how Gesing was treating the girl, but he could not help but know about the existence of those reasons why Gesing might sometimes treat the child not especially affectionately. Living in the city, Kroneberg did not take any radical measures in order to raise the moral level of the child; at least, we do not know of any. It appears to us to have been thoroughly proven that in Petersburg the switch was not employed, and instead, blows were inflicted on the child's face—blows that left marks in the form of bruises. This was the first measure which Kroneberg considered necessary to take in order to make the child forget all the bitterness of her origins and existence! His further actions took place at the dacha. He rented the dacha in order to help the ill Gesing, in order to give her and the child the possibility of breathing clean air. And here Kroneberg takes measures other than slaps in the face, which leave marks which I consider to be proven, since the defendant does not deny, didn't deny earlier, and now affirms that this happened. And Gesing testified at the preliminary investigation that blows were in fact inflicted and that bruises then remained on the girl's face. At the dacha Kroneberg resorted to a switch. Both at the preliminary investigation and in the indictment, the reasons for the punishment by the switch are not quite the same as they have been presented here at the inquest. There it was a question of the fact that the girl was constantly sleeping, that she was dirty [nechistoplotna], and that at the time of the punishment Kroneberg was in a nervous state. Here, however, to all this was added another circumstance which, because of its importance, has become the main reason for the severity of the punishment, namely, that illness about which Doctor Suslova testified. Moreover, Kroneberg says that he was offended because his daughter, for whom he had done so much, was on intimate terms with the servants. You heard the testimony of Titova, who lived at the dacha, and of Bibina, the mother of the caretaker. From this testimony we see that they are simple people, uneducated people, and that they truly felt pity for the child. It would seem that there is nothing criminal in the fact that simple people treated the girl affectionately; what is so offensive, what could be such a cause for indignation? If in the given case these people engaged in some kind of bad actions with the girl, that is another matter; but there has been no mention of this. Meanwhile, Kroneberg testifies that there were some sort of fights among him, his daughter, and the servants merely because the servants treated the girl with affection. As for the other reason, adduced by Suslova, this is in fact a very important reason, it could make it necessary for any father to take more strict measures against the child. But the torture of which Kroneberg is accused stands independently of the goal with which that torture was undertaken. If someone punishes his child even with the goal of breaking him or her of that vice about which Suslova spoke, and in doing so causes the child's torture, then despite the cause, he must be held responsible for that torture, since, as the Senate elucidates, in the crime of torture the goal with which it is undertaken is not of essential significance.

From the testimony of Titova and Bibina it is clear that the punishment with the switch was repeated not once but several times. By the way, the question of whether the witnesses were correct about how many times the girl was beaten is completely irrelevant in view of the fact that Kroneberg himself does not deny that he beat his daughter first three times and that the fourth time he punished her with that switch that the expert Florinskii quite correctly called "spitz-rutens." The point is not how many times she was beaten, but that she was beaten several times and that the beating was conducted with cruelty. According to Kroneberg's statement, the thrice-repeated beating with a switch, from which marks remained, did not lead to a good result, and he punished his daughter on July 25, as he himself says, very severely, and he beat her hard, beside himself. The simple people surrounding Kroneberg reacted to this fact with special pity and reported it to the police. The preliminary investigation began. Everything was confirmed and the proof of it is the expert examinations, repeated one after the other over the course of several days. The witnesses Balashova and Mik-hailova, brought in as witnesses at the examination of the girl on July 29, who therefore saw the girl soon after her punishment, told us about the impression that the marks on the girl's body produced on them. They say that the marks inflicted on Mariia Kroneberg by her father were very severe and that they, the witnesses, felt a particular pity for the girl. The doctor who conducted the ex-amination on July 29 testifies to the existence of these marks and says that these marks were severe. Several days later, another examination of the girl was car-ried out, namely, the examination of the marks on her face. This examination proved (I'll even cede three or four scars to the defense) that on her face, be-sides marks of older origin, there were bruises, purple marks, and scars, which by their appearance could not belong to the time to which the mother-of-pearl-colored scar belongs. This examination took place on July 31. The detailed ex-amination of the girl was on August 11, that is, seventeen days after the last pun-ishment. From this examination, and also from the conclusions of the experts at the trial, it is clear that on the girl's body there were marks which indicated di-rectly that the punishment was, in the words of some, rather harsh, and in the words of others—severe; but in the minutes, however, it is said that it was severe and moreover the kind of punishment that exceeded the bounds of those mea-sures called measures of domestic correction. It was also attested that if such punishment were to continue, it would have harmful results for the child's health. Several of the witnesses called by the defense refute the existence of spots and bruises on the girl's face; but I must say that the testimony of these wit-nesses did not produce the results the defendant expected. Thus de Lorne, de Troulle, and Linn say that they saw the girl on July 24 and 26, and that there were no marks on her face, while at the examination on July 31 a great number of bruises and other marks were found. Finally, Linn testifies that he didn't see any spots at all on the girl's face; I in my turn asked him whether he noticed a mother-of-pearl-colored scar, and he answered in the negative. From this I con-clude that he did not examine the girl especially attentively, and it is impossible to concede that he could not see those bruises that must have been on the girl, judging by the minutes of the July 31 examination. On the other hand, Kroneberg himself, both at the preliminary investigation and here at the trial, explained that he inflicted blows on his daughter's cheeks; this is confirmed both by the witnesses' testimony and by the minutes of the examination, and thus, in view of the fact that the circumstances of the trial, both as regards the marks on the face and in general, do not at all change that which was discovered at the preliminary investigation, I maintain the accusation in the form in which it was presented in the court's indictment, the conclusions of which appear to me to have been completely proven at the trial, both by the defendant's explanation and by the witnesses' testimony and the conclusion of the expert witnesses; it has been proven without a doubt that blows were inflicted on the girl's cheeks and that bruises were left as a result; that there was a punishment with a switch, which by its external appearance is not at all the kind of switch that is usually employed to punish one's children. I cannot admit—and I think you will agree with me—that beating a seven-year-old child on the cheeks to the point of bruising can be called a measure for domestic correction, much less punishment with the kind of switch that lies before you, gentlemen of the jury. At the preliminary investigation particular attention was paid to the fact that the kerchiefs and linen submitted for the case by the witnesses had traces of blood on them. I do not have any basis for affirming that these bloody spots were produced by the beatings inflicted by Kroneberg on his daughter—I completely believe that they were stained with blood from the girl's nose. But, gentlemen of the jury—Kroneberg, as the father of his daughter, more than anyone else, had the opportunity to notice that the girl's nose was bleeding and could have taken measures in a timely manner to clear up this illness. You know that the witnesses de Combe also speak of this disorder of the nose. Thus if Kroneberg knew, and he couldn't help but know, that the girl's nose was painful, then beating her in the face indiscriminately could be called cruel; to beat her on the cheeks meant to cause even more bleeding; Kroneberg knew that the girl's nose would bleed at the slightest touch, and despite this, he continued to beat his daughter, not paying attention to the fact that he could be causing severe pain thereby. I ask you, gentlemen of the jury, is this not cruel treatment? As for the marks on her face and the traces of the thrice-repeated punishment with the switch, I consider it necessary to direct your attention to the testimony of the witness Gesing, given at the preliminary investigation. There she said that marks remained both on the girl's face and on her body after the punishment with the switch, and here she testifies that she did not speak about this. To the defense attorney's question, however, Gesing answered that the testimony was translated for her word for word and that the judicial investigator himself questioned her and read her the testimony. For my part, I do not see the slightest basis for suspecting the judicial investigator of writing down precisely this part of the testimony not in the way Gesing gave it, since she does not deny the other parts of her testimony. There is no proof that the investigator had such an attitude toward the case, and therefore it seems to me that it was improper to hint such a thing. The minutes of Gesing's testimony, consequently, appear to be legitimate and completely reliable. So how can we explain such a contradiction on the part of Gesing? I assume that she could have either forgotten what she said earlier, or this contradiction is the result of that intimate relationship with Kroneberg about which you have heard. Thus, after each beating with the switch, marks remained, and Kroneberg, as the witnesses state, subjected his daughter to punishment very often.

I will move on to the event of July 25. What in particular did the child do on that day for which she had to be subjected to such a punishment? Gesing says that Mariia Kroneberg was a great liar, that she was constantly stealing things;

but the question arises, what exactly did she steal? She stole prunes, sugar, and various sweets. I suppose, gentlemen of the jury, that this could happen with any of our children. If you, returning home from this trial, see that your child has gone into your study and in your absence taken some sweet which was kept there and maybe was prepared for the child himself, would you really consider that a theft, and moreover, in relation to a child who was only seven years old? Here they have tried to prove to you that the girl was planning to steal money, but where is the proof of this? They say that the girl herself told them this; but after all, you consider her a liar, so why in one case do you not believe her, and in another you believe her unconditionally? Why, without verifying her statement, would you immediately begin beating her cruelly, and with the kind of switch that is called "spitzrutens"; can the punishment of a seven-year-old child with such a switch really not be acknowledged as cruelty? We have a society for the protection of animals, the goal of which consists in, to the extent possible, putting an end to the tortures inflicted on animals and placing them in more advantageous circumstances. If, therefore, we are made indignant by inhuman treatment of animals, can any of us not be made indignant by the act of a father or mother who beats his or her child, and beats him cruelly with thick branches? I suppose that each of us, if we saw such treatment, would try to persuade the parent that one cannot treat one's children so cruelly. Gesing, by the way, says that they punished the girl because she stole sweets from the trunk and broke a crochet hook. Gesing punished the girl, making her stand on her knees, and that, it seems to me, was quite enough. Why did she have to relate all this to Kroneberg, whose character Gesing must have known? It was not a secret from her that Kroneberg was nervous and irritable in the highest degree. If Gesing had been the mother of the child, she would not have said anything to a father with such a character. In his turn Kroneberg did not try to find out or ask about whether the girl really wanted to steal money and give it to the cook; he didn't pay any attention to the fact that from the very essence of the child's words it was clear that it was a lie, because the girl doesn't speak Russian and Titova doesn't speak French; the question arises, in what language could Titova have had a talk with the girl? Kroneberg didn't pay any attention to any of this, and resorted to cruel punishment. During this punishment, Gesing asked Kroneberg to break off a twig that was sticking out on the end of the switch, but he didn't want to do this for the reason that the twig would make the blow more severe. Kroneberg does not deny the existence of this twig, and he also says that he beat the girl hard, beat her helter-skelter, and that afterward he himself cried. If you, gentlemen of the jury, take into account all these circumstances of the case, if you analyze them in detail, you will agree with me that Kroneberg's treatment of his daughter was too cruel, was of the kind that is covered by the crime provided for by Statute 1489 of the Code of Punishment. I repeat, gentlemen of the jury, that the goal with which the punishment is carried out must be removed from consideration. So what does Kroneberg adduce in his defense? He says that he was concerned to raise the moral level of his child, that he had adopted her. In fact, this kind of action is worthy of imitation and example. To adopt a child does not, however, mean to do everything for her. If Kroneberg took on all the rights of a father, then he was obliged also to take on all the obligations, not only in the child's upbringing, but in her general treatment. He was obliged to understand her position, to behave himself truly as a father, not only as regards punishment, but not to permit himself to subject the child to such punishments for which one may end up in the dock. Whether you agree with me or not, gentlemen of the jury, whether you pronounce one or another verdict, that is a matter for your conscience, but I consider it necessary in concluding my speech to repeat again that I share completely in the conclusions of the indictment, and I deem that the treatment was too cruel, that it was torture, and since Kroneberg does not deny that he inflicted these injuries on the girl—he must be subjected to punishment for such actions.

January 29, 1876

Defense Attorney Spasovich: Gentlemen of the jury! Although we are seasoned people and accustomed to controversies like the present one, still, when you take the case you are defending to heart, you involuntarily feel fear and disquiet. I will not conceal that I am experiencing such feelings now: I am afraid, gentlemen of the jury, not of the court's decision, not of the prosecutor's accusation, which although it is very serious is at the same time restrained—I am afraid of an abstract idea, a phantom, I am afraid that the crime as it is entitled has as its subject a weak, defenseless creature. The very words "torture of a child," in the first place, arouse a feeling of great compassion for the child, and in the second place, a feeling of just as strong indignation in relation to the one who was her tormentor. I, gentlemen of the jury, am not an advocate of the switch, I understand completely that one may carry out a system of education from which the switch is excluded, but nevertheless, I consider it just as unlikely that corporal punishment will be completely and unconditionally eradicated as it is unlikely that in court you would cease to act for the cessation of criminal acts and violations of the justice that must exist both at home in the family and in the state. In the normal order of things, normal measures are taken. In the present incident, a measure was taken that was undoubtedly abnormal; but if you carefully investigate the circumstances that provoked this measure, if you take into consideration the nature of the child, the temperament of the father, the goals he was guided by in punishing her, then you will understand a great deal in this incident, and once you understand—you will acquit, because a deep understanding of a case inevitably leads to the fact that a great deal will be explained and will seem natural, not requiring a criminal remedy. Such is my task: to explain the incident. I will try to convey the circumstances of the case just as they were, without exaggerating or diminishing anything. I must begin, gentlemen of the jury, with the love affair to which the girl owes her existence.

Kroneberg is the son of a well-known banker in Warsaw. He himself has no personal fortune of his own, and is completely dependent on his father, a highly respected person but also a very strict person, who educated his children in the severe school of subordination. In 1863 the defendant graduated from gymnasium and entered Warsaw University at the very time of sedition, when almost all the young people to a man were agitated; in order to avoid the danger, his father sent him abroad to Brussels. This made Kroneberg almost a foreigner; that is, although he is a Russian national, born in the Polish Kingdom, he is more a German and even more a Frenchman. From Brussels Kroneberg returned to Warsaw in 1867, completed a master of law degree, which corresponds to our candidate's diploma; then he set off again to complete further scholarly courses in the universities of Bonn and Heidelberg. In this interval of time, between Brussels and Bonn, while living in Warsaw in 1867, he became intimate with a woman who was older than he, a widow with children. This woman understood that they were not compatible in age, that Kroneberg's parents would never consent to a marriage. She herself took the initiative in their breakup. Kroneberg didn't even suspect that she was pregnant by him. He was terribly distressed and sad and looked for some kind of distraction, some kind of field of activity. When the Franco-Prussian War began, he set off for France, entered the ranks of the French army, participated in twenty-three battles, received the medal of the Legion of Honor, attained the rank of second lieutenant, and retired after the end of the war. His experiences caused him to forget about the woman he had once loved. In 1872 he encountered her in Warsaw, when she was already married; at this point he learned that there was a child belonging to him in Geneva. The birth of this child had been accompanied by the following circumstances: the pregnant mother naturally wished that the birth not be made public; she went abroad and gave birth in Geneva. According to the laws there, an illegitimate child is registered in the name of the mother, unless the father is present and acknowledges the child. The mother could not take the child with her, and left it to be cared for by peasants in exchange for monetary compensation. Since she herself had gotten married a second time, it was as if between her and the child had been erected a stone wall which did not admit the slightest possibility for this mother to caress her child, or for the child to seek her out. When Kroneberg found out that the child was alive, he immediately conceived the firm intention of finding her and providing for her. The question arises: but how? The answer to this question depends greatly on the laws under which a person lives; the laws in turn have an effect on mores; on the other hand, mores are also reflected in laws. The interaction of laws and mores is perhaps nowhere more powerfully manifested than in the relationship of parents to their illegitimate children. Take for example our way of life. The law is strict with regard to illegitimate children: they have no rights, and it is not even defined whether there is fatherly authority over them. So how then are parents of illegitimate children to provide for them? If the parents are the least bit tender-hearted, if it goes against their grain to give their child up to a foundling home, then the sole means of providing for the child consists in money: to send the child somewhere out of the way to be brought up, to see him secretly, without witnesses, not letting the child find out whose he is; and if expressions of affection are to be admitted, then only secretly, without witnesses. Such is the relationship that necessarily results from the existing system of laws; this system cannot help but have an influence on mores; that is, parents, knowing that they cannot do any more for the child, rest content in their conscience when they have done all that the law allows, when they have given their child money as a dowry when they send them into some sort of educational institution.

But, gentlemen of the jury, within the boundaries of our empire there is a country—the Kingdom of Poland, which has its own special laws. When the Kingdom of Poland was the Principality of Warsaw, the Napoleonic Code was introduced there in 1808. In 1825, in the reign of Alexander I, certain parts of this code having to do with family rights, namely in the first and third books, were revised. This 1825 edition of the code is in effect to this day. In volume 19 of the Diary of Laws is contained the law of 1836, according to which the family rights of the inhabitants of the Kingdom of Poland are governed by the laws of the kingdom when these inhabitants resettle within the boundaries of the Russian Empire. The 1825 code establishes between parents and illegitimate children the following relationship: according to Statute No. 101, a father may at any time acknowledge a child as his own; this is done by means of noting the father's name in the register of civil status. As a result of this acknowledgment, according to Statute No. 303, the parent takes upon himself the legal obligation to educate, support, and provide for the child, that is, the same obligation a father has toward legitimate children. According to Statute No. 756 and following, such a child even inherits from his parents on the following basis: if there are legitimate children, they receive one third of what the legitimate children receive; if the brothers or parents survive the deceased, the illegitimate children receive one half; if more distant relatives survive, they receive three fourths. If no regular heirs exist, they receive the entire estate. Of course, parental authority over the children corresponds to these rights. This authority is twofold: it is expressed, in the first place in guardianship, which belongs to the mother; if the mother cannot be the guardian, then to the father; in the second place, in the right to punish the children. Besides this, there is Statute No. 339, which is extremely important and the significance of which I will allow myself to explain to you; it consists in the following: parents who are dissatisfied with the behavior of their children may punish them by means that do not injure their health and do not hinder scholarly progress. For abusing this authority, parents are given a reprimand in the presence of a civil tribunal of the first instance in camera, etc. . . .

Presiding Judge: Would you be so good as not to mention punishment? You may refer to the law, but not speak about punishment.

Defense Attorney Spasovich: This is not a punishment; it is only a measure available to a civil court according to a civil code. I consider it my duty to state that according to Statute No. 339, no punishment is stipulated for exceeding the authority to punish, and all that can be done is to take away parental authority and give the children to another person to be brought up at the parent's expense. Kroneberg is a holder of a master's degree in law: he knew his laws, he understood what he could do for the child and wanted to do the maximum that he could do according to the law. He turned for advice to lawyers in Geneva, who advised him to register his acknowledgment of the child. He took pains to make the acknowledgment as strong as possible, so that his acknowledgment would be in force in the boundaries of the Kingdom of Poland. Of course, he understood very well that he did not yet have his own fortune. But in giving the child his name, he was assured that if some misfortune were to overtake him, his parents and relatives would take care of a little girl bearing the name Kroneberg, that as a last resort his daughter would be accepted in one of the government foundling institutions in France, as the daughter of a holder of the Legion of Honor. Kroneberg took the girl from the peasants who had been bringing her up and where she could not receive any kind of education, and brought her to a home that seemed to him as proper as could be, to the Pastor de Combe, whose wife was the girl's godmother. Thus passed the years 1872, 1873, and 1874, up until the beginning of 1875. During these years, several changes took place in the intentions, the occupations, and the position of Kroneberg.

There are people who by nature are more inclined to family life; there are people who can live their whole lives as bachelors. Kroneberg belongs precisely to the first category of people who are inclined toward marriage; he very nearly got married in 1872, in 1873 he also intended to, but the match fell apart, and a major obstacle was the fact that he declared the existence of a natural daughter; the second obstacle was Kroneberg's father, who would not allow a marriage to be arranged without his participation and consent. In Paris Kroneberg became acquainted with the unmarried woman Gesing. When he was faced with a journey to St. Petersburg in 1874, to a completely alien city where he would be completely alone, he accepted Gesing's proposal to go with him, and he took her with him. You were able to judge to what extent Mrs. Gesing resembles or does not resemble a woman of the demimonde, with whom one engages in only a passing affair. Of course she is not Kroneberg's wife, but their relationship does not exclude either love or respect. You have seen whether this woman is heartless toward the child and whether she loves the child or not. She wished to do all kinds of good things for the child. In the testimony of the witnesses against the defendant, even the most unfavorable, as for example, of Titova, there is not a word against Mrs. Gesing. In 1874 they came to St. Petersburg, and in 1875 Mrs. Gesing fell ill; she was greatly attached to the defendant and she herself began to insist: "Take the child, it will be fun for you and for me; I will take care of her and bring her up." Kroneberg did not yet have a firm intention of taking the child at that time, but he decided to go to Geneva to have a look . . . In Geneva he was struck: the child, whom he visited unexpectedly, at a time that hadn't been announced, was found to be wild and didn't recognize her father. Kroneberg was dissatisfied with her upbringing and immediately settled accounts with Mme de Combe and brought the child to St. Petersburg. They came on April 28; they lived for a while in the Hotel Demuth, then settled in the city, and finally in June they moved to the dacha. All of May Kroneberg was busy with the affairs of the Vistula Railroad, which did not give him a moment's leisure. At the dacha the event took place that gave rise to this case. Various reasons for this event came together, both internal and external, contained both in the child and in the father, and also in the various influences on the child.

Before I pass to an account of the reasons for the catastrophe of July 25, I must analyze in more detail the very external fact for which Kroneberg is being tried—the fact of the beating of the little girl, attested both by the material evidence and by the witnesses' testimony. The marks that were the object of investigation may be subdivided into marks on the face, marks on the arms and extremities, marks on the back parts of the body, and blood spots on linen. Each of these traces much be analyzed separately, and above all *the marks on the face.* When one looks attentively into the child's face, that face indeed is covered [ispisano] in all directions by thin scars, covered in some places by hair, so that they are just barely visible. These marks were identified by Mr. Cherbishevich as ineradicable disfigurements on the face, with which I could agree only if each person went around armed with two microscopes. Since the girl was examined as a result of being beaten with a switch, one naturally assumes that the marks on the face must have been produced by such a beating. I think that precisely this idea was adopted involuntarily by the examining doctors, especially Mr. Cherbishevich, that it became a preconceived idea and hindered the investigation. The minutes of the examination must be analyzed separately, because they do not coincide with each other. If one lumps them together, as has been done in the indictment, then the result is something coherent, but if you analyze them separately, then it is evident that each of the investigating doctors pulled in a different direction, so that in their conclusions they diverged from each other to an immeasurable distance. Mr. Cherbishevich, having analyzed the marks on her face, divided them into, first, white scars and welts; second, yellow-brown and yellow spots; and third, scabs. The welts on the left temple and left cheek he admitted to be the only marks that could be considered to be old. He observed yellow and yellow-brown spots, but not purple or bluish-purple spots. I must note that not one of the doctors found such blue and purple spots. Mr. Cherbishevich found yellow and yellow-brown spots on the whole length of the temple, on the nose, on the right cheek, and there were scabs in the nostril and under the nose. All these marks and scabs were recognized as of recent origin. Several of these marks, in the opinion of Cherbishevich, were very characteristic of marks undoubtedly caused by a switch, namely: the small lengthwise welts, parallel to the entire length of the nose. Such was the conclusion of Doctor Cherbishevich, who saw the girl on July 31. About ten days later, the girl was examined by four doctors: Cherbishevich and another three. A completely different conclusion was reached. Several of those marks that Mr. Cherbishevich recognized as being recent were now relegated to the category of very old; thus, for example, the yellow spot on the temple had turned into a welt with a mother-of-pearl tint, which could not have been formed any earlier [sic] than six months before, that is, when the girl was not yet in St. Petersburg. The marks on the bridge of the nose were also attributed to more than six months before. Not one of the marks on the face was recognized as characteristic of a mark from a switch; only one very small mark on the cheek was noted by Professor Florinskii as one that could have been produced by a switch, but even then not reliably. Despite the fact that the second expert opinion was more tempered and cautious than the first, it still went too far in its assumptions, which can only serve as proof of how difficult it is to explain the origin of injuries based only on external appearances and not on the basis of factual data. The doctors who examined the girl on August 11 presumed that the pink marks on her nose and cheeks had arisen recently, while later it was learned from the de Combe couple, Jenny Geks, and Doctor Faucon that each of these marks, not excluding the welts on the nose and cheeks, was three or four years old. Thus, as far as the marks on the face are concerned, there is not one of them of which it could be said that it was produced by a blow inflicted by the father. The question of the slaps in the face and the bruises that may have been the result of the slaps remains open. Kroneberg did slap the child; that is definite, he himself admits that he struck the girl in the face about three or four times. I admit that a slap in the face cannot be considered worthy of approbation as part of a father's treatment of a child. But I also know that there are very respected systems of pedagogy, for example, the English and the German, which consider a blow of the hand on the cheek to be no more severe than, and perhaps in certain respects even preferable to, beating with a switch. The reasons why the slap in the face is considered a particularly offensive blow lie in mores, in the past. If we follow the history of the origins of this idea, we will find them in those chivalric times when knights wore helmets with visors, and it was impossible to hit them in the face when they were in their usual garb, and such blows were rained only on peasants and villeins [feudal serfs]. If we analyze parental authority, it is difficult to say that it in no case extends to the slap in the face. From a stranger a blow in the face can become a deadly insult, but not from a father. I suppose that you cannot recognize slaps to be torment or torture if these slaps did not produce visible injuries on the face. The question arises: what were the consequences of the blows in the face? In the present instance, did they leave spots or bruises on the face? Even if spots remained from them, you heard the testimony of Professor Korzhenevskii about the fact that this girl has a tendency to scrofula, and how, with a scrofulous constitution, with an abundance of lymph, the lightest blow, a pinch, a mere pressure, will produce spots on the body. You heard that the marks on the elbows were almost undoubtedly formed merely because they held her by the arms during the punishment. Thus the bruises could have been produced even by weak blows. But I do not see any basis for admitting that there were any bruises. Who speaks of them? Titova; but even she didn't see any bruises either in the city or at the dacha until July 25; she supposedly observed them only after July 25. Please note, gentlemen of the jury, that Agrafena Titova is that woman who, together with Bibina, brought the switch and the linen to the judicial investigator; they acted together, they instigated the prosecution of Kroneberg together. If these bruises had existed, then someone other than Titova would have seen them. Recall the testimony of the witnesses Kovalevskii, Valevskii, Linn, who deny the existence of bruises. The prosecutor, in order to weaken Linn's testimony, reprimands him for not noticing the scar on her temple; that means he did not look attentively at the girl; but, gentlemen of the jury, after all, that scar is under her hair; the only way one could notice it would be to make a special effort to look at her and turn her hair back. After the beating, on the next day, on Saturday, July 26, Kroneberg had a governess, Mrs. de Lorne, to give lessons to the girl, and she did not notice anything resembling bruises. But it is said that Mrs. Gesing did not deny the bruises in the testimony she gave to the investigator, and only now does she testify to the contrary. I suppose that of the two testimonies, it would be more possible not to believe the one given at the preliminary investigation; it is true, the investigator translated it for her, but, in the first place, she was probably agitated, just as now, that is, she was in a nervous state that did not dispose her to weighing the words that were being read to her. In the second place, I cannot help but say that that investigation was a bit inflated, that certain circumstances were brought forward in it that have now significantly receded into the background. That is why I suppose that the bruises on the face have not been proven even by the testimony of Gesing. I now move to the marks on the arms and legs; these marks arose simply from the fact that the girl was held during the punishment. Then there follow the marks of blood on the slip and handkerchiefs. This blood was produced by the most natural means: from a nosebleed. The slip is completely clean on the back, only on the breast are there a few drops; the new handkerchiefs are also strewn with drops. It is obvious that there is a direct, immediate connection between the blood on the slip and on the handkerchiefs. Perhaps the slaps in the face hastened the flow of this blood from the scrofulous scab in the nostril, but this is not at all an injury: even without a wound and a knock this blood would have flowed a bit later. Thus this blood does not contain in itself anything that should dispose one against Kroneberg. At the minute when he inflicted the blow, he might not have remembered, he might not even have known, that the child suffered from nosebleeds. All the data about the nosebleeds was gathered later, when the investigation began. There remain the marks on the back parts of the body. These marks were investigated three times: first, on July 29, by Mr. Lansberg; the second time, on August 5, by Mr. Florinskii alone; and on August 11, by four doctors, including both Lansberg and Florinskii. Despite the fact that Mr. Lansberg's opinion is unfavorable toward Kroneberg, for his defense I will adopt many data from his minutes of July 29. Mr. Lansberg positively attested that on the back parts of the girl's body there were no welts, no lacerations in the skin, but only dark-purple subcutaneous spots and the same sort of red stripes. Most of these spots were on the left buttocks area passing onto the left thigh. Without having found any traumatic marks or even any scratches, Mr. Lansberg testified that the stripes and spots did not present any life-threatening danger. Six days later, on August 5, during the examination of the girl by Professor Florinskii, he noticed no spots, but only stripes—some smaller, some larger; but he did not at all admit that these stripes constituted any sort of significant injury, although he admitted that the punishment had been severe, especially in view of the instrument with which the child was punished. At the examination of August 11 by four doctors, they found on the buttocks some pink skin with traces of scabs that had fallen off, from which one could deduce the existence of wounds, if we did not have the minutes of Lansberg's examination of the girl on July 29, from which it is clear without a doubt that there were no wounds at all. The origin of these scabs was explained best of all by Professor Korzhenevskii, who described them as a local necrosis of the skin, which was shed and replaced by new skin. This skin injury was most superficial and external; but with the child's organization, with a multiplicity of lymphatic vessels, the beating inevitably left visible traces. Such is the conclusion of Mr. Korzhenevskii. As for the question of whether the punishment in the present case was severe, it seems to me that the expert was completely correct in saying: this is not my business to decide whether it was severe or not. The very question turns out to be not a medical question but a pedagogical one, and in order to answer it by means of expert opinion, one needs not medical men but high-school inspectors and teachers. A medical man cannot determine either the limits of a father's authority or the severity of an incorrect punishment. The marks on the back parts undoubtedly were produced by the switch. This switch is here; the branches were pulled off several days before the punishment by Kroneberg, who wished to frighten the child with them, because the measures he had used up to that point had not produced the appropriate impression on the child. In tearing off these rowanberry branches, perhaps he did not know that he would in fact have to use them. Then there came a moment of anger, completely just and legitimate anger, and the punishment was carried out. It seems to me that from the entire investigation you cannot come to any other conclusion than that he punished his daughter with this instrument only once. He himself says that he punished her about three times over fairly large intervals of time, with small twigs that could not leave any marks. The severe punishment for which Kroneberg is being tried, the punishment that exceeded the bounds of the usual, as the indicting authority says, was only on July 25. That it was only one punishment is confirmed by all the circumstances of the case. We cannot even speak of any preceding punishments. Only Bibina alone says that the girl was beaten every day; but this is refuted by all the data, it is refuted by Valevskii, who heard crying three or four times, it is refuted by Mrs. Gesing, by everyone in the house, and without doubt one has only to look at the child, at her healthy aspect, in order to be assured that if she had been beaten every day for a month and a half, the girl could not look this way. She often screamed at the dacha; but she's no mean screamer [ona krichat' gorazda], she screams when they make her stand in a corner or on her knees. No one was present at these punishments. Titova participated in the punishment only once, namely July 25.

In order to finish with the external aspect of the crime, I have only to dwell on those final conclusions, expressed in scientific terms, which were given by the gentlemen experts. Mr. Lansberg concluded that he considers the injuries to be, although not life-threatening, nevertheless *grave*. When we asked why he calls these injuries grave, he replied that he calls them that according to his inner conviction, according to his subjective view, that he was not at all governed by volume 13 of the Code of Laws, moreover, that he was carrying out a forensic medical examination for the first time in his life. Meanwhile, it is hardly necessary to prove that a *grave* sign is not as subjective as Lansberg represents it to be, that it does not depend on a personal opinion, that there are several general grounds for dividing injuries into grave and slight. It was these grounds that Professors Florinskii and Korzhenevskii indicated. If the tissue is damaged, damaged deeply, then this is a grave injury; in the contrary case, it is not. The practice of the court of appeals, to which the indictment refers, expounded for the guidance of courts what should be considered grave and slight injuries. It turns out that it is not a medical term but a legal term, a delimitation introduced into the law in order to exact more or less severe penalties; from the law it enters into forensic medicine, and medical men, in taking courses in forensic medicine, study among other things the grounds for sorting injuries into grave and slight. In the classic 1872 decision on the subject of injuries, No. 1072, the case of Loktev, it was said by the criminal appeals department of the Senate that the characteristic feature of grave injuries consists in the fact that such injuries cause illness, a prolonged disorder of the organism, the impossibility of working for a certain period of time. The question arises: was this sign apparent in the present case? No, it was not there at all, it was not there to such an extent that on the next day the little girl was playing, did her lessons, and no one noticed any changes in her; the doctors who observed her on July 29 and July 31 did not find any symptoms of illness in her. Mr. Lansberg himself, in my opinion, committed a deviation, because, while he wrote in his minutes "grave injuries," in court he explained that he considered not the injury but only the punishment to be grave; in a word, he acted in the role of a pedagogue who evaluates the relative gravity of a child's punishment. I think that no matter how you analyze the case, in conscience you will certainly come to the conclusion that the injuries were in any case very slight. Slight injuries do not even enter into the realm of actions within the jurisdiction of the district court: they are decided by a justice of the peace. In the following examinations, the doctors who offered different conclusions defined these injuries in the following way: they say that this punishment exceeds the bounds of the usual. This definition would be excellent if we could define what is a usual punishment; but as long as such a definition doesn't exist, anyone would find difficulty in saying whether it exceeded the bounds of the usual. Let us assume that it is so; then what does it mean? That this punishment, in the majority of cases, is inapplicable to children; but even with children there may be extraordinary cases. Will you really not admit that fatherly authority may be, in exceptional cases, in such a position that it must use more severe measures than usual, which do not resemble those usual measures that are used every day? But let us assume that the gentlemen experts, in predetermining a criminal question, came to the conclusion that Mr. Kroneberg abused his fatherly authority. In such a case, try him for abusing his authority. But he is being tried for something completely different—he is being tried for torture and torment inflicted on a child. In order to understand where this formulation of the indictment comes from, I must touch on the law and again the same appeals practice on which the indictment dwells.

In the law, on the subject of beatings, in Statute 142 of the regulations for justices of the peace, types of violence are specially defined that include mild beatings as well; but then in the Code of Punishment there is a huge lacuna on this account, and it speaks only of severe, life-threatening beatings and other types of torture in Statute 1489. Among these types of crimes, there is apparently an interval and a large interval, because not all severe beatings are life-threatening. There have, meanwhile, been cases where it would have been strange to impose a penalty as if for violence. In Tiflis, a certain Caucasian prince painfully beat a civil servant who had made advances to his wife; in Riazan or Kursk, a second lieutenant was beaten up by his comrades; the husband of Vysotskaia tormented his wife by putting a noose on her neck and then pulling at the rope and tying the rope to a table. In all such cases there was no danger to life, but nonetheless, to impose a penalty as if for violence would be beyond the power of the authorities. That is why the Senate interpreted Statute 1489 in such a way that the adjective "life-threatening" applied only to beatings and not to tortures and torments. At the same time, however, the Senate understood that the concept of torture and torment was too indefinite. If I pinch someone, if I severely burn his hand and arrange for a person to lie in bed covered with insects, and he doesn't sleep all night, if I do some other little nasty thing, can that really be recognized here as torture or torment? That is why the governing Senate, in the same decisions to which the indicting authority refers, determined, on the other hand, that tortures and torments are to be understood as such an encroachment on a personality or on the personal inviolability of a man that is accompanied by torment and cruelty. In tortures and torments, in the opinion of the Senate, physical sufferings must without fail present a more intense, more prolonged degree of suffering than in ordinary beatings, even severe ones. If one cannot call the beating severe, and torture must be more severe than severe beatings, if not one expert called it severe, except Lansberg, who himself repudiated his own conclusion, then the question arises, how can one subsume this action under the concept of torture and torment? I believe that this is unthinkable.

I, gentlemen of the jury, up to this time have only been occupied with one side of the case, which for you is of much less importance than the other side, the internal side, the motives that forced Kroneberg to act. I know that the Senate in its decision, to which the presenter of the indictment referred, says that the goal as such is not important as long as the torments were severe and prolonged; I believe that if the person being tried before you were that very person in whose case that decision was handed down, that is, that very Caucasian prince who beat the supposed lover of his wife, then you nevertheless would take into consideration the circumstance of whether the malice on the part of the tormentor was a completely unfounded one, purely for the pleasure of looking at another person's sufferings, or whether the anger was a just one, with a rational cause. This inner motive, this cruelty not only of suffering, but also the cruelty of the heart of the tormentor, has a huge significance when a father is being tried for the fact that he cruelly punished his daughter—that is, that he used a means of domestic correction on an exaggerated scale. The question arises: was there a reason for the use of this extraordinary measure? Consequently, the main question resides not in those bruises and stripes on the body about which the witnesses testified, but in the correspondence between the reason that called forth the punishment and the punishment itself. If you enter into an analysis of these reasons, then I believe that you will pity the daughter, and you will also pity the father. The little girl, as you could see yourselves, is unusually sharp [shustraia], unusually quick on the uptake, lively as a flame, as quick to blaze up as gunpowder, with a powerful imagination, well developed physically; it is true, she has a certain tendency toward scrofula, but in general her health is in a blooming state. This is a good side of her both physically and morally; but there is also a dark side, a bad side, which partly depends, perhaps, on her nature and partly on her upbringing. She was raised among peasant children without supervision; de Combe did not reeducate her; when her father brought her to live with him, he found many defects in her: untidiness, a lack of knowledge of how to behave, the beginnings of illness from her bad habit, but the main thing that made the father indignant—was her constant, even purposeless lying. Whether correctly or not, Kroneberg considers that lying is the mother of all other vices and that all people's defects mainly stem from the fact that they are not truthful. For him, truthfulness is an absolute obligation without exception. In a letter written in July 1871 to Mrs. de Combe, long before he took his daughter, he expresses the opinion that lying is a baseness of the mind and heart (*lâcheté de coeur et d'esprit*). That is why from the very beginning Kroneberg tried above all to eradicate this vice of lying; perhaps he set about eradicating it too zealously—he is a bad pedagogue, he admits that himself. The girl, meanwhile, did not obey, did not fear either her father or Gesing, did not obey her governesses either. While they were in the city, everything worked out somehow; but they moved to the dacha and all the circumstances of her upbringing changed for the worse. The dacha lay between Udel'naia and Pargolovo Stations, completely isolated; her father came home only in the evenings and left in the mornings; Gesing is an ill woman, occupied with her treatment, not very active. The child is frisky, she goes running to the caretaker and the servants, she strikes up an acquaintance with them and falls under the bad influence of the servants and learns various nasty tricks and thievery. At first these small thefts pass unnoticed, others are suspected, but she is not suspected of carrying off things, all they notice is that the child is wild and struggles from their grasp. The father beat her slightly about two or three times, but this had no effect at all: the girl had gotten used to beatings at the de Combes'. On July 25 the father comes to the dacha and for the first time finds out by surprise that the child had been rummaging in Gesing's trunk, had broken a crochet hook and gotten at some money. I don't know, gentlemen, whether it is possible to regard such actions by one's daughter with indifference? People may say: "So what? Can you really exact such a severe penalty for a few prunes, some sugar?" I believe that from prunes to sugar, from sugar to money, from money to banknotes is a direct path, an open highway. It is the same thing as the habit of lying: once it has taken root, it grows more and more, like that wild burdock that covers the fields if it is not rooted out and weeded out. When they discovered this bad habit, combined with all the girl's other defects, when the father found out that she was thieving, he in fact became very angry. I think that each of you would have become just as angry, and I think that to prosecute a father because he punished his child painfully but justly does a disservice to the family, a disservice to the state, because the state is only strong when it is founded on a strong family. Since in former times they used to say of a father who stopped his child in time, "he is saving his son from the gallows"—

we say in such cases that the father is saving his son from hard labor and deportation, and his daughter from becoming a debauched [rasputnaia] woman. If the father became indignant, he was completely within his rights, he beat her painfully, harder than is usually done; he was driven out of his wits, then he began to sob and fell onto the bed in a nervous fit. After this crisis, which was the result of such natural causes, there is no basis for drawing the conclusion that is drawn in the present case, that if such a punishment were to be repeated more often, and for a longer period of time, it could have a harmful effect on the child's health. And what if it wasn't repeated? After all, one can say the same of any measure; to withhold food from a person for the course of six hours means nothing, but to withhold food for six days would mean to starve him to death; to pull one tooth is nothing, but to pull all the teeth in the jaw could kill a person from the pain alone. Consequently, the conclusion that if such a punishment were multiplied by many times, it would produce such-and-such results, in the present case leads nowhere, has no practical significance and must be completely dismissed. I admit, gentlemen of the jury, that Kroneberg punished the girl hard, painfully, so that the marks of the punishment remained visible; he made two logical mistakes which were reflected in the very act: in the first place, he acted too zealously; he assumed that one could at one time, with one blow uproot all the evil that had been sown for years and cultivated for years in the soul of the child. But this is impossible to do, one must act slowly and have patience. The other mistake was that he acted not as a cautious judge, that is, having caught the child in a theft to which she confessed, he did not investigate the circumstances that inclined the girl toward theft; he did not properly look into the fact that from the girl the trail led to the persons surrounding her; he simply asked why and for whom she had taken the money. The girl answered with stubborn silence, then a few months later she said that she had wanted to take the money for Agrafena. If he had investigated the circumstances of the theft in more detail, he perhaps would have come to the conclusion that the corruption that had insinuated itself into the girl could be laid to the account of the people close to her. The very silence of the girl attests that the child did not want to betray the people with whom she was on good terms. But human nature is strange; everyone in the house is convinced that, after all, the last punishment had a good effect on the child; despite the fact that the investigation has shaken the fatherly authority of Kroneberg, the punishment produced the effect that she lies less often and there is hope that she will come to greater and greater improvement.

In conclusion I will permit myself to say that in my opinion the entire indictment of Kroneberg has been formulated completely incorrectly, that is, in such a way that the questions posed to us cannot at all be decided. I believe that you will all admit that there is such a thing as a family, there is such a thing as fatherly authority by nature, and in the present case by law as well, an authority that extends also to illegitimate children; you will admit that parents have the right to punish their children. I think that you also cannot deny that your authority here in court stems from the same source—you are also carrying out a sort of corporal punishment, in a different form, corresponding to a more mature age. Consequently, you cannot deny a father's authority, deny his right to punish in such a way that the punishment has an effect, without also denying your own authority, the authority of the criminal court. What is the father being tried for? For abusing his authority; the question arises: where is the boundary to this authority? Who can determine how many blows a father can inflict and in what instances he can inflict them without harming the child's organism in the course of the punishment? If this was an abuse, then you must try him for excess, for excess [za izlishek, za ekstsez]. If you are trying a person who, in being forced to defend himself, inflicted an unnecessary blow on the attacker and killed him, would you really try him for murder? No, you would try him only for excessive force. If you try a person for the most severe insult that he inflicted on another person who had insulted him, you will deduct the last insult he himself received from the one he inflicted; but in the present case you are being required to punish not according to a difference but according to a sum, not for an abuse of authority, not for the fact that this punishment exceeded the bounds of the usual, but [according to a statute intended] for a torture inflicted by a stranger on a grown person. If you ponder this strange formulation of the question, you, gentlemen of the jury, will have to say that within such limits you cannot impose a penalty. If the question is posed as a question of excess, you can decide it, but if you are being forced to judge on the basis of a sum, then you will act more imprudently than Kroneberg did when he punished his daughter. Kroneberg at least knew what kind of branches he was binding together into a switch with which he would punish her, and he after all punished her in such a way that it did not have an effect on the girl's health; but you do not know the dimensions of that large, perhaps iron switch . . .

Presiding Judge: Would you be so good as not to mention punishment?

Spasovich: I have finished.

Kroneberg: Everything that I said, gentlemen of the jury, is true. I completely deny that the marks on my little girl's face were inflicted by me. I did in fact punish her hard one time with a soft switch. I will not lie. When my daughter comes of age, she will become convinced that she had an unfortunate but honorable father.

The court's decision is already well known.

Notes

INTRODUCTION

1. The approach of reconstructing the scientific thought of Dostoevsky's time was pioneered by James L. Rice, whose major focus is Dostoevsky's epilepsy and theories of epilepsy's causes and consequences in his time (*Dostoevsky and the Healing Art: An Essay in Literary and Medical History* [Ann Arbor: Ardis, 1985]). Liza Knapp adopts a similar approach in gathering contemporaneous texts on natural science as part of her exploration of Dostoevsky's "metaphysics of inertia" (*The Annihilation of Inertia: Dostoevsky and Metaphysics* [Evanston: Northwestern University Press, 1996]). My own work in tracing Dostoevsky's sources on sexuality has been greatly aided by the historical studies of Laura Engelstein (*The Keys to Happiness: Sex and the Search for Modernity in Fin-de-Siècle Russia* [Ithaca: Cornell University Press, 1992]) and Dan Healey (*Homosexual Desire in Revolutionary Russia: The Regulation of Sexual and Gender Dissent* [Chicago: University of Chicago Press, 2001]).

2. Sigmund Freud, "Dostoevsky and Parricide," in *The Standard Edition of the Complete Psychological Works of Sigmund Freud*, ed. James Strachey (London: Hogarth Press and Institute of Psycho-Analysis, 1953–74), 21:175–96.

3. Joseph Frank, "Freud's Case-History of Dostoevsky," in his *Dostoevsky: The Seeds of Revolt, 1821–1849* (Princeton: Princeton University Press, 1976), 379–91. See also James L. Rice, *Freud's Russia: National Identity in the Evolution of Psychoanalysis* (New Brunswick: Transaction, 1993), and V. K. Kantor, "Freid contra Dostoevskii," *Tolstoi ili Dostoevskii? Filosofsko-esteticheskie iskaniia v kul'turakh Vostoka i Zapada*, ed. V. E. Bagno, St. Petersburg: Nauka, 2003, 197–207.

4. A. Kashina-Evreinova, *Podpol'e geniia: Seksual'nye istochniki tvorchestva Dostoevskogo* (Petrograd: Tret'ia Strazha, 1923; reprint ed., Leningrad: Atus, 1991).

5. Kashina-Evreinova, *Podpol'e geniia*, 52, 53–54. Kashina-Evreinova is of course following the lead of N. K. Mikhailovskii, who labeled Dostoevsky a "cruel talent" in his 1882 book by that name.

6. T. Enko, *F. Dostoevskii—Intimnaia zhizn' geniia* (Moscow: OOO MP Geleos, OAO BI-GAZ-SI, 1997).

7. Joseph Frank, *The Seeds of Revolt; Dostoevsky: The Years of Ordeal, 1850–1859* (Princeton: Princeton University Press, 1984); *Dostoevsky: The Stir of Liberation, 1860–1865* (Princeton: Princeton University Press, 1986); *Dostoevsky: The Miraculous Years, 1865–1871* (Princeton: Princeton University Press, 1995); and *Dostoevsky: The Mantle of the Prophet, 1871–1881* (Princeton: Princeton University Press, 2002).

8. Elizabeth Dalton, *Unconscious Structure in "The Idiot": A Study in Literature and Psychoanalysis* (Princeton: Princeton University Press, 1979). See also Joe Andrew, "The Law of the Father and *Netochka Nezvanova*," in his *Narrative and Desire in Russian Literature, 1822–49: The Feminine and the Masculine* (New York: St. Martin's, 1993), 214–26; and Daniel Rancour-Laferriere, *The Slave Soul of Russia: Moral Masochism and the Cult of Suffering* (New York: New York University Press, 1995), which includes many references to Dostoevsky. A. L. Bem produced what he billed as a Freudian reading of some of Dostoevsky's works in 1938, but thanks to Bem's intellectual rigor and scrupulousness the study does not end up by being very Freudian at all (*Dostoevskii: Psikhoanaliticheskie etiudy* [Berlin: Petropolis, 1938; reprint ed., Ann Arbor: Ardis, 1983]). Bem offers an interesting critique of Freud's study of Dostoevsky (11–12). For a collection of essays that approach the subject of sexuality in Russian culture from a variety of perspectives, see Jane T. Costlow and Stephanie Sandler, eds., *Sexuality and the Body in Russian Culture* (Stanford: Stanford University Press, 1993).

9. Dalton, *Unconscious Structure,* 177.

10. The model for my approach is the subtle analysis carried out by Robert Louis Jackson in his collection of essays *Dialogues with Dostoevsky: The Overwhelming Questions* (Stanford: Stanford University Press, 1993). Many of the essays in his book are also concerned with the sexual awakening of children.

CHAPTER ONE

1. For a discussion of Dostoevsky's treatment of sexuality, see Robert Louis Jackson, "In the Darkness of the Night: Tolstoy's *Kreutzer Sonata* and Dostoevsky's *Notes from the Underground*," in his *Dialogues with Dostoevsky,* 212–14. Olga Meerson deals sensitively with Dostoevsky's techniques of rhetorical tabooing, although sexual taboos are not at the forefront of her concerns (*Dostoevsky's Taboos* [Dresden: Studies of the Harriman Institute and Dresden University Press, 1998]).

2. Robert Louis Jackson, "Dostoevsky and the Marquis de Sade: The Final Encounter," in *Dialogues with Dostoevsky,* 144–45.

3. Quoted by Dostoevsky in F. M. Dostoevskii, *Polnoe sobranie sochinenii,*

ed. V. G. Bazanov et al., 30 vols. (Leningrad: Nauka, 1972–90), 19:97. All citations of Dostoevsky's writings are from this edition. All translations are mine. The history of the debate is outlined in the commentary to Dostoevsky's essays, 19:292–95, 300–8.

4. V. Kirpotin, "Dostoevskii o 'Egipetskikh nochakh' Pushkina," *Voprosy literatury*, 1962, no. 11:112–21, 117. See also Joseph Frank, *Stir of Liberation*, 86–87; and Lewis Tracy, "Decoding Puškin: Resurrecting Some Readers' Responses to *Egyptian Nights*," *Slavic and East European Journal* 37, no. 4 (1993): 456–71.

5. V. Komarovich, "Dostoevskii i 'Egipetskie nochi' Pushkina," *Pushkin i ego sovremenniki: Materialy i issledovaniia,* no. 29–30 (Petrograd: Rossiiskaia Akademiia nauk, 1918): 36–48, 45n.

6. Komarovich, "Dostoevskii i 'Egipetskie nochi,'" 44.

7. Leslie O'Bell, *Pushkin's "Egyptian Nights": The Biography of a Work* (Ann Arbor: Ardis, 1984), 151. Translation adapted from O'Bell, 25.

8. Near the end of his essay Dostoevsky quotes a letter (actually an unpublished article) by N. N. Strakhov, who calls the Russian audience "barbarians" and "Puritans" (19:138).

9. Monika Greenleaf, *Pushkin and Romantic Fashion: Fragment, Elegy, Orient, Irony* (Stanford: Stanford University Press, 1994), 5.

10. In his discussion of the debate, for example, Jackson takes Dostoevsky's arguments at face value ("Dostoevsky and the Marquis de Sade," 145, 147–48, 318n6).

11. Frank, *Stir of Liberation,* 87–88. See also Komarovich, "Dostoevskii i 'Egipetskie nochi,'" 42; and Kirpotin, "Dostoevskii o 'Egipetskikh nochakh,'" 119–21.

12. Alyosha obsessively visits "various Josephines and Minnas," i.e., prostitutes. At one point he confesses to Ivan that before coming to visit the virginal Katia, he succumbed to a certain Alexandrine his father introduced him to after dinner (3:349). Compare Dostoevsky's letter of November 16, 1845, to his brother Mikhail: "The little Minnas, Klaras, and Mariannas have become unbelievably pretty, but they cost a terrible lot of money" (letter to M. M. Dostoevskii, 28.1: 116).

13. Valkovskii's lover appears to be a version of the Marquise de Merteuil, heroine of *Les liaisons dangereuses* by Choderlos de Laclos (1782), who also combines a semblance of virtue with actual depravity. Another possible source is the inhabitants of "one of the corrupt convents in Sade's novels" (Jackson, "Dostoevsky and the Marquis de Sade," 157). On the connection to Laclos, see also R. G. Nazirov, "Tragediinoe nachalo v romane F. M. Dostoevskogo 'Unizhennye i oskorblennye,'" *Filologicheskie nauki*, 1965, no. 4:27–39, 36.

14. Robert Louis Jackson, "Some Considerations on 'The Dream of a Ridiculous Man' and 'Bobok,' from the Aesthetic Point of View," in his *The Art*

of Dostoevsky: Deliriums and Nocturnes (Princeton: Princeton University Press, 1981), 301. For more on the *petit-jeu* in *The Idiot,* see chapter 2 of the present volume.

15. Dostoevsky's use of the rather inappropriate word "chistoserdechie" in this passage is yet another clue that points to the organic connection between the restaurant scene and the "Egyptian Nights" polemic, since Dostoevsky's first contribution to the polemic was entitled "Obraztsy chistoserdechiia."

16. See the discussion by Robin Feuer Miller of Dostoevsky's treatment of the confession as "a problematic, double-edged form" in her *Dostoevsky and "The Idiot": Author, Narrator, and Reader* (Cambridge, Mass.: Harvard University Press, 1981), 176–82.

17. The issues discussed in this chapter were raised in a 1989 article by Gary Saul Morson, who also uses Valkovskii's story of the French exhibitionist as a touchstone for Dostoevsky's treatment of "scandalous" subject matter. Morson comes to a somewhat different conclusion than I do, and argues that Dostoevsky is guilty of the charge of artistic exhibitionism: "What is most disturbing about Dostoevsky is that his novels follow the same logic, have much of the same appeal, as operates in the scandalous scenes. In effect, they *are* scandalous scenes . . . Dostoevsky understands above all how corrupting this experience can be . . . And yet [he] himself, with full knowledge, uses this same technique that he knows to be corrupting" (Morson, "Prosaics, Criticism, and Ethics," *Formations* 5, no. 2 [Summer-Fall 1989]: 77–95, 79, 80). As I hope to demonstrate in this book, Dostoevsky's struggle constantly to ground such scenes in a moral framework and ethically responsible point of view saves them from being equivalent to the escapades of Valkovskii's flasher.

18. This of course recalls the "nravstvennaia von'" ("moral stink," 21:51) of the confessing corpses in "Bobok." Janine Langan has aptly described the way in which Dostoevsky implicates the reader: "The human propensity for more or less angelic pornography haunts Dostoevsky's novels . . . One could almost say that Dostoevsky's novels are a lifelong attempt to arouse, unmask, exorcise and reorient his and our violent pornographic pulsions, the black, Karamazov smut that he sees as fueling all literature" (Langan, "Icon vs. Myth: Dostoevsky, Feminism, and Pornography," *Religion and Literature* 18, no. 1 [Spring 1986]: 63–72, 65). Morson rejects such a defense of Dostoevsky's artistic practice, because "most readers may not learn the moral lesson but may still taste the pleasure of sin, which is to say they may learn the opposite lesson" (Morson, "Prosaics, Criticism, and Ethics," 81).

19. Sigmund Freud, "Three Essays on the Theory of Sexuality" (1905), in *Freud on Women: A Reader,* ed. Elisabeth Young-Bruehl (New York: Norton, 1990), 89–145, 101.

20. The editors of the Academy edition of Dostoevsky's works recognize a self-reference and a kind of prophecy here: "It is precisely such a point of view

that Dostoevsky the artist adheres to in the 1860s and 1870s, depicting monstrous deviations in the psyche and behavior of his characters, who advocate the 'ideal of Sodom' or tragically experience in their souls the struggle between the 'ideal of Sodom' and the 'ideal of the Madonna'" (19:301).

21. There is an indication that near the end of his life Dostoevsky regarded his own works as being, like the *Medici Venus*, inappropriate for adolescents. In a letter of August 18, 1880, to N. L. Osmidov, Dostoevsky offers advice about appropriate reading for Osmidov's daughter (her age is not mentioned but it appears she is quite young). After explaining how reading Sir Walter Scott had helped him develop his imagination in a healthy way and to struggle against "seductive, passionate, and debauching impressions," Dostoevsky goes on to recommend not just Scott but all of Dickens, *Don Quixote*, all of Pushkin, Gogol, Turgenev, and Goncharov. In passing he says, "As for my works, I don't think all of them would be suitable for her" (30.1:212).

22. Jackson and others have identified interesting philosophical relationships between Dostoevsky and Sade. Besides Jackson's essay cited earlier, see P. Bitsilli, "K voprosu o vnutrennei forme romana Dostoevskogo. Prilozhenie III: De-Sad, Laklo i Dostoevskii," in his *Izbrannye trudy po filologii*, ed. V. N. Iartseva (Moscow: Nasledie, 1996), 533–38; F. Kaufman, "Dostoevskij a Markiz de Sade," *Filosofický časopis* (Prague), 1968, no. 3:384–89; and Sergei Kuznetsov, "Fedor Dostoevskii i Markiz de Sad: Sviazi i pereklichki," in *Dostoevskii v kontse XX veka*, ed. K. A. Stepanian (Moscow: Klassika plius, 1996), 557–74. See also Viktor Erofeev, "Metamorfoza odnoi literaturnoi reputatsii: Markiz de Sad, Sadizm i XX vek," *Voprosy literatury*, 1973, no. 6:135–68.

23. A. G. Dostoevskaia, *Vospominaniia*, ed. L. P. Grossman (Moscow-Leningrad: Gosudarstvennoe izdanie, 1925), 64. Cited in Jackson, "Dostoevsky and the Marquis de Sade," 146. Cited here in my own translation.

24. See Dostoevsky, 5:306; 9:126, 134, 138.

25. William C. Brumfield, "*Thérèse philosophe* and Dostoevsky's Great Sinner," *Comparative Literature* 32 (1980): 238–52. See also Robert Darnton, *The Forbidden Best-Sellers of Pre-Revolutionary France* (New York: W. W. Norton, 1996), 85–114; and Anne Richardot, "*Thérèse philosophe:* Les charmes de l'impénétrable," in *Faces of Monstrosity in Eighteenth-Century Thought*, ed. Andrew Curran, Robert P. Maccubbin, and David F. Morrill; special issue of *Eighteenth-Century Life* 21, n.s., no. 2 (May 1997): 89–99. Darnton provides translated excerpts of *Thérèse philosophe* in his book, 249–99.

26. [Boyer d'Argens, Jean-Baptiste], *Thérèse philosophe, ou Mémoires pour servir à l'histoire du P. Dirrag et de Mlle Eradice*, facsimile of the Paris (?) edition, ca. 1780, intro. Jacques Dupilot, 2 vols. (Geneva: Éditions Slatkine, 1980), 1:7.

27. Darnton, *Forbidden Best-Sellers*, 96, 103. See chapters 4 and 5 of the present volume for a discussion of eighteenth- and nineteenth-century attitudes toward masturbation as reflected in Dostoevsky's works.

28. *Thérèse philosophe,* 2:1.

29. Ibid., 2:25.

30. Richardot, "Les charmes," 92.

31. Richardot, "Les charmes," 94; Henry Abelove, "Some Speculations on the History of Sexual Intercourse during the Long Eighteenth Century in England," in his *Deep Gossip* (Minneapolis: University of Minnesota Press, 2003), 21–28, 27 (the essay was first published in 1989). Richardot points out that the only sexual practice that meets with disapproval in *Thérèse philosophe* is (heterosexual) anal intercourse, because it seems "hyperbolically penetrative" ("Les charmes," 99n10).

32. See, for example, the scene in which an elderly madam and a fat priest attempt intercourse after a drinking bout and end up vomiting into each other's mouths (*Thérèse philosophe,* 2:41–44).

33. E. N. Opochinin, "Ustnyi rasskaz F. M. Dostoevskogo: Iz arkhiva E. N. Opochinina," ed. M. Odesskaia, *Novyi mir,* 1992, no. 8:211–17.

34. Opochinin, "Ustnyi rasskaz," 216.

35. Ibid., 213–14.

36. Svidrigailov shows a keen interest in what is now called sadomasochism (6:216) and in pedophilia (6:369). He also argues for the mysterious nature of "normal" adult heterosexual relationships: "Never vouch for what takes place between a husband and wife or a lover and his mistress. There is always a little corner there that always remains unknown to the whole world and is known only to those two" (6:368).

37. In 1972 the theater critic Kenneth Tynan (who was a devotee of spanking) deplored the oversimplification that Freudianism had introduced into thinking about sexuality: "Psychoanalysis, so far from dissolving the guilt attached to sexual fetishes, has in fact intensified it. To the Victorian an interest in spanking was an eccentricity; to the Freudian it is evidence of a pre-genital fixation; it is an offense against the sacrosanct ideal of the Exclusively Genital Orgasm. Freud hypothesized an ideal sexual act, from which all deviations were heresies to be purified by confession and rooted out in the annealing fires of analysis . . . In other words, the new orthodoxy finds many more things anathema than the old" ("The Journals of Kenneth Tynan," *New Yorker,* August 7, 2000, 48–59, 52–53).

38. Compare a recent statement by the playwright Arthur Miller: "Didn't Plato deal with this problem, that basically art is amoral? The artist's ability to embrace whatever he is interested in often contradicts his own opinion" (*New York Times,* April 15, 2004, E3).

39. Brumfield, "*Thérèse philosophe* and Dostoevsky's Great Sinner," 242.

40. See Robert Louis Jackson's subtle analysis of how Dostoevsky confronts the "complex boundary-mentality of twelve or thirteen year olds" in a section of the December 1876 issue of *A Writer's Diary* ("Dostoevskij's 'Anecdote from a Child's Life': A Case of Bifurcation," *Russian Literature* 25 [1989]: 127–40).

CHAPTER TWO

1. Nazirov, "Tragediinoe nachalo," 27–28.
2. Ibid., 31.
3. Ibid., 29.
4. William Woodin Rowe, *Dostoevsky: Child and Man in His Works* (New York: New York University Press, 1968), 23.
5. See Rowe: "Dostoevsky's apparent interest in such a situation can be construed to reflect the agitation typical of his more overt treatments of pedophilia" (*Child and Man*, 16).
6. See Nina Pelikan Straus's discussion of the theme of rape in *Crime and Punishment: "Crime and Punishment: 'Why Did I Say "Women!"?'"* in her *Dostoevsky and the Woman Question: Readings at the End of a Century* (New York: St. Martin's, 1994), 19–36. Carol Flath offers a provocatively revisionist reading of Svidrigailov's character, in the chapter on *Crime and Punishment* in her book in preparation on the topic of "secrets, sacraments, and sexuality." I would like to thank Carol Flath for sharing her manuscript with me. On the theme of prostitution in *Crime and Punishment* and Dostoevsky's use of French precursor texts, see Priscilla Meyer's forthcoming book, *How the Russians Read the French: Lermontov, Dostoevsky, Tolstoy.* On Raskol'nikov and Svidrigailov as doubles, see Laura A. Curtis, "Raskolnikov's Sexuality," *Literature and Psychology* 37, no. 1–2 (1991): 88–106.
7. The sensuously rich description of the beautiful young blonde lying in a satin-lined coffin surrounded by flowers is quite evocative of the anecdote of the necrophiliac supposedly recounted by Dostoevsky to E. N. Opochinin (see chapter 1 earlier).
8. Donald Rayfield, "Dumas and Dostoevskii—Deflowering the Camellia," in *From Pushkin to Palisandriia: Essays on the Russian Novel in Honor of Richard Freeborn,* ed. Arnold McMillin (New York: St. Martin's, 1990), 70–82, 70. See also M. S. Al'tman, "'Idiot' Dostoevskogo i 'Dama s kameliiami' Diuma," in his *Dostoevskii: Po vekham imen* (Saratov: Izdanie Saratovskogo universiteta, 1975), 58–67; and Olga Matich, "What's to Be Done about Poor Nastja: Nastas'ja Filippovna's Literary Prototypes," *Wiener slawistischer Almanach* 19 (1987): 47–64, 51–52. On Nastas'ia Filippovna, see Miller, *Dostoevsky and "The Idiot,"* 112–15; and Diana Lewis Burgin, "The Reprieve of Nastasja: A Reading of a Dreamer's Authored Life," *Slavic and East European Journal* 29, no. 3 (1985): 258–68.
9. On the similarities in the characters of Nelli and Nastas'ia Filippovna, see Nazirov, "Tragediinoe nachalo," 37, 39.
10. The implied rape of the girl in the coffin in Svidrigailov's vision is also termed an "amazing" event: "[Her heart was] insulted by an offense that horrified and amazed [udivivsheiu] this young, childish consciousness" (6:391).
11. On the connections between Nastas'ia Filippovna's story and Karamzin's

"Poor Liza" ("Bednaia Liza," 1792), see Matich, "What's to Be Done." L. A. Levina argues that Myshkin's fatal mistake is that he fails to take seriously Nastas'ia Filippovna's loss of innocence, the extent to which Totskii has truly debauched her (Levina, "Nekaiushchaia Magdalina, ili pochemu kniaz' Myshkin ne mog spasti Nastas'iu Filippovnu," in *Dostoevskii v kontse XX veka,* ed. Stepanian, 343–8).

12. Brumfield, *"Thérèse philosophe* and Dostoevsky's Great Sinner," 245.

13. *Thérèse philosophe,* 2:12.

14. Ibid.

15. Ibid., 1:10.

16. Ibid., 1:10–11.

17. Compare Morson: "Generally speaking, the characteristic falsity of confessions in Dostoevsky . . . derives from the self-exposing logic of exhibitionism" (Morson, "Prosaics, Criticism, and Ethics," 79).

18. Al'tman, "'Idiot,'" 59.

19. Rayfield, "Dumas and Dostoevskii," 72–73.

20. Alexandre Dumas fils, *Camille (The Lady of the Camellias)* (New York: Signet, 1972), 93.

21. According to Laura Engelstein, a 1901 study indicated that "the average peasant woman began menstruating between the ages of sixteen and seventeen" (Engelstein, *Keys to Happiness,* 182n70). It is likely that gentry women would begin menstruating somewhat earlier, but it seems clear that sixteen would be considered a safe boundary age between girlhood and womanhood. For an analysis of Dostoevsky's pre-Siberia story "A Christmas Party and a Wedding" ("Elka i svad'ba," 1849), in which a man casts lascivious glances on an eleven-year-old girl whom he marries when she becomes sixteen, see Robert Louis Jackson, "Dostoevsky in Chekhov's Garden of Eden: 'Because of Little Apples,'" in his *Dialogues with Dostoevsky,* 83–103.

22. For the textual history of "At Tikhon's," see Dostoevsky, *Polnoe sobranie sochinenii,* 12:237–46. See also A. S. Dolinin, "'Ispoved' Stavrogina.' (V sviazi s kompozitsiei 'Besov')," *Literaturnaia mysl',* 1922, no. 1:139–62; B. V. Fedorenko, "Iz razyskanii o Dostoevskom. 2. Iz tvorcheskoi istorii romana F. M. Dostoevskogo 'Besy,'" in *Novye aspekty v izuchenii Dostoevskogo: Sbornik nauchnykh trudov,* ed. V. N. Zakharov (Petrozavodsk: Izdatel'stvo Petrozavodskogo Universiteta, 1994), 265–94; and G. F. Kogan, "Iz istorii sozdaniia 'Ispovedi Stavrogina,'" *Izvestiia Akademii nauk. Seriia literatury i iazyka* 54, no. 1 (1995): 65–73. The chapter has attracted a great deal of attention among Russian scholars in the post-perestroika era, when it became much more possible to speak frankly about sexual matters. Several of these studies focus on the rumors that Dostoevsky himself committed "the sin of Stavrogin." See Iu. Kariakin, "Khram bez kupola ('Besy' bez glavy 'U Tikhona')," in his *Dostoevskii i kanun XXI veka* (Moscow: Sovetskii pisatel', 1989), 319–34; Vitalii Svintsov, "Dostoevskii i

stavroginskii grekh," *Voprosy literatury,* 1995, no. 2:111–42; Vitalii Svintsov, "Dostoevskii i 'otnosheniia mezhdu polami,'" *Novyi mir,* 1999, no. 5:195–213 (English translation, "Dostoevsky and 'Relations between the Sexes,'" *Russian Studies in Literature* 38, no. 4 [Fall 2002]: 7–34); Irina Rodnianskaia, "Mezhdu Konom i Dostoevskim: Replika Vitaliiu Svintsovu," *Novyi mir,* 1999, no. 5:213–15 (English translation, "Between Kon and Dostoevsky: A Reply to Vitalii Svintsov," *Russian Studies in Literature* 38, no. 4 [Fall 2002]: 35–38); Tat'iana Kasatkina, "Kak my chitaem russkuiu literaturu: O sladostrastii," *Novyi mir,* 1999, no. 7:170–82; and M. N. Zolotonosov, "Seks 'ot Stavrogina': Pornosoficheskii kommentarii k 'otrechennoi' glave iz romana 'Besy,'" in his *Slovo i telo: Seksual'nye aspekty, universalii, interpretatsii russkogo kul'turnogo teksta XIX–XX vekov* (Moscow: Ladomir, 1999), 9–78. For a reading that takes full account of the centrality to *The Devils* of the image of the "violated female," see Straus, *Dostoevsky and the Woman Question,* 81–96. In her attempt to demonstrate that Stavrogin represents an image of a homosexual or bisexual, Irene Zohrab raises the possibility that Dostoevsky originally intended for the raped child in Stavrogin's confession to be a boy: "'Mann-Männliche' Love in Dostoevsky's Fiction (An Approach to *The Possessed*): With Some Attributions of Editorial Notes in *The Citizen.* First Installment," *Dostoevsky Journal* 3–4 (2002–3): 113–226.

23. Zohrab draws a parallel between Stavrogin's pamphlets and the confessional pamphlets of the "Urning" (homosexual) Karl Heinrich Ulrichs, published in Germany in the 1860s and 1870s (Zohrab, "'Mann-Männliche' Love," 122–24, 147–50). Her hypothesis is intriguing, but Dostoevsky's primary reference is clearly to the political activities within the novel, especially the buried printing press that serves as the pretext for luring Shatov to his murder.

24. See Susanne Fusso, "Maidens in Childbirth: The Sistine Madonna in Dostoevskii's *Devils,*" *Slavic Review* 54, no. 2 (Summer 1995): 261–75, 266. Zolotonosov links the Tikhon of "At Tikhon's" to the Tikhon in the "Life of a Great Sinner" who reads *Thérèse philosophe,* as well as to the French novel's incontinent priests and monks: "Dostoevsky seems to be alluding to the possibility of an analogy between Tikhon and the lustful holy fathers described in that novel" (Zolotonosov, "Seks 'ot Stavrogina,'" 69n34). On religious models for Tikhon, see Margaret Ziolkowski, "Dostoevsky and the Kenotic Tradition," in *Dostoevsky and the Christian Tradition,* ed. George Pattison and Diane Oenning Thompson (Cambridge: Cambridge University Press, 2001), 31–40.

25. A recent article by Sergei Bocharov is a magnificent summation of Russian critical meditations on Stavrogin, as well as a literary history of the Stavrogin characterological type that traces it back to Evgenii Onegin and forward to Aleksandr Blok (Bocharov, "Frantsuzskii epigraf k 'Evgeniiu Oneginu' [Onegin i Stavrogin]," *Moskovskii pushkinist* 1 [1995]: 212–50). Some of the key texts are collected in F. M. Dostoevskii, *"Besy": Antologiia russkoi kritiki,* ed. L. I. Saras-

kina (Moscow: Soglasie, 1996). Mikhail Bakhtin assesses Stavrogin's confession (apparently in Dostoevsky's first version) as being "intensely oriented toward another person [i.e., Tikhon], without whom the hero could not manage but whom at the same time he despises and whose judgement he does not accept . . . [It] is deprived of any finalizing force and tends toward that same vicious circle that marked the speech of the Underground Man" (Bakhtin, *Problems of Dostoevsky's Poetics*, ed. and trans. Caryl Emerson [Minneapolis: University of Minnesota Press, 1984], 244). Bakhtin's verdict on the confession's failure to achieve its goal of redemption for Stavrogin does not, in my view, detract from the directness and honesty of Stavrogin's account of his crime, at least in Dostoevsky's first version of the text. On Stavrogin's text as a work of literature, see Liudmila Saraskina, *Fedor Dostoevskii: Odolenie demonov* (Moscow: Soglasie, 1996), 407–19; and Adam Weiner, *By Authors Possessed: The Demonic Novel in Russia* (Evanston: Northwestern University Press, 1998), 107–8. Weiner sees Stavrogin's text as revealing in him "the sin of proudly conveying in a literary form that which should have been humbly—which is to say privately and *orally*—confessed" (268n40; emphasis in original).

26. Rowe, *Child and Man*, 209.

27. Svintsov, "Dostoevskii i stavroginskii grekh," 133; Svintsov, "Dostoevskii i 'otnosheniia mezhdu polami,'" 207. Rodnianskaia, "Mezhdu Konom i Dostoevskim," 214. For Zolotonosov, the scene is a version of the mythic "rite of initiation of a youth [the youth being Stavrogin] upon achieving sexual maturity" (Zolotonosov, "Seks 'ot Stavrogina,'" 11). He also claims (with no textual evidence) that "the sexual episode in the chapter 'At Tikhon's' involved not the usual deflowering, but fellatio" (37).

28. On the concept of the "threshold dialogue" that according to Mikhail Bakhtin forms an important part of the legacy of Menippean satire for Dostoevsky, see Bakhtin, *Problems of Dostoevsky's Poetics*, 111, 116, 128.

29. Straus calls this "the revolutionary's fist-clench," "a protest against masculinist cruelty" (Straus, *Dostoevsky and the Woman Question*, 88).

30. Jean-Jacques Rousseau, *Confessions*, trans. J. M. Cohen (Harmondsworth: Penguin, 1975), bk. 3, pp. 108–9. It is implied early in the novel that Stavrogin's tutor, Stepan Trofimovich Verkhovenskii, initiated him into the practice during nocturnal visits: "Stepan Trofimovich knew how to touch the deepest chords in his friend's heart and to call forth in him the first, still indefinite, sensation of that eternal, holy melancholy [tosku], which some chosen souls, having tasted and known it, will never exchange for cheap satisfaction. (There are even some fanciers who value this melancholy more than the most radical satisfaction, even if such were possible)" (10:35). It is fitting, given the nineteenth-century view of the physical consequences of masturbation, that when Stavrogin goes to boarding school at age fifteen, he is "frail and pale, strangely quiet and pensive." The narrator adds, in an aside that is fully consistent with Stavrogin's claim that

he gave up masturbating at age sixteen, "Later he was distinguished by extraordinary physical strength" (10:35). For more on Rousseau and masturbation, see chapter 4 in the present volume.

31. For detailed descriptions of the kind of examinations carried out on victims of rape and rape-murder in nineteenth-century Russia, see V. Merzheevskii, *Sudebnaia ginekologiia. Rukovodstvo dlia vrachei i iuristov* (St. Petersburg: B. G. Ianpol'skii, 1878), 76–203.

32. In Merzheevskii's catalog of case histories, suspicion of rape often arises when a young girl is known to have been alone recently with an older male relative or acquaintance (Merzheevskii, *Sudebnaia ginekologiia*, 76–203 passim).

33. Some critics have argued that Dostoevsky changed his mind about the chapter, since he himself made no attempt to include it in the separate edition of the novel. This has been convincingly refuted by Iu. Kariakin: he points out that the sole edition of *The Devils* that appeared in Dostoevsky's lifetime appeared only a few weeks after the journal publication in the *Russian Herald* was completed, and Dostoevsky began work as the editor of *The Citizen* soon afterward. Thus he would have had no time for reworking the text, and no possibility of including the chapter at that point without causing an open break with Katkov (Kariakin, "Khram bez kupola," 328–29). Dolinin makes a similar point ("'Ispoved' Stavrogina,'" 145).

34. Kariakin, "Khram bez kupola," 322. Kariakin sees Dostoevsky's defense of Pushkin as "a magnificently precise self-evaluation of the chapter 'At Tikhon's'" (323). See also Saraskina, *Odolenie demonov*, 241–47.

35. The word I have translated as "obscene" here is "klubnichnoe," derived from "klubnika," "strawberries." The word, used in the same sense of "obscenity, lewdness" in the 1860s and 1870s by M. E. Saltykov-Shchedrin and P. V. Boborykin, is derived from Nikolai Gogol's novel *Dead Souls* (*Mertvye dushi*, 1842), in which a lecherous lieutenant refers to his seduction of peasant women as "making use of little strawberries" (N. V. Gogol', *Polnoe sobranie sochinenii*, 14 vols. [Moscow: Akademiia nauk SSSR, 1937–52], 6:66).

36. V. G. Avseenko, "Literaturnoe obozrenie," *Russkii vestnik* 121 (January 1876): 506–7; cited in V. N. Zakharov, "Fakty protiv legendy," in his *Problemy izucheniia Dostoevskogo* (Petrozavodsk: Petrozavodskii gosudarstvennyi universitet, 1978), 105.

37. Dostoevsky continues, "From what sources. Stavrogin (an unbeliever, and the triumph of living life, the reproach for a single filthy act)." *Literaturnoe nasledstvo*, vol. 83, pp. 555–56, cited in Zakharov, "Fakty protiv legendy," 106.

38. There were some political difficulties associated with publishing later parts of *Crime and Punishment* after D. V. Karakozov's attempt on the tsar's life in April 1866 (*Polnoe sobranie sochinenii*, 7:323).

39. Zakharov, "Fakty protiv legendy," 75–109. See also the articles by Svintsov in note 22 of this chapter; and Robert Louis Jackson, "A View from the Un-

derground: On Nikolai Nikolaevich Strakhov's Letter about His Good Friend Fyodor Mikhailovich Dostoevsky and on Leo Nikolaevich Tolstoy's Cautious Response to It," in his *Dialogues with Dostoevsky*, 104–20. See also L. M. Rozenblium, *Tvorcheskie dnevniki Dostoevskogo* (Moscow: Nauka, 1981), 44–45. Anna Grigor'evna Dostoevskaia addresses the rumors in her memoirs (*Vospominaniia*, 285–92). Jackson offers some intriguing speculations on the possibility of Dostoevsky's guilt in his analysis of an episode in the December 1876 issue of *A Writer's Diary* ("Dostoevskij's 'Anecdote from a Child's Life,'" 137–40).

40. Dolinin, "'Ispoved' Stavrogina,'" 146. I would qualify Dolinin's statement to acknowledge that the theme does recur episodically in Dostoevsky's later work, but I agree with him that it is never again treated with such focus and intensity.

41. Saraskina's interpretation coincides with my own: "The insistence with which Dostoevsky returned to the theme of violence done to a little girl, the fearlessness with which he tried to free himself from the captivity of censorship, the revisions he was ready to introduce into the proofs of the chapter in order to save it, and the risk of 'spoiling his career' that he recognized before his editors and critics did, displayed the daring of an artist and the passion of a master, not the filth of a pervert who disguises an 'incident from life' with the window-dressing of piquant belles-lettres" (Saraskina, *Odolenie demonov*, 436).

42. Kariakin, "Khram bez kupola," 329–30.

CHAPTER THREE

1. The term "pseudo-autobiography" is Andrew Wachtel's. It refers to "a first-person retrospective narrative based on autobiographical material in which the author and the protagonist are not the same person" (Wachtel, *The Battle for Childhood: Creation of a Russian Myth* [Stanford: Stanford University Press, 1990], 3).

2. Igor' Volgin discusses Sirotkin's homosexuality in his *Propavshii zagovor: Dostoevskii i politicheskii protsess 1849 g.* (Moscow: Libereia, 2000), 282–83. James L. Rice analyzes Dostoevsky's prison experience, in particular what he reads as "homosexual anxiety" in Dostoevsky's letters of the period, in connection with the story "The Peasant Marei" (Rice, "Psychoanalysis of 'Peasant Marei': Some Residual Problems," in *Russian Literature and Psychoanalysis*, ed. Daniel Rancour-Laferriere [Amsterdam: John Benjamins, 1989], 245–61).

3. Jacques Catteau, *Dostoyevsky and the Process of Literary Creation*, trans. Audrey Littlewood (Cambridge: Cambridge University Press, 1989), 254. Rudolf Neuhäuser contrasts Arkadii's chaotic narrative with the novel's underlying symmetrical spatiotemporal patterns (Littlewood, *F. M. Dostojevskij: Die grossen Romane und Erzählungen. Interpretationen und Analysen* [Vienna: Böhlau, 1993], 118–35). Thorough analyses of the genesis of *A Raw Youth* through Dostoevsky's notebooks and drafts are provided by Catteau and by L.

M. Rozenblium, "Tvorcheskaia laboratoriia Dostoevskogo-romanista," in *Literaturnoe nasledstvo*, vol. 77: *F. M. Dostoevskii v rabote nad romanom "Podrostok." Tvorcheskie rukopisi*, ed. I. S. Zil'bershtein and L. M. Rozenblium (Moscow: Nauka, 1965), 7–56. See also Rozenblium, *Tvorcheskie dnevniki Dostoevskogo;* and Fyodor Dostoevsky, *The Notebooks for "A Raw Youth,"* ed. Edward Wasiolek, trans. Victor Terras (Chicago: University of Chicago Press, 1969). The most comprehensive study of *A Raw Youth* is Horst-Jürgen Gerigk, *Versuch über Dostoevskijs "Jüngling": Ein Beitrag zur Theorie des Romans* (Munich: Wilhelm Fink, 1965). See also the reading by Joseph Frank, *Mantle of the Prophet*, 149–96; and E. N. Semyonov, *Roman Dostoevskogo "Podrostok" (Problematika i zhanr)* (Leningrad: Nauka, 1979).

4. In a series of articles, Irene Zohrab explores the possible routes by which Dostoevsky could have become familiar with the phenomenon of same-sex desire (see notes 22 and 23 of chapter 2). She identified Trishatov as a homosexual character in "Dostoevsky and Meshchersky and 'Homosexual Consciousness,'" *Australian Slavonic and East European Studies* 12, no. 1 (1998): 115–34, 131–34. (I regret that when the original version of this chapter was published in *Russian Review* in 2000, I was unaware of Zohrab's work and did not cite it.) See also her later article, "Dostoevsky and the 'Other' Meshchersky: Refashioning Masculinities on the Pages of *The Citizen* (with a Decoding of a Section from *The Adolescent*)," *Soviet and Post-Soviet Review* 28, no. 3 (2001 [2002]): 333–62. On the history of legal punishment for homosexuality in Russia, see Engelstein, *Keys to Happiness*, 57–64; and Healey, *Homosexual Desire in Revolutionary Russia*, 21–22, 79–81. Healey points out that Article 995 was only episodically enforced (78).

5. In her interesting chapter on *A Raw Youth*, Olga Meerson argues that the novel traces Arkadii's progress from being an emotional exhibitionist who fails to respect the secrets of others (what she calls "zero-tabooing") to being a person who is expert in tabooing, who *"has no choice* but to keep silent about the scandalousness of this fallen world and of himself in it" (*Dostoevsky's Taboos*, 165; emphasis in original).

6. Simon Karlinsky, "Russia's Gay Literature and History (11th–20th Centuries)," in *Gay Roots: Twenty Years of Gay Studies*, ed. W. Leyland (San Francisco: Gay Sunshine, 1991), 89. Karlinsky adduces *Notes from the House of the Dead* as an example of Dostoevsky's ignorance of homosexual desire. But although there was a limit to how explicit Dostoevsky could be, in his description of the prisoner Sirotkin he indicates his awareness of homosexual behavior and of male prostitution. (Perhaps this behavior does not meet the definition of "gayness" because of its semi-involuntary character. See John Boswell, *Christianity, Social Tolerance, and Homosexuality: Gay People in Western Europe from the Beginning of the Christian Era to the Fourteenth Century* [Chicago: University of Chicago Press, 1980], 43–46.)

7. Michael Katz, "Dostoevsky's Homophilia/Homophobia," in *Gender and*

Sexuality in Russian Civilization, ed. Peter I. Barta (London: Routledge, 2001), 239–53. I wish to thank Michael Katz for sharing his work with me before publication. Some of the best work on Dostoevsky's interest in the varieties of sexual desire has been done by Robert Louis Jackson (see, for example, "Dostoevsky and the Marquis de Sade," in his *Dialogues with Dostoevsky*, 144–61). Jackson's subtle reading of the homoerotic theme encoded in Dostoevsky's early story "A Christmas Party and a Wedding" is a model for my approach to *A Raw Youth* (Jackson, "Dostoevsky in Chekhov's Garden of Eden: 'Because of Little Apples,'" in *Dialogues with Dostoevsky*, 101–3). Volgin argues for the homosexuality of some minor Dostoevsky characters, notably Kalganov in *The Brothers Karamazov* (Volgin, *Propavshii zagovor*, 282–90). In his article Katz also discusses one of the few clear cases of female-female eroticism in Dostoevsky, an episode in "Netochka Nezvanova" (1848–49). See also Victor Terras, *A Karamazov Companion: Commentary on the Genesis, Language, and Style of Dostoevsky's Novel* (Madison: University of Wisconsin Press, 1981), 187.

8. See W. E. Mosse, "Imperial Favourite: V. P. Meshchersky and the *Grazhdanin*," *Slavonic and East European Review* 59, no. 4 (October 1981): 529–47; and Iu. G. Oksman, ed., *Vospominaniia E. M. Feoktistova* (Leningrad: Priboi, 1929), 244–48. Zohrab has scoured Meshcherskii's journal *The Citizen* for homoerotic references. While the idea is a promising one, at times her zeal leads her astray, as when she reads the word "kurtizan" ("courtier") as referring to "male courtesan," implying a sexual dimension that is absent in the journal's text (Zohrab, "Dostoevsky and Meshchersky," 126–27). On Meshcherskii's view of Dostoevsky, see V. P. Meshcherskii, *Moi vospominaniia*, pt. 2 (1865–1881) (St. Petersburg: Tipografiia kniazia Meshcherskogo, 1898), 176–78, 181–82.

9. S. Iu. Vitte, *Vospominaniia*, ed. A. L. Sidorov (Moscow: Izdatel'stvo sotsial'no-ekonomicheskoi literatury, 1960), 3:580, 582, 459. In regard to Alexander III, Witte repeats three times that because of Meshcherskii's reputation, the tsar could not invite him to visit openly but had to receive him "s zadnego khoda" or "s zadnego kryl'tsa" ("from the back door," "from the back porch"). These expressions, besides their more innocuous meanings, are also a euphemism for anal penetration. The coyness with which Witte uses the phrases leaves little doubt as to his meaning.

10. See B. O. Unbegaun, *Russkie familii* (Moscow: Progress, 1989), 19, 347. Prince P. V. Dolgorukov insisted in his genealogical works that the correct form was Dolgorukov, but Unbegaun calls this "a matter rather of the process of unification than of the historical authenticity of either form" (347). See P. V. Dolgorukov, *Rossiiskaia rodoslovnaia kniga* (St. Petersburg: Karl Vingeber, 1854), 86–87.

11. N. G. Pustygina has assembled the textual evidence for Dostoevsky's interest in Dolgorukov in her article "O familii Dolgorukov v romane F. M. Dostoevskogo 'Podrostok,'" *Uchenye zapiski Tartuskogo gosudarstvennogo univer-*

siteta: Problemy tipologii russkoi literatury, no. 645 (1985): 37–53. (I would like to thank Nina Perlina for providing me with a copy of this article.)

12. "Materialy dlia biografii A. Pushkina," *Poliarnaia zvezda. Zhurnal A. I. Gertsena i N. P. Ogareva v vos'mi knigakh, 1855–1869,* facsimile edition (Moscow: Nauka, 1968), bk. 6, pp. 132–40; A. Ammosov, *Poslednie dni zhizni i konchina Aleksandra Sergeevicha Pushkina. So slov byvshego ego litseiskogo tovarishcha i sekundanta Konstantina Karlovicha Danzasa* (St. Petersburg: Izd. F. A. Isakova, 1863); "Pis'mo A. S. Pushkina k kavalerist-devitse N. A. Durovoi, s poslesloviem barona F. A. Biulera," *Russkii arkhiv* (1872): 204. According to P. E. Shchegolev, the accusations published by Ammosov in 1863 "were reprinted in many Russian journals and newspapers and were widely disseminated both in Russia and abroad" (Shchegolev, *Duel' i smert' Pushkina. Issledovanie i materialy,* 2nd ed. [Petrograd: Literaturnaia knizhnaia lavka, 1917; reprint ed. Ann Arbor, 1975], 416). Pustygina points out the similarities between the "scandalous story" of the anonymous letters and the plot of *A Raw Youth* (Pustygina, "O familii Dolgorukov," 40).

13. Stella Abramovich, *Predystoriia poslednei dueli Pushkina. Ianvar' 1836–ianvar' 1837* (St. Petersburg: Rossiiskaia akademiia nauk, 1994), 76. See also Iu. M. Lotman, "O dueli Pushkina bez 'tain' i 'zagadok,'" in his *Pushkin. Biografiia pisatelia. Stat'i i zametki 1960–1990. "Evgenii Onegin." Kommentarii* (St. Petersburg: Iskusstvo-SPB, 1995), 375–88; and I. S. Sidorov, "Eshche raz ob anonimnom 'diplome' i kn. P. V. Dolgorukove," *Moskovskii pushkinist* 1 (1995): 208–11. For arguments in favor of Dolgorukov's guilt, see B. L. Modzalevskii, "Kto byl avtorom anonimnykh paskvilei na Pushkina?" in *Novye materialy o dueli i smerti Pushkina,* ed. B. L. Modzalevskii, Iu. G. Oksman, and M. A. Tsiavlovskii (Petersburg: Atenei, 1924), 13–49; and Anna Akhmatova, "Gibel' Pushkina" (1958), in her *Sochineniia,* vol. 3, ed. G. P. Struve, N. A. Struve, and B. A. Filippov (Paris: YMCA, 1983), 269–70, 277–79. Pustygina does not (and perhaps could not) mention Dolgorukov's homosexuality in her otherwise meticulous article.

14. Healey, *Homosexual Desire in Revolutionary Russia,* 48; see also 30–31. The transition to capitalism is one of Dostoevsky's major themes in *A Raw Youth.* See my article "The Weight of Human Tears: *The Covetous Knight* and *A Raw Youth,*" in *Alexander Pushkin's Little Tragedies: The Poetics of Brevity,* ed. Svetlana Evdokimova (Madison: University of Wisconsin Press, 2003), 229–42.

15. I. L. Kasper, *Prakticheskoe rukovodstvo k sudebnoi meditsine,* ed. V. O. Merzheevskii et al. (St. Petersburg: V. I. Golovin, 1872), an adaptation of Johann Ludwig Casper, *Practisches Handbuch der gerichtlichen Medizin, nach eigenen Erfahrungen,* 2 vols. (Berlin, 1857–58); V. M. Tarnovskii, *Izvrashchenie polovogo chuvstva. Sudebno-psikhiatricheskii ocherk. Dlia vrachei i iuristov* (St. Petersburg: M. M. Stasiulevich, 1885). See also Engelstein, *Keys to Happiness,* 131–33, 152–55, 156; and Healey, *Homosexual Desire in Revolutionary Russia,*

82–86. The Casper-Merzheevskii text includes a detailed discussion of the question, can an epileptic fit be faked? (416–18). If Dostoevsky read this text, this passage may well have influenced his treatment of Smerdiakov in *The Brothers Karamazov*. For a thorough discussion of Dostoevsky's own epilepsy and the medical practice of the time, see James L. Rice, *Dostoevsky and the Healing Art*.

16. Kasper, *Prakticheskoe rukovodstvo*, ed. Merzheevskii, 252.

17. Ibid., 252, 253, 254.

18. Tarnovskii, *Izvrashchenie*, 52–53.

19. Kasper, *Prakticheskoe rukovodstvo*, ed. Merzheevskii, 213. Tarnovskii also adduces tales of blackmail by homosexuals (*Izvrashchenie*, 29, 72–73). See also Healey, *Homosexual Desire in Revolutionary Russia*, 28–29, 31, 38.

20. Kasper, *Prakticheskoe rukovodstvo*, ed. Merzheevskii, 214; Tarnovskii, *Izvrashchenie*, 73.

21. Ayşe Agiş has pointed out that Trishatov's name may be meant to evoke the French "tricher," "to cheat or trick."

22. A. F. Koni, *Na zhiznennom puti: Iz zapisok sudebnogo deiatelia*, vol. 1 (St. Petersburg: Trud, 1912), 152–53. My attention was drawn to this source by a reference in Healey.

23. Koni, *Na zhiznennom puti*, 1:155.

24. Ibid., 1:154.

25. Compare this with Tarnovskii on the pernicious influence of "closed educational institutions": "The weaker students try to imitate the well-grown, strong, daring student. Incited by his example, by the desire not to be left behind by the others, to display one's mettle, the poor youths force themselves to overcome their revulsion from the filthy act, inflame their imaginations with thoughts of women, and at the same time abandon themselves to pederasty" (Tarnovskii, *Izvrashchenie*, 45). Arkadii's story of Lambert's verbal seduction echoes the memoirs of the homosexual F. F. Vigel', published in Moscow in 1864. Vigel' recalls his upbringing in the home of the Golitsyns, a prominent aristocratic family: "Since there is no good without evil, in that same home (I have to admit with sorrow) I first became acquainted with vice and debauchery . . . The elder of my little companions [Prince Pavel Sergeevich Golitsyn], younger than me, as I said, began to talk to me in a kind of language that at first seemed incomprehensible; I blushed from shame and horror, when I understood him, but soon after that I began to listen to him with pleasure" (F. F. Vigel', *Vospominaniia*, pt. 1 [Moscow: Katkov, 1864], 136).

26. Tarnovskii, *Izvrashchenie*, 9.

27. René Girard, *Deceit, Desire, and the Novel: Self and Other in Literary Structure*, trans. Yvonne Freccero (Baltimore: Johns Hopkins Press, 1965); Eve Kosofsky Sedgwick, *Between Men: English Literature and Male Homosocial Desire* (New York: Columbia University Press, 1985), 25–26.

28. For a Girardian analysis of *A Hero of Our Time*, as well as a discussion of

Girardian desire in the works of other nineteenth-century Russian writers, including Dostoevsky, see Natasha Reed, "Reading Lermontov's 'Geroj nashego vremeni': Problems of Poetics and Reception" (Ph.D. dissertation, Harvard University, 1994). In a probing article, Jostein Børtnes uses the Girardian model to explore the homoerotic dimensions of the relationship between Myshkin and Rogozhin in *The Idiot*. I would like to thank Jostein Børtnes for sharing this article with me before publication. Jostein Børtnes,"Male Homosocial Desire in *The Idiot*," *Severny sbornik: Proceedings of the NorFA Network in Russian Literature*, ed. Peter Alberg Jensen and Ingunn Lunde (Stockholm: Almqvist & Wiksell, 2000), 103–20. Also available at http://www.hf.uib.no/i/russisk/jostein/male homosdes.pdf. See also Katz, "Dostoevskii's Homophilia/Homophobia," 245.

29. Nineteenth-century Russian medical science believed that homosexual tendencies could be overcome by an act of will. Tarnovskii explains: "As the patient forces himself through willpower to overcome more and more easily his instinctive, abnormal attraction to men, his aversion to women decreases, and in many cases we have observed, youths with pronounced sexual perversion became able at 25 or 30 to have relations with women, get married, and have children" (Tarnovskii, *Izvrashchenie*, 27). Arkadii seems to be on this path by the end of *A Raw Youth*.

30. Tarnovskii, *Izvrashchenie*, 46. Compare the words of one society wife, as relayed in his memoirs by S. Iu. Witte. In reference to V. P. Meshcherskii, a well-known homosexual and Dostoevsky's employer at the journal *The Citizen* (see the discussion of Meshcherskii in note 9 of this chapter), she said, "He comes to see my husband when he is in St. Petersburg, but I don't receive him since he is a dirty person [chelovek griaznyi]" (Witte, *Vospominaniia*, 3:576). As with Trishatov, the "dirt" here is not meant literally.

31. See Tarnovskii, *Izvrashchenie*, 10; and Kasper, *Prakticheskoe rukovodstvo*, ed. Merzheevskii, 212.

32. Tarnovskii, *Izvrashchenie*, 10.

33. *Literaturnoe nasledstvo*, vol. 77, *F. M. Dostoevskii v rabote nad romanom "Podrostok": Tvorcheskie rukopisi* (Moscow: Nauka, 1965), 402. In the *Polnoe sobranie sochinenii* the epithet is partly censored (16:408). Trishatov was originally intended to be a prince (17:116, 117).

34. Michel Foucault, *The History of Sexuality*, vol. 1: *An Introduction*, trans. Robert Hurley (New York: Vintage, 1990), 43.

35. As far as I can determine, Zohrab is the first scholar to discuss Trishatov's homosexuality. In a personal communication, Liia Mikhailovna Rozenblium, editor of the drafts of *A Raw Youth* for *Literaturnoe nasledstvo*, expressed her concurrence in my opinion that the character of Trishatov is meant to be a portrait of a homosexual man (September 1996).

36. L. N. Tolstoi, *Sobranie sochinenii v dvadtsati tomakh*, ed. N. N. Akopovaia et al. (Moscow: Khudozhestvennaia literatura, 1963), 8:208.

37. Compare the description of Sirotkin in *Notes from the House of the Dead:* "lichiko chisten'koe, nezhnoe" ("a clean, tender little face," 4:39). Variants of the text of *A Raw Youth* show that Dostoevsky worked carefully on the epithets used to describe Trishatov (17:115–20).

38. Liza Knapp has related the idea of decomposition in *A Raw Youth* to the second law of thermodynamics and what she calls "the poetics of entropy." See the chapter "Death by Ice: The Poetics of Entropy in *The Adolescent*," in her *Annihilation of Inertia*, 131–71. In a personal communication, Liia Mikhailovna Rozenblium suggested to me that Dostoevsky would have regarded Trishatov's homosexuality as one of the forces of disorder (September 1996).

39. In chapter 6 I will return to the subject of "accidental families."

40. D. S. Likhachev, *Poetika drevnerusskoi literatury*, 2nd ed. (Leningrad: Khudozhestvennaia literatura, 1971), 351.

41. Nathan Rosen, "Breaking Out of the Underground: The 'Failure' of *A Raw Youth*," *Modern Fiction Studies* 4, no. 3 (Autumn 1958): 225–39, 236, 238–39.

42. Alexander Welsh, *George Eliot and Blackmail* (Cambridge, Mass.: Harvard University Press, 1985), 9. (Welsh also points out that in the earliest prosecutions for blackmail in England, "the threatened accusation was that of buggery" [9].) For an interpretation of *A Raw Youth* based on rhetorical devices of reticence (what Arkadii calls "figury umolchaniia"), see Nina Perlina, "Rethinking Adolescence," in *Celebrating Creativity: Essays in Honour of Jostein Børtnes*, ed. Knut Andreas Grimstad and Ingunn Lunde (Bergen: University of Bergen, 1997), 216–26. See also Ingunn Lunde, "'. . . ia gorazdo umnee napisannogo': On Apophatic Strategies and Linguistic Experiments in Dostoevsky's *A Raw Youth*," *Slavonic and East European Review* 79, no. 2 (January 2001): 264–89.

43. The phrase "dori-no-si-ma chin-mi" is from the second strophe of the Cherubim Hymn, a sixth-century Greek text used in all Orthodox traditions to pray for "putting aside all worldly cares" to be worthy of communion. I wish to thank Alexander Lehrman for providing this information and the translation of the phrase as used in Anglophone Orthodox services. See A. Gozenpud, *Dostoevskii i muzykal'no-teatral'noe iskusstvo* (Leningrad: Sovetskii kompozitor, 1981), 145–46.

44. Steven Paul Scher, *Verbal Music in German Literature* (New Haven: Yale University Press, 1968), 8.

45. Scher, *Verbal Music*, 151.

46. Gozenpud, *Dostoevskii i muzykal'no-teatral'noe iskusstvo*, 145. Jacques Catteau concurs in this opinion (*Dostoyevsky and the Process of Literary Creation*, 32). A. S. Dolinin, who offers a detailed comparison of Trishatov's scene to Goethe's *Faust*, also loses sight of Trishatov's authorship and speaks only of Dostoevsky's (Dolinin, *Poslednie romany Dostoevskogo: Kak sozdavalis' "Podros-*

tok" i "Brat'ia Karamazovy" [Moscow-Leningrad: Sovetskii pisatel', 1963], 179–80). A. L. Bem calls Trishatov's creation "a distinctive contamination of Goethe's text with [Jules] Barbier's libretto to Gounod's opera" (Bem, *"Faust" v tvorchestve Dostoevskogo* [Prague: Russkii svobodnyi universitet v Prage, 1937; reprint ed., Ann Arbor: University Microfilms, 1967], 23). I have not been able to identify any elements of Trishatov's scene that are in Barbier's libretto but not in Goethe as well, and in every case Trishatov's scene is closer to Goethe than to Barbier. (Charles Gounod, *Faust: A Lyric Drama in Five Acts,* libretto by Jules Barbier and Michel Carré after the Tragedy by Johann Wolfgang von Goethe [New York: Broude Brothers, n.d.; opera first performed 1859 in Paris].)

47. Gerigk, *Versuch über Dostoevskijs "Jüngling,"* 136.

48. There is some question whether the "Evil Spirit" who speaks to Gretchen in the cathedral is meant to be identified with Mephistopheles or is rather the inner voice of Gretchen's conscience (see, for example, Cyrus Hamlin's notes to *Faust,* trans. Walter Arndt [New York: W. W. Norton, 1976], 93n). Zohrab sees allusions to A. N. Apukhtin in Trishatov's opera plan (Zohrab, "Dostoevsky and Meshchersky," 133).

49. It seems unfair, then, to compare Trishatov's unrealized opera invidiously with the completed works of other composers, as Gozenpud and Catteau do.

50. J. W. von Goethe, *Goethes Faust: Der Tragödie erster und zweiter Teil. Urfaust,* ed. Erich Trunz (Hamburg: Christian Wegner, 1963), 121, lines 3828–31.

51. Goethe, *Goethes Faust,* 142, line 4504.

52. The text of the Russian translation of part 1 of *Faust* that Dostoevsky owned uses the same word, "gnushat'sia," that Dostoevsky uses to characterize Alphonsine's disgust at Trishatov. Gretchen says to Faust, "Kak zhe ty gnushat'sia mnoi ne stal?" ("How is it that you are not disgusted by me?": *Faust. Tragediia. Soch. Gete,* trans. M. Vronchenko [St. Petersburg: Fisher, 1844], 227). The Russian text of the Evil Spirit's speech in the cathedral is also evocative of Alphonsine's reaction to Trishatov: "Ot tebia otvrashchaiut / Ugodniki lik svoi. Protivno im, chistym, / Podat' tebe ruku!" ("The saints turn / Their countenances from you. / The pure ones find it revolting / To give you their hand!" 188).

53. Goethe, *Goethes Faust,* 354, lines 11762–63, 11767–77. Bem argues convincingly in *"Faust" v tvorchestve Dostoevskogo* that Dostoevsky was familiar with part 2 of *Faust.*

54. J. W. von Goethe, *Goethe's Faust,* trans. Barker Fairley (Toronto: University of Toronto Press, 1970; reprinted 1985), 199. I have slightly modified the translation.

55. Goethe, *Goethes Faust,* 355, lines 11797–800.

56. Goethe, *Faust,* trans. Fairley, 200.

57. Goethe, *Goethes Faust,* 359, lines 11949–52.

58. Goethe, *Goethes Faust,* 354, lines 11780–82; Goethe, *Faust,* trans. Fairley, 200.

59. Sergei Durylin, "Ob odnom simvole u Dostoevskogo. Opyt tematicheskogo obzora," in his *Dostoevskii* (Moscow: Gosudarstvennaia Akademiia Khudozhestvennykh nauk, 1928), 187. See also N. M. Lary, *Dostoevsky and Dickens: A Study of Literary Influence* (London: Routledge and Kegan Paul, 1973), 154–55. In her article cited in note 42 of this chapter, Lunde offers an interesting interpretation of the symbolism of the slanting ray.

60. Charles Dickens, *The Old Curiosity Shop,* introduced by Peter Washington (New York: Alfred A. Knopf, 1995), 27.

61. Dickens, *Old Curiosity Shop,* 223.

62. See Durylin, "Ob odnom simvole," 163–98; Knapp, *Annihilation of Inertia,* 131–71 passim.

63. Dickens, *Old Curiosity Shop,* 394–99. See the analysis by Dolinin, *Poslednie romany Dostoevskogo,* 182–84.

64. Dickens's Nell attracts the unwanted attentions of the dwarf Quilp (*Old Curiosity Shop,* 45, 72–73, 86); Dostoevsky's Nelli is nearly raped in a brothel by the obese Arkhipov (3:276); see the discussion in chapter 2 earlier. See also Lary, *Dostoevsky and Dickens,* 46–47.

65. See Bem, *"Faust,"* 4–5.

66. On part 1 of *A Raw Youth,* see my article "The Weight of Human Tears."

67. Joseph Frank argues that the anticlimactic nature of the narrative of *A Raw Youth* was dictated by Dostoevsky's relationship with the Populist editors of *Otechestvennye zapiski* (*Notes of the Fatherland*), the journal in which the novel was first published (Frank, *Mantle of the Prophet,* 171). Frank rejects the approach, pioneered by Gerigk and followed by me here, that reads Arkadii's story as "a crisis of puberty," seeing such an interpretation as an attempt "to substitute our own, sexually hyperconscious twenty-first-century outlook for that of Dostoevsky" (174). For more on *A Raw Youth* as a dramatization of "the hell of puberty," see Gerigk's comparison of Dostoevsky's novel to J. D. Salinger's *The Catcher in the Rye,* in his *Die Russen in Amerika: Dostojewskij, Tolstoj, Turgenjew und Tschechow in ihrer Bedeutung für die Literatur der USA* (Stuttgart: Guido Pressler, 1995), 403–19.

68. Lawrence Lipking, *The Life of the Poet: Beginning and Ending Poetic Careers* (Chicago: University of Chicago Press, 1981).

69. Lipking, *Life of the Poet,* 15. Meerson points out the importance for Dostoevsky of "educating oneself by reading or rereading the written work" (Meerson, *Dostoevsky's Taboos,* 150n4).

70. Lipking, *Life of the Poet,* 48.

71. Ibid., 20.

72. Gary Saul Morson relates this passage to Dostoevsky's notion of time: "Dostoevsky defined his art, and true realism, in terms of the present and pres-

entness; he detected a range of falsities in those who, like Tolstoy, chose either to give the present the finish of the past (*Anna Karenina*) or the past the openness of the present (*War and Peace*)" (Morson, *Narrative and Freedom: The Shadows of Time* [New Haven: Yale University Press, 1994], 180). Morson is developing an alternative to poetics, which he calls "tempics," as a way of understanding works like *A Raw Youth, The Idiot,* and *War and Peace,* which are "written in an open, processual temporality sensed by the reader *as* he reads" (Morson, "Tempics and *The Idiot*," in *Celebrating Creativity,* 132).

73. Compare this with Rosen: "It is as if the chaos of the first novel stood in some vital relation to the order of the second" ("Breaking Out of the Underground," 226). Rosen sees the creation of Dolgorukii as an indispensable step toward creating Dmitrii Karamazov. His explanation for the difference in form between *A Raw Youth* and *The Brothers Karamazov,* however, is less than fully satisfactory: "Once the image of Dolgoruky was mastered, Dostoevsky could concentrate his creative power on the problem of structure" (239). Edward Wasiolek has correctly identified the novel's recapitulation of the earlier Dostoevsky: "It is a grab bag of old themes, devices, and psychologizing. Very little is new, and there is a little bit of everything that Dostoevsky had dealt with before" (Wasiolek, *Dostoevsky: The Major Fiction* [Cambridge: MIT Press, 1964], 137). While I agree with Wasiolek's characterization, I see this repetition as a legitimate artistic strategy, not a mistake.

CHAPTER FOUR

1. See Irene Zohrab's articles (cited in notes 22 and 23 of chapter 2 and note 4 of chapter 3) for valuable work on "decoding" references to taboo forms of sexuality in Dostoevsky's writings.

2. See also Arkadii's remark early in the novel: *"I have heard from depraved people* that very often a man, when having sex with a woman, begins without saying a word, which is of course the height of monstrous and nauseating behavior" (13:11; emphasis mine).

3. Jean-Jacques Rousseau, *Emile; or, On Education,* trans. and ed. Allan Bloom (New York: Basic Books, 1979), bk. 4, p. 333.

4. Rousseau, *Emile,* 334.

5. Rousseau, *Confessions,* bk. 3, p. 109. For an excellent discussion of the role of the imagination in Rousseau's attitude toward masturbation, see Vernon A. Rosario II, "Phantastical Pollutions: The Public Threat of Private Vice in France," in *Solitary Pleasures: The Historical, Literary, and Artistic Discourses of Autoeroticism,* ed. Paula Bennett and Vernon A. Rosario II (New York: Routledge, 1995), 101–30. The masturbatory nature of the dreamer's reveries appears in Dostoevsky's pre-Siberia works such as "White Nights" ("Belye nochi," 1848) and "Petersburg Chronicle" ("Petersburgskaia letopis'," 1847). See the

analysis of "White Nights" by Carol Flath in her forthcoming book on "secrets, sacraments, and sexuality" in Dostoevsky.

6. Thomas W. Laqueur, *Solitary Sex: A Cultural History of Masturbation* (New York: Zone Books, 2003), 210; on Rousseau, see 42–44. For a succinct summary of Laqueur's argument, see the review by Stephen Greenblatt, "Me, Myself, and I," *New York Review of Books,* April 8, 2004, 32–36.

7. Greenblatt, "Me, Myself, and I," 35.

8. G. I. Arkhangel'skii, "Zhizn' v Peterburge po statisticheskim dannym," *Arkhiv sudebnoi meditsiny i obshchestvennoi gigieny,* 1869, no. 2 (June): pt. 3, pp. 33–85; no. 3 (September): pt. 3, pp. 84–143. My attention was directed to this source by a reference in Engelstein, *Keys to Happiness.*

9. Arkhangel'skii, "Zhizn' v Peterburge," no. 2:71–72.

10. Ibid., no. 2:72.

11. See also a later speech by Arkadii's father, Versilov: "You're always secretive, at the same time that your honest appearance and red cheeks clearly attest that you could look everyone in the eyes with complete innocence" (13:90).

12. See chapter 1 for a more extensive discussion of *Thérèse philosophe* and Dostoevsky's interest in it. For more on *Thérèse philosophe* in relation to eighteenth-century medical texts on masturbation, see Théodore Tarczylo, *Sexe et liberté au siècle des Lumières* (Paris: Presses de la Renaissance, 1983), 222–27.

13. "Ia s nego riasku stashchu," "ona mne govorila odnazhdy, chto ona kogda-nibud' tebia s"est," "khotela ego proglotit'." Compare Lise's words in the chapter "A Lady of Little Faith": "Vot on vdrug menia teper' boitsia, ia ego s"em, chto li?" ("Suddenly he's afraid of me now; does he think I'm going to eat him up?" 14:55). Grushenka's peremptory requests that Rakitin bring Alyosha to her ("privedi da privedi!" 14:74) are echoed by Dmitrii's words when he asks Katerina Ivanovna's half sister to send her to him to be seduced: "prishlite mne . . . vashu institutku sekretno" ("send me your schoolgirl on the sly," 14:103). Katerina Ivanovna's "extraordinary desire" ("chrezvychainoe zhelanie," 14:133) to see Alyosha is a high-toned version of Grushenka's crude requests.

14. Knapp, *Annihilation of Inertia,* 198–205.

15. See Donna Orwin's discussion of this scene in the context of religious psychology: "Did Dostoevsky or Tolstoy Believe in Miracles?" in *A New Word on "The Brothers Karamazov,"* ed. Robert Louis Jackson (Evanston: Northwestern University Press, 2004), 125–41. See also the Freudian reading of this scene by Slobodanka Vladiv-Glover: "Dostoyevsky, Freud, and Parricide; Deconstructive Notes on *The Brothers Karamazov,*" *New Zealand Slavonic Journal,* 1993, 7–34, 26. My student Rebecca F. Smith suggested in a seminar on *The Brothers Karamazov* that the role of Zosima in Alyosha's consummation introduces a potentially homoerotic dimension to the scene. Catherine Ciepiela has pointed out in a private communication that it is the "spell" of Zosima's words that precipitates

Alyosha's ecstasy. She cites Nathan Rosen's discussion of Zosima's "verbal leg-erdemain" ("Style and Structure in *The Brothers Karamazov*," in Fyodor Dosto-evsky, *The Brothers Karamazov*, trans. Constance Garnett, rev. and ed. Ralph E. Matlaw [New York: Norton, 1976], 841–51, 849 [the article was first published in 1971]). On Alyosha as a hagiographic hero, see V. E. Vetlovskaia, *Poetika romana "Brat'ia Karamazovy"* (Leningrad: Nauka, 1977), 161–83. An English translation of this passage is available as "Alyosha Karamazov and the Hagiographic Hero" in *Dostoevsky: New Perspectives*, ed. Robert Louis Jackson, trans. Nancy Pollak and Susanne Fusso (Englewood Cliffs, N.J.: Prentice-Hall, 1984), 206–26.

16. Peter Gay, *The Bourgeois Experience: Victoria to Freud*, vol. 1: *Educa-tion of the Senses* (New York: Oxford University Press, 1984), 317. Jane Caplan relates this development to the rise of capitalism: "One may speculate that the prohibitions on masturbation came to prominence at this time as one theme in a many-sided discourse on individual continence and self-restraint, correspond-ing to the development of a capitalist mode of production which was highly individualist, and which emphasised restraint on spending in favour of accumu-lation" (Caplan, "Sexuality and Homosexuality," in *Women in Society: Inter-disciplinary Essays*, ed. Cambridge Women's Studies Group [London: Virago, 1981], 165n4). Laqueur greatly expands on the economic analogy (*Solitary Sex*, 280–302).

17. Michael R. Katz calls Smerdiakov "the final and fullest exploration of the male homosexual stereotype in Dostoevsky's fiction," citing Smerdiakov's fastid-iousness and aversion to women (Katz, "Dostoevskii's Homophilia/Homopho-bia," 247–48).

18. Gary Saul Morson, "Verbal Pollution in *The Brothers Karamazov*," in *Fyodor Dostoevsky's "The Brothers Karamazov*," ed. Harold Bloom (New York: Chelsea House, 1988), 88.

19. Engelstein, *Keys to Happiness*, 226. The edition of Tissot that I was able to consult is S.-A.-A.-D. Tissot, *L'onanisme, dissertation sur les maladies pro-duites par la masturbation, par Mr. Tissot, Doct. med.*, 8th ed. (Lausanne: Franç. Grasset et Comp., 1785). I also consulted two Russian editions: *Onanizm ili ras-suzhdenie o bolezniakh, proiskhodiashchikh ot rukobludiia. Soch. G. Tisso-tom . . . perevedennoe s poslednego original'nogo izdaniia, protiv prezhnego zna-chitel'no umnozhennoe i ispravlennoe. V trekh chastiakh* (St. Petersburg: V tipografii Imperatorskogo Vospitatel'nogo Doma, 1822); and *Onanizm ili ras-suzhdenie o bolezniakh, proiskhodiashchikh ot rukobludiia, Sochinenie Doktora Tissota. S frantsuzskogo perevel doktor meditsiny Aleksandr Nikitin* (St. Peters-burg: V tipografii Iv. Selezneva, 1845). On Tissot and other early writers on mas-turbation, see Laqueur, *Solitary Sex*, 13–62, 85–87, 192–213, 223–39; Gay, *Bourgeois Experience*, 294–309; Ludmilla Jordanova, "The Popularisation of Medicine: Tissot on Onanism," *Textual Practice* 1 (1984): 68–80; Roy Porter, "Forbidden Pleasures: Enlightenment Literature of Sexual Advice," in *Solitary*

Pleasures, 75–98; Rosario (on Tissot's relationship with Rousseau), "Phantastical Pollutions," 103–7; and Tarczylo, *Sexe et liberté,* 108–39.

20. Tissot, *L'onanisme,* 8; Russian edition (1822), 2; Russian edition (1845), 6.

21. See, for example, the 1845 Russian edition: "People of both sexes who indulge in masturbation have the common symptom of becoming indifferent to hymeneal pleasures . . . One man devoted to masturbation who entered into marriage felt such great repulsion for it that he fell into ennui and the deepest melancholy [zadumchivost'], from which he could hardly be cured" (31; p. 50 of 1822 edition).

22. Rice discusses the sexual etiology of epilepsy and its implications for Dostoevsky in *Dostoevsky and Healing Art,* 121.

23. Charles Dickens, *David Copperfield* (New York: Modern Library, 1998), 206 (chapter 15). On the importance of *David Copperfield* for Dostoevsky, see Lary, *Dostoevsky and Dickens,* 2, 119–23. Vladimir Golstein also compares Smerdiakov to Uriah Heep, but not with reference to masturbation (Golstein, "Accidental Families and Surrogate Fathers: Richard, Grigory, and Smerdiakov," in *A New Word on "The Brothers Karamazov,"* 90–106, 102).

24. Laqueur, *Solitary Sex,* 63–64.

25. Dickens, *David Copperfield,* 206, 211. For more on the masturbatory significance of the hand in Dickens, see William A. Cohen, "Manual Conduct in *Great Expectations,*" in his *Sex Scandal: The Private Parts of Victorian Fiction* (Durham: Duke University Press, 1996), 26–72.

26. Morson, "Verbal Pollution," 93.

27. The puns were first noted by V. Trenin and N. Khardzhiev, "Maiakovskii o kachestve stikha," in their *Poeticheskaia kul'tura Maiakovskogo* (Moscow: Iskusstvo, 1970), 325n5. M. S. Al'tman offers a more detailed analysis in his *Dostoevskii: Po vekham imen,* 222–23. For more on Dostoevsky's use of sexual puns, see G. A. Levinton, "Dostoevskii i 'nizkie' zhanry fol'klora," special issue of *Literaturnoe obozrenie, spetsial'nyi vypusk: Erotika v russkoi literature, ot Barkova do nashikh dnei, Teksty i kommentarii* (Moscow: Literaturnoe obozrenie, 1992), 46–53.

28. In his Freudian interpretation of Lise's crisis, Nathan Rosen makes the important point that, although Lise does not appear again after this scene, the narrator's later references to her performing a series of selfless deeds suggest that she may be on the way to recovery from her demonic madness. "The Madness of Lise Khokhlakova in *The Brothers Karamazov,*" *Dostoevsky Studies,* n.s., vol. 6 (2002): 154–62, 161.

29. See Thomas Laqueur's discussion of masturbation ("the solitary vice") and prostitution ("the social evil") as "social pathologies that visited destruction on the body in the same way that in ages past blasphemy or lechery produced monsters": "The problem with both masturbation and prostitution was essen-

tially quantitative: doing it alone and doing it with lots of people rather than doing it in pairs . . . The paradoxes of commercial society that had already plagued Adam Smith and his colleagues, the nagging doubts that a free economy might not sustain the social body, haunt the sexual body" (Laqueur, *Making Sex: Body and Gender from the Greeks to Freud* [Cambridge, Mass.: Harvard University Press, 1990], 227, 232–33). For more on the solitary nature of masturbation, see Laqueur, *Solitary Sex*, 222–35. On Freud's reevaluation of masturbation as a necessary stage of sexual development, see Laqueur, *Solitary Sex*, 56, 71–76; on Freud's inability to completely overcome the older view, see 366–67.

CHAPTER FIVE

1. Gary Saul Morson, "Introductory Study: Dostoevsky's Great Experiment," in Fyodor Dostoevsky, *A Writer's Diary*, trans. and annotated by Kenneth Lantz, 2 vols. (Evanston: Northwestern University Press, 1993), 1:61. See also the commentary to the January 1876 issue of *A Writer's Diary* in Dostoevsky's complete works: "The resonance of the 'theme of children' [in the first two chapters of the issue] grows stronger, it constantly takes on new overtones and acquires a deeper and more capacious philosophical meaning: for children are not just the present but also the future of Russia, therefore society has a particularly great responsibility toward them" (22:280–81). For a probing analysis of Dostoevsky's treatment of the theme of childhood innocence in the 1876 *Writer's Diary*, see Jackson, "Dostoevskij's 'Anecdote from a Child's Life.'"

2. See the description by A. F. Kistiakovskii of boys imprisoned with adults in the Lithuanian Castle: "The juvenile criminals came into contact with the adult convicts in the kitchen, while doing heavy labor, in the workshops, in the infirmary, when called out to the prison office to meet their relatives and friends . . . The juveniles were positively offended if they were called not *convicts* and *rogues* but *pupils, foster children, students* . . . Nearly every one of the juvenile prisoners under investigation, after receiving his indictment, went immediately to the infirmary to learn *thievish-roguish* wisdom there from the hardened convicts" (Kistiakovskii, *Molodye prestupniki i uchrezhdeniia dlia ikh ispravleniia s obozreniem russkikh uchrezhdenii* [Kiev: V universitetskoi tipografii (I. I. Zavadzkogo), 1878], 134).

3. Rovinskii of course contradicts here his earlier assurance to Dostoevsky that indulgence in nasty habits was impossible in the colony.

4. Kh. D. Alchevskaia, "Dostoevskii," in *F. M. Dostoevskii v vospominaniiakh sovremennikov*, ed. V. E. Vatsuro et al., 2 vols. (Moscow: Khudozhestvennaia literatura, 1990), 2:327.

5. Alchevskaia, "Dostoevskii," 2:330, 331.

6. The basic information on the case is drawn from the notes to Dostoevsky's complete works (22:346) and from the newspaper account on which Dos-

toevsky primarily relied (*Golos* [*The Voice*], 1876, January 24, 25, 26, 27, 28, and 29). The accused is identified as "Kronenberg" in court documents and in the first installment in *The Voice*, but the name was spelled "Kroneberg" in subsequent installments and in *A Writer's Diary*. To avoid confusion I will use the latter spelling. Other non-Russian surnames in the trial account, such as "Gesing," have been transliterated according to my best conjecture. On Dostoevsky's notes toward his account of the case, see Rozenblium, *Tvorcheskie dnevniki Dostoevskogo*, 234–37.

7. Gary Rosenshield, "The Imprisonment of the Law: Dostoevskii and the Kroneberg Case," *Slavic and East European Journal* 36, no. 4 (1992): 415–34, 415, 429. After the manuscript of this book was completed, Rosenshield's book on Dostoevsky's view of the jury trial appeared: *Western Law, Russian Justice: Dostoevsky, the Jury Trial, and the Law* (Madison: University of Wisconsin Press, 2005). An expanded version of Rosenshield's essay on the Kroneberg case appears in his book as chapter 1. Harriet Murav has also written on the Kroneberg case in the context of Dostoevsky's other articles on legal issues in *A Writer's Diary* (Murav, "Legal Fiction in Dostoevsky's *Diary of a Writer*," *Dostoevsky Studies* 1, no. 2 [1993]: 155–73) and *Russia's Legal Fictions* (Ann Arbor: University of Michigan Press, 1998), 125–55. In her book, Murav briefly mentions Mariia Kroneberg's masturbation (129–30).

8. Gary Rosenshield, "Western Law vs. Russian Justice: Dostoevsky and the Jury Trial, Round One: The Kroneberg Trial," *Graven Images: A Journal of Culture, Law, and the Sacred* 1 (1994): 117–35, 128. Murav notes that in Dostoevsky's account, Bibina becomes the child's "true parent" ("Legal Fiction," 166). See also the discussion by Joseph Frank, *Mantle of the Prophet*, 291–93. For a detailed rhetorical analysis of Spasovich's summation and of the responses by Dostoevsky and Saltykov-Shchedrin, see V. V. Vinogradov, *O khudozhestvennoi proze* (Moscow-Leningrad: Gosudarstvennoe izdatel'stvo, 1930), 106–87. See also V. A. Tunimanov, "Publitsistika Dostoevskogo. 'Dnevnik Pisatelia,'" in *Dostoevskii—Khudozhnik i myslitel': Sbornik statei*, ed. A. L. Grishunin et al. (Moscow: Khudozhestvennaia literatura, 1972), 165–209.

9. Rosenshield, "Dostoevsky and the Jury Trial," 130.

10. Kroneberg is so disdainful of and ignorant about his servants that he refers to Bibina as the caretaker's wife, although she is identified as his mother by several other witnesses, including the caretaker himself (January 24, 26).

11. Rosenshield notes this parallel in a different context, the larger context of blaming the victim, as Fetiukovich blames Fyodor Karamazov: "Both defenses involve a casuistic—in the now older, pejorative sense—legalistic attempt to redefine their clients' actions as legally nonculpable" (Rosenshield, "Dostoevsky and the Jury Trial," 121). For a brilliant analysis of the attorneys' discourse at the trial of Dmitrii Karamazov, see Kate Holland, "The Legend of the *Ladonka* and the Trial of the Novel," in *A New Word on "The Brothers Karamazov*," 192–99.

12. Aleksandr Smirnov, *Pervaia russkaia zhenshchina-vrach* (Moscow: Medgiz, 1960), 152. Smirnov includes a bibliography of other sources on Suslova. A typical member of the generation of radical youth, Suslova was under police surveillance in the early 1860s. See *Literaturnoe nasledstvo*, vol. 71: *Vasilii Sleptsov: Neizvestnye stranitsy* (Moscow: Akademii nauk SSSR, 1963), 449–53.

13. Smirnov, *Pervaia russkaia zhenshchina-vrach*, 152.

14. Ibid., 153–55.

15. See A. S. Dolinin's publication of A. P. Suslova's diaries, *Gody blizosti s Dostoevskim. Dnevnik. Povest'. Pis'ma* (1928; reprint ed., New York: Serebrianyi vek, 1982). The major primary and secondary documents on Apollinaria Suslova have been assembled by Liudmila Saraskina in her remarkable work *Vozliublennaia Dostoevskogo. Apollinariia Suslova: Biografiia v dokumentakh, pis'-makh, materialakh* (Moscow: Soglasie, 1994).

16. Smirnov, *Pervaia russkaia zhenshchina-vrach*, 156.

17. Smirnov, *Pervaia russkaia zhenshchina-vrach*, 156. Suslova's Swiss husband, F. F. Erisman, came with her to Russia and did valuable work in the area of hygiene and sanitation, with particular attention to the needs of the poor. See Smirnov, *Pervaia russkaia zhenshchina-vrach*, 161–65; and N. A. Semashko, "Na zare russkoi gigieny i sanitarii (F. F. Erisman)," *Sovetskoe zdravookhranenie*, 1944, no. 4–5:26–32. Suslova and Erisman were divorced in 1874. She was married again to Professor A. E. Golubev, with whom she remained until her death. She had no children.

18. See also K. Rozova: "In 1868 Suslova returned to Russia and worked in St. Petersburg mainly in obstetrics and gynecology" (Rozova, "Pervaia russkaia zhenshchina vrach," *Fel'dsher i akusherka*, 1945, no. 3:48–52, 52).

19. Nadezhda Suslova's stories are "Rasskaz v pis'makh," *Sovremennik*, 1864, no. 7; "Fantazerka. Povest'," *Sovremennik*, 1864, no. 9; and "Iz nedavnego proshlogo. Rasskaz," *Vestnik Evropy*, 1900, no. 6. For a discussion of Suslova's fiction in the context of Russian radicalism, see Peter C. Pozefsky, "Love, Science, and Politics in the Fiction of *Shestidesiatnitsy* N. P. Suslova and S. V. Kovalevskaia," *Russian Review* 58 (July 1999): 361–79.

20. See the letter from Nadezhda to Apollinaria from Zurich in 1865, in which she quotes large chunks of Sand's novel *Lélia* in order to express her feelings (Saraskina, *Vozliublennaia Dostoevskogo*, 272–73).

21. N. Suslova-Erisman, review of *O vospitanii detei v pervye gody zhizni*, by Mar'ia Manasseina (St. Petersburg, 1870), in *Arkhiv sudebnoi meditsiny i obshchestvennoi gigieny*, 1870, bk. 4:21–31, 25–26. Smirnov points to another diagnostic remark in this article as "unusually new and bold" and supported by later discoveries, i.e., Suslova's claim that the cause of conjunctivitis in infants is not bright sunlight but an infection from the mother's vagina (as a result of gonorrhea) at the time of birth (Smirnov, *Pervaia russkaia zhenshchina-vrach*, 161–62).

22. I have chosen to translate "soznat'sia" as "confess," although some readers of this chapter have suggested that the sense of guilt and confession is not as strong in the word "soznat'sia" as it is in the word "priznat'sia." The dictionary of Vladimir Dal' gives the following definition for "soznat'sia": "priznat'sia, ne otrekat'sia, ne otpirat'sia, povinit'sia; vyskazat', po ubezhden'iu svoemu istinu" ("to confess, not to disavow, not to deny, to accept guilt; to express the truth according to one's conviction"). (Dal', *Tolkovyi slovar' zhivogo velikorusskago iazyka,* 4th edition., ed. Baudouin de Courtenay, 4 vols. [St. Petersburg-Moscow: M. O. Vol'f, 1904], 4:366.) It seems that there is no ideal one-word English translation of "soznat'sia"; it exists somewhere between the words "to admit," which does not necessarily entail culpability, and "to confess," which places more stress on guilt and less on the cognitive dimension of the utterance. The linguist Sergei Bunaev agrees with me that "soznat'sia v bolezni" is an ambivalent statement that places responsibility for the illness upon the sufferer.

23. M. E. Saltykov-Shchedrin, chapter 5 of *Nedokonchennye besedy* (*"Mezhdu delom"*), in his *Polnoe sobranie sochinenii,* ed. V. Ia. Kirpotin et al., vol. 15 (Moscow: Khudozhestvennaia literatura, 1940), 368. This essay was originally published under the title "Otrezannyi lomot'" (signed "A Young Man") in *Otechestvennye zapiski,* 1876, no. 3. According to V. Gol'diner, it appeared "soon after Dostoevsky's article" ("Saltykov-Shchedrin i Dostoevskii ob advokature," *Sovetskaia iustitsiia,* 1961, no. 1:19–21, 21).

24. Saltykov-Shchedrin, *Nedokonchennye besedy,* 15:369, 371, 372, 379.

25. N. V. Gogol', *Polnoe sobranie sochinenii,* 5:70 (scene 8). Dostoevsky refers to this passage at 22:156, 251–52, and 24:135, 140, and 143.

26. Suslova-Erisman, review of Manasseina, 22. See also Suslova's autobiographical story "Iz nedavnego proshlogo": "The extreme difficulty of [raising children] frightened my timidity. I thought that on that path, with all the best intentions, only out of ignorance, frivolity, and lack of skill, which are hard to avoid, one could lead an inexperienced, just-beginning life astray into a dark forest, and the hugeness of the moral responsibility for the fate of one's pupils pushed me away from this occupation" (N. Suslova,"Iz nedavnego proshlogo," *Vestnik Evropy,* 1900, no. 6:624–73, 627). Nadezhda's feelings were apparently shared by Apollinaria. She records in her diary of May 1865 a conversation with a French doctor who assures her that after the treatment he has just administered she will still be able to have children (she was probably being treated for ovarian cysts). Suslova says that she is not at all consoled by this news. "'But why?' he asked. 'All women want to have children.' 'Because I don't know how to bring them up,' I said" (Saraskina, *Vozliublennaia Dostoevskogo,* 245; on her ovarian cysts, *Vozliublennaia Dostoevskogo,* 365).

27. An 1867 article on Suslova compares her to the pioneering American physician Elizabeth Blackwell ("Pervaia russkaia zhenshchina-medik," *Zhenskii*

vestnik, 1867, no. 8:82–84, cited in Saraskina, *Vozliublennaia Dostoevskogo*, 201). Blackwell campaigned against masturbation as "a model for unbridled sexuality generally" (Laqueur, *Solitary Sex*, 66; see also 49).

28. See note 22 in this chapter.

29. Tissot, *Onanizm ili rassuzhdenie* (1845), 30. Laqueur discusses the attention paid in the eighteenth century particularly to the problems of children and women masturbating (Laqueur, *Solitary Sex*, 199–203, 229, 339–58).

30. V. Ditman, "Tainyi porok," *Pedagogicheskii sbornik, izdavaemyi pri Glavnom upravlenii voenno-uchebnykh zavedenii*, 1871, bk. 3 (March): 367–75; bk. 4 (April): 551–56; bk. 5 (May): 654–63. My attention was drawn to this source by the discussion of it in Engelstein, *Keys to Happiness*, 227–28. Engelstein traces Russian attitudes toward masturbation into the twentieth century.

31. Ditman, "Tainyi porok," bk. 3:369. When I presented this chapter as a talk at Brandeis University, Joan Chevalier suggested that Mariia Kroneberg's obsessive masturbation beginning at the age of four would today be considered a possible indication that she had been sexually abused. Given the neglect in which the child was raised, this seems a likely possibility, but there is no documentary evidence for it.

32. Ditman, "Tainyi porok," bk. 4:554. One would expect that given this advice, virtually all parents would suspect their small children of masturbation.

33. See Tissot in the 1845 Russian edition: "The face, the mirror of the condition of soul and body, is the first to show the internal disorder of the body. The fullness and freshness of the face, without which beauty produces no impression on us, disappear first of all. Then there immediately follow a gauntness and pallor of the face; the eyes become sunken and lose their gleam and sharpness: finally the whole composition of the body becomes hideous" (Tissot, *Onanizm ili rassuzhdenie*, 30). See also Laqueur, *Solitary Sex*, 64–65.

34. Ditman, "Tainyi porok," bk. 3:375. If we take Ditman seriously, then the "rosy cheeks" of Arkadii Dolgorukii and Alyosha Karamazov are no guarantee that they have abstained from masturbation (see chapter 4).

35. Ditman, "Tainyi porok," bk. 4:551. By 1913, a collection of articles for educators included an essay translated from English that retreated very far from the doctrine of Tissot: "In recent times the general opinion of doctors has come down to the idea that this habit, if it is not abused too often, does not cause the organism any particularly serious physical harm" (Klara Shmit, "O prepodavanii v obshchestvennykh shkolakh faktov, otnosiashchikhsia k polovomu voprosu," in *Polovoe vospitanie. Sbornik statei uchitelei, roditelei i vospitatelei* [Moscow: Vil'de, 1913], 95).

36. Ditman, "Tainyi porok," bk. 4:554–55.

37. Ibid., bk. 4:556.

38. Laqueur, *Solitary Sex*, 46.

39. L. Martineau, *Leçons sur les déformations vulvaires et anales produites par la masturbation, le saphisme, la défloration, et la sodomie* (Paris: Adrien Delahaye et Émile Lecrosnier, 1884), 55–56.

40. Compare Murav: "For Dostoevsky, the villain of the Kroneburg case was not so much the abusive father, as the defense lawyer and his 'talent,' that is, his skillful rhetoric" (Murav, "Legal Fiction," 159). Murav also points out that in the later Kornilova case, Dostoevsky repeated Spasovich's strategy of explaining away the beating of a child as being necessary to rid her of a bad habit (in this case bedwetting; Murav, "Legal Fiction," 163). See also her *Russia's Legal Fictions,* 125–44.

41. Saltykov-Shchedrin, *Polnoe sobranie sochinenii,* 15:372.

42. Dal', *Tolkovyi slovar',* 3:1627.

43. In his notes Dostoevsky mentions the possibility of a trial in camera, but ignores Spasovich's motion even here (24:149).

44. Yuz Aleshkovsky (b. 1929) is the author of *The Hand (Ruka,* 1980), *Kangaroo (Kenguru,* 1981), and many other novels of late twentieth-century Russian life that virtuosically employ a broad range of Russian discourses, including high literary language, prison slang, and obscenity.

45. Marina Kostalevsky has made a similar point about Fetiukovich, the defense attorney in *The Brothers Karamazov* for whom Spasovich served as a model. Fetiukovich is labeled an "adulterer of thought" ("preliubodei mysli"). As Kostalevsky says of his abuse of the very process of thinking, "Thought itself becomes an object of desire, and the process of thinking turns into a sensual process. In other words, Fetyukovich engages in a bit of mental masturbation" (Kostalevsky, "Sensual Mind: The Pain and Pleasure of Thinking," in *A New Word on "The Brothers Karamazov,"* 200–9, 203). Kostalevsky's essay is a provocative analysis of the interaction between cognitive and sensual spheres in Dostoevsky.

46. V. Sazhin, "Ruka pobeditelia: Vybrannye mesta iz perepiski V. Belinskogo i M. Bakunina," in *Literaturnoe obozrenie, spetsial'nyi vypusk,* 39.

47. Laqueur, *Solitary Sex,* 62.

48. Compare this with Freud's view, in Laqueur's account: "Adolescence, in particular, became the crux, a fraught time between 'natural' infantile auto-eroticism and its sad holdover into maturity, the period when masturbation went from being a sign of 'budding sexuality' full of promise to being an indication that its practitioner was unable to have a proper love object and, more generally, to make peace with the demands of society" (Laqueur, *Solitary Sex,* 73–74). Dostoevsky would agree with Freud here on the need to grow out of the masturbatory phase. As we have seen in chapter 4, however, he would have regarded that phase not as a normal and necessary stage of "budding sexuality," but as an addiction to a "nasty habit" weighted with moral and physical danger.

49. E. N. Opochinin, "Iz 'Besed s Dostoevskim,'" in *Dostoevskii v vospominaniiakh sovremennikov,* 2:383.

50. Opochinin, "Iz 'Besed,'" 2:383–34.

CHAPTER SIX

1. Harriet Murav points out: "Whatever woman is in Dostoevsky—absence, image, memory trace, a blank space, albeit a Christological blank space—she is not a speaking subject" (Murav, "Reading Woman in Dostoevsky," in *A Plot of Her Own: The Female Protagonist in Russian Literature,* ed. Sona Stephan Hoisington [Evanston: Northwestern University Press, 1995], 44–57, 51). Murav argues that it is only in *A Writer's Diary* that "women deliberate, plan, have ideas, and commit crimes, even the unthinkable crimes against children, the kind that Dostoevsky's heroes commit" ("Reading Woman," 55).

2. This was a programmatic decision on Turgenev's part. As he wrote to K. K. Sluchevskii (April 14, 1862), "All the real *negators* I have known, without exception (Belinsky, Bakunin, Herzen, Dobrolyubov, Speshnev, etc.), came from comparatively good and honest parents. A great idea is contained therein: it removes from the *men of action,* the negators, every suspicion of *personal* dissatisfaction, personal irritation. They go their way only because they are more sensitive to the demands of national life" (Ivan Turgenev, *Fathers and Sons,* ed. Ralph E. Matlaw [New York: Norton, 1966], 185).

3. I am following here Northrop Frye's model of comedy in *Anatomy of Criticism: Four Essays* (Princeton: Princeton University Press, 1957), 163–71. Turgenev was no doubt familiar with many of the classical and Shakespearean texts on which Frye based his model.

4. See the admirably succinct discussion of Dostoevsky's view of the Russian family in W. J. Leatherbarrow, *Fyodor Dostoevsky: "The Brothers Karamazov"* (Cambridge: Cambridge University Press, 1992), 21–30. See Liza Knapp, *Annihilation of Inertia,* 131–71. The question of the historical and sociological accuracy of Dostoevsky's view of the family is beyond the scope of this essay. I suspect that Dostoevsky greatly exaggerated the magnitude of the changes in the Russian family from the 1840s to the 1870s. On the problem of child abandonment (mainly by peasant and working-class women and families, who tend not to be the subject of Dostoevsky's fictional works), see David L. Ransel, *Mothers of Misery: Child Abandonment in Russia* (Princeton: Princeton University Press, 1988). On Dostoevsky's "Fathers and Sons," see Semyonov, *Roman Dostoevskogo "Podrostok,"* 127–62.

5. Harriet Murav sees Dostoevsky in *A Writer's Diary* as creating a new order by rhetorically constructing himself first as a "child" and then as a "father," "whose offspring are his readers" (Murav, "Legal Fictions," 164–73). See also

her *Russia's Legal Fictions,* 125–44. Vladimir Golstein discusses Dostoevsky's concept of the family and his preoccupation with abandoned children in his article "Accidental Families," 90–106. For an article that focuses not on fathers but on mothers, see Liza Knapp, "Mothers and Sons in *The Brothers Karamazov:* Our Ladies of Skotoprigonevsk," in *A New Word on "The Brothers Karamazov,"* 31–52.

6. Irina Paperno, *Chernyshevsky and the Age of Realism: A Study in the Semiotics of Behavior* (Stanford: Stanford University Press, 1988), 157. See also Edward Hallett Carr, *The Romantic Exiles: A Nineteenth-Century Portrait Gallery* (New York: Frederick A. Stokes, 1933); T. A. Bogdanovich, *Liubov' liudei shestidesiatykh godov* (Leningrad: Academia, 1929); and Richard Stites, *The Women's Liberation Movement in Russia: Feminism, Nihilism, and Bolshevism 1860–1930* (Princeton: Princeton University Press, 1978), esp. 19–25, 41–47, and 89–99.

7. A. Gertsen [Herzen], *Povesti i rasskazy* (Moscow: Khudozhestvennaia literatura, 1967), 106.

8. Herzen, *Povesti,* 106.

9. "Polin'ka Saks" is also mentioned in *The Devils,* when the radical Pyotr Verkhovenskii commends Mavrikii Nikolaevich for tolerating his fiancée's affair with Stavrogin (10:409, 410).

10. See the excellent discussion of Liza Herzen's suicide in Irina Paperno, *Suicide as a Cultural Institution in Dostoevsky's Russia* (Ithaca: Cornell University Press, 1997), 178–82. See also Murav, "Reading Woman," 52–56; and Carr, *Romantic Exiles,* 347–62.

11. Diane Oenning Thompson, *"The Brothers Karamazov" and the Poetics of Memory* (Cambridge: Cambridge University Press, 1991), 165. Thompson points out that the Devil himself (in Ivan's dream) has, like Verkhovenskii, Versilov, and Karamazov, allowed his own children to be "brought up somewhere far away, by some kind of aunts" (168 in Thompson, 15:71 in Dostoevsky).

12. Golstein calls this "the movement from false fathers to the true, usually surrogate ones" ("Accidental Families," 91).

13. Golstein offers a new interpretation of Grigorii as a neglectful, abusive "father" to Smerdiakov who bears great responsibility for Smerdiakov's crime ("Accidental Families").

14. Sibling hostility as well as love surfaces in both novels. In a brilliant set piece, Arkadii's half brother, Versilov's legitimate aristocratic son, treats him like a footman (13:397–401). Ivan and Dmitrii are locked in rivalry over a woman, and Smerdiakov (who may or may not be the Karamazovs' brother but who certainly thinks he is) hates Ivan, Dmitrii, and Alyosha. The ancient history of brotherly hostility is evoked in *The Brothers Karamazov* through references to the stories of Cain (14:206, 211) and Joseph (14:266).

15. Stepan Verkhovenskii says something remarkably similar about Fed'ka

near the end of the novel: "I'll tell him the whole truth, that I am to blame . . . and that *for ten years* I suffered for his sake, more than he suffered out there in the army" (10:481).

16. Friedrich Schiller, *Five Plays*, trans. Robert David MacDonald (London: Absolute Classics, 1998), 167. The German text reads: "Die Gesetze der Welt sind Würfelspiel worden, das Band der Natur ist entzwei, die alte Zweitracht ist los, der Sohn hat seinen Vater erschlagen" (Friedrich Schiller, *Dramen*, ed. Benno von Wiese [Frankfurt: Büchergilde Gutenberg, 1959], 180). The fullest analysis of the use of Schiller in *The Brothers Karamazov* is D. Tschiževskij [Chizhevsky], "Schiller und *Die Brüder Karamazov*," *Zeitschrift für slavische Philologie* 4 (1929): 1–42. A partial translation of this can be found in Dostoevsky, *The Brothers Karamazov*, ed. Matlaw, 794–807.

17. For a brilliant analysis of the discourse of the defense and prosecuting attorneys, see Holland, "Legend of the *Ladonka*," 192–99. See also the extensive discussion of Dmitri's trial (including the use of Spasovich as a model for Fetiukovich), in Rosenshield, *Western Law, Russian Justice*, 131–253.

18. Dmitrii and Grigorii seem to agree in part with Fetiukovich, Dmitrii when he calls Grigorii "my own father" ("otets rodnoi," 14:414), and Grigorii when he is more shocked by Dmitrii's beating of himself than by his beating of Fyodor: "'He dared to hit me!' Grigorii uttered gloomily and distinctly. 'He "dared" to hit his father too, let alone you!' Ivan Fyodorovich remarked, curling his lip. 'I washed him in a trough . . . he dared to hit me!' Grigorii repeated" (14:129).

19. See Rosenshield, "Dostoevsky and the Jury Trial," 121, 124.

20. Fetiukovich, like Fyodor, has read *The Robbers*, which includes the following speech by Franz von Moor, the character to whom Fyodor compared Dmitrii: "'He's your father!' He gave you life, you are his flesh and blood!—he must be sacred to you. Another artful notion! Why did he make me? Not out of love for *me*, as I had yet to become *me*. Did he know me, before he made me? Was it *me* he wished for, as he made me? . . . Can I recognize a love not founded on respect for my own self? . . . And what's so sacred about that? the actual process by which I was made? The animal satisfaction of animal desires . . . There you have it, the whole abracadabra [Hexerei] used to set up some sort of holy fog round the subject, to exploit the timidity of our natures" (Schiller, *Five Plays*, 79; Schiller, *Dramen*, 95). See Terras, *A Karamazov Companion*, 432. Dostoevsky expressed approval of this speech in the notes toward his account of the Kroneberg case: "I consider the reasoning of this debauched man to be correct" (24:136). Later Franz uses the same argument to justify murder: "If a man's birth is the product of animal compulsion or mere chance, who can call the negation of that birth any great matter?" (*Five Plays*, 149; *Dramen*, 162).

21. Dostoevsky highlighted his own qualifications as a father by using the example of his own children, although not identified as such, to illuminate the

psychology of children in the essay (22:66, 70; see notes, 22:352, 354). For Spasovich's entire speech, see the appendix in the present volume.

22. See Rosenshield, "Imprisonment of the Law," 427. The idea of the family as the foundation of the state probably goes back to Hegel's *Philosophy of Right* (1821). Compare the discussion by Murav, *Russia's Legal Fictions*, 138–39.

23. See Thompson's discussion of Alyosha's love for Fyodor and the effect it has on the latter (*Poetics of Memory*, 171–73).

24. A full discussion of gender issues in Dostoevsky is beyond the scope of this book. The best treatment of gender in Dostoevsky is to be found in Nina Pelikan Straus's thorough study *Dostoevsky and the Woman Question*. See also Murav, "Reading Woman"; and Andrew, *Narrative and Desire in Russian Literature*.

25. For an interpretation of *The Brothers Karamazov* that uses Freud's "scientific myth of the father of the primal horde" as a framework, see Michael Holquist, "How Sons Become Fathers: *The Brothers Karamazov*," in his *Dostoevsky and the Novel* (Princeton: Princeton University Press, 1977), 165–91. See also Vladiv-Glover, "Dostoyevsky, Freud, and Parricide." Igor' P. Smirnov argues for the (Freudian) Oedipal character of Russian realism of the 1840s through the 1880s, and for Dostoevsky's "Oedipal attack" on the authority of both nihilism and anti-nihilism in *The Devils* (Smirnov, *Psikhodiakhronologika: Psikhoistoriia russkoi literatury ot romantizma do nashikh dnei* [Moscow: Novoe literaturnoe obozrenie, 1994], 81–130). Smirnov stresses that Turgenev's anti-nihilism in *Fathers and Sons* is based on the championing of "family happiness" (115–16), while in *The Devils*, "family life [rodovaia zhizn'] is depicted as impossible" (124).

26. Sophocles, *Oedipus the King*, in *Greek Tragedies*, ed. David Grene and Richmond Lattimore, vol. 1 (Chicago: University of Chicago Press, 1960), 154. Fyodor's accusations of Dmitrii in the elder's cell are an echo of the prophecy that haunted Oedipus's father Laius: "the thing he feared, / death at his son's hands" (142).

27. Turgenev used an Oedipal motif once removed, by having Bazarov compete (rather halfheartedly) with his nonbiological "fathers" Nikolai and Pavel Kirsanov for the favors of Nikolai's peasant mistress. He presents a more truly Oedipal situation (in the Freudian sense) in his 1860 novella *First Love (Pervaia liubov')*.

28. Milan Kundera, *The Unbearable Lightness of Being*, trans. Michael Henry Heim (New York: Harper and Row, 1984), 177.

29. John E. Toews, "Having and Being: The Evolution of Freud's Oedipus Theory as a Moral Fable," in *Freud: Conflict and Culture*, ed. Michael S. Roth (New York: Knopf, 1998), 67. For Dostoevsky the father-son conflict is not only a sexual and moral one but also an economic one. Both Stepan and Fyodor compete with their sons over the income from their mothers' estates. The status of

the family as the bulwark of the institution of private property was a key reason for its targeting by Russian radicals. See Pyotr's ravings to Stavrogin: "As soon as there's family or love, there's the desire for property" (10:323). The famous 1870 manifesto "From the Russian Revolutionary Society to Women," perhaps authored by Nechaev (who was the model for Pyotr), makes the same connection but in reverse causal order: "Only after destroying private property can we destroy the legal family" (*Literaturnoe nasledstvo,* vol. 41–42: *A. I. Gertsen II* [Moscow: Akademiia nauk SSSR, 1941], 149). A thought-provoking article that reviews the Oedipal theory in the light of modern evolutionary models sees parent-offspring conflict as "a gender-blind disagreement about resource allocation" (Martin Daly and Margo Wilson, "Is Parent-Offspring Conflict Sex-Linked? Freudian and Darwinian Models," *Journal of Personality* 58, no. 1 [March 1990]: 163–89). For a further critique of the Oedipal theory, see Malcolm Macmillan, *Freud Evaluated: The Completed Arc* (Cambridge: MIT Press, 1997), 500–4, 650–51.

30. Toews, "Having and Being," 69.

31. Toews, "Having and Being," 71. For a review of the history of Freud's abandonment of the seduction theory, see Macmillan, *Freud Evaluated,* 222–27, 636–40.

32. Frederick Crews et al., *The Memory Wars: Freud's Legacy in Dispute* (New York: New York Review of Books, 1995), 57.

33. Crews, *Memory Wars,* 22.

34. "Honor your father and your mother, so that your days may be long in the land that the Lord your God is giving you" (Exodus 20:12).

35. Paperno, *Chernyshevskii and the Age of Realism,* 157.

36. Opochinin, "Ustnyi rasskaz," 213.

37. Crews, *Memory Wars,* 139.

Bibliography

Abelove, Henry. "Some Speculations on the History of Sexual Intercourse During the Long Eighteenth Century in England." In his *Deep Gossip*, 21–28. Minneapolis: University of Minnesota Press, 2003.

Abramovich, Stella. *Predystoriia poslednei dueli Pushkina. Ianvar' 1836–ianvar' 1837.* St. Petersburg: Rossiiskaia Akademiia nauk, 1994.

Akhmatova, Anna. "Gibel' Pushkina" (1958). In her *Sochineniia*, vol. 3, ed. G. P. Struve, N. A. Struve, and B. A. Filippov, 262–85. Paris: YMCA, 1983.

Alchevskaia, Kh. D. "Dostoevskii." In *F. M. Dostoevskii v vospominaniiakh sovremennikov*, ed. V. E. Vatsuro et al. 2 vols. 2:325–42. Moscow: Khudozhestvennaia literatura, 1990.

Al'tman, M. S. *Dostoevskii: Po vekham imen.* Saratov: Izdanie Saratovskogo universiteta, 1975.

Ammosov, A. *Poslednie dni zhizni i konchina Aleksandra Sergeevicha Pushkina. So slov byvshego ego litseiskogo tovarishcha i sekundanta Konstantina Karlovicha Danzasa.* St. Petersburg: Izd. F. A. Isakova, 1863.

Andrew, Joe. "The Law of the Father and *Netochka Nezvanova*." In his *Narrative and Desire in Russian Literature, 1822–49: The Feminine and the Masculine*, 214–26. New York: St. Martin's, 1993.

Arkhangel'skii, G. I. "Zhizn' v Peterburge po statisticheskim dannym." *Arkhiv sudebnoi meditsiny i obshchestvennoi gigieny*, 1869, no. 2 (June): pt. 3, pp. 33–85; no. 3 (September): pt. 3, pp. 84–143.

Bakhtin, Mikhail. *Problems of Dostoevsky's Poetics.* Edited and translated by Caryl Emerson. Minneapolis: University of Minnesota Press, 1984.

Bem, A. L. *Dostoevskii: Psikhoanaliticheskie etiudy.* Berlin: Petropolis, 1938; reprint ed., Ann Arbor: Ardis, 1983.

———. *"Faust" v tvorchestve Dostoevskogo.* Prague: Russkii svobodnyi universitet v Prage, 1937; reprint ed., Ann Arbor: University Microfilms, 1967.

Bitsilli, P. "K voprosu o vnutrennei forme romana Dostoevskogo. Prilozhenie III: De-Sad, Laklo i Dostoevskii." In his *Izbrannye trudy po filologii*, ed. V. N. Iartseva, 533–38. Moscow: Nasledie, 1996.

Bocharov, S. G. "Frantsuzskii epigraf k 'Evgeniiu Oneginu' (Onegin i Stavrogin)." *Moskovskii pushkinist* 1 (1995): 212–50.

Bogdanovich, T. A. *Liubov' liudei shestidesiatykh godov.* Leningrad: Academia, 1929.

Børtnes, Jostein."Male Homosocial Desire in The Idiot." In *Severny Sbornik: Proceedings of the NorFA Network in Russian Literature,* ed. Peter Alberg Jensen and Ingunn Lunde, 103–20. Stockholm: Almqvist & Wiksell, 2000.

Boswell, John. *Christianity, Social Tolerance, and Homosexuality: Gay People in Western Europe from the Beginning of the Christian Era to the Fourteenth Century.* Chicago: University of Chicago Press, 1980.

[Boyer d'Argens, Jean-Baptiste]. *Thérèse philosophe, ou Mémoires pour servir à l'histoire du P. Dirrag et de Mlle Eradice,* facsimile of the Paris (?) edition, ca. 1780. Introduced by Jacques Dupilot. Geneva: Éditions Slatkine, 1980.

Brumfield, William C. "*Thérèse philosophe* and Dostoevsky's Great Sinner." *Comparative Literature* 32 (1980): 238–52.

Burgin, Diana Lewis. "The Reprieve of Nastasja: A Reading of a Dreamer's Authored Life." *Slavic and East European Journal* 29, no. 3 (1985): 258–68.

Caplan, Jane. "Sexuality and Homosexuality." In *Women in Society: Interdisciplinary Essays,* ed. Cambridge Women's Studies Group, 149–67. London: Virago, 1981.

Carr, Edward Hallett. *The Romantic Exiles: A Nineteenth-Century Portrait Gallery.* New York: Frederick A. Stokes, 1933.

Casper, Johann Ludwig Casper [I. L. Kasper]. *Prakticheskoe rukovodstvo k sudebnoi meditsine.* Edited by V. O. Merzheevskii et al. St. Petersburg: V. I. Golovin, 1872.

Catteau, Jacques. *Dostoyevsky and the Process of Literary Creation.* Translated by Audrey Littlewood. Cambridge: Cambridge University Press, 1989.

Cohen, William A. "Manual Conduct in Great Expectations." In his *Sex Scandal: The Private Parts of Victorian Fiction,* 26–72. Durham: Duke University Press, 1996.

Costlow, Jane T., and Stephanie Sandler, eds. *Sexuality and the Body in Russian Culture.* Stanford: Stanford University Press, 1993.

Crews, Frederick, et al. *The Memory Wars: Freud's Legacy in Dispute.* New York: New York Review of Books, 1995.

Curtis, Laura A. "Raskolnikov's Sexuality." *Literature and Psychology* 37, no. 1–2 (1991): 88–106.

Dal', Vladimir. *Tolkovyi slovar' zhivogo velikorusskago iazyka.* 4th ed. 4 vols. Edited by Baudouin de Courtenay. St. Petersburg-Moscow: M. O. Vol'f, 1904.

Dalton, Elizabeth. *Unconscious Structure in "The Idiot": A Study in Literature and Psychoanalysis.* Princeton: Princeton University Press, 1979.

Daly, Martin, and Margo Wilson. "Is Parent-Offspring Conflict Sex-Linked? Freudian and Darwinian Models." *Journal of Personality* 58, no. 1 (March 1990): 163–89.

Darnton, Robert. *The Forbidden Best-Sellers of Pre-Revolutionary France.* New York: W. W. Norton, 1996.

Dickens, Charles. *David Copperfield.* New York: Modern Library, 1998.

———. *The Old Curiosity Shop.* Introduced by Peter Washington. New York: Alfred A. Knopf, 1995.

Ditman, V. "Tainyi porok." *Pedagogicheskii sbornik, izdavaemyi pri Glavnom upravlenii voenno-uchebnykh zavedenii,* 1871, bk. 3 (March): 367–75; bk. 4 (April): 551–56; bk. 5 (May): 654–63.

Dolgorukov, P. V. *Rossiiskaia rodoslovnaia kniga.* St. Petersburg: Karl Vingeber, 1854.

Dolinin, A. S. "'Ispoved' Stavrogina.' (V sviazi s kompozitsiei 'Besov')." *Literaturnaia mysl'*, 1922, no. 1:139–62.

———. *Poslednie romany Dostoevskogo: Kak sozdavalis' "Podrostok" i "Brat'ia Karamazovy."* Moscow-Leningrad: Sovetskii pisatel', 1963.

Dostoevskaia, A. G. *Vospominaniia.* Edited by L. P. Grossman. Moscow-Leningrad: Gosudarstvennoe izdanie, 1925.

Dostoevskii, F. M. *"Besy": Antologiia russkoi kritiki.* Edited by L. I. Saraskina. Moscow: Soglasie, 1996.

———. *Polnoe sobranie sochinenii v tridtsati tomakh.* Edited by V. G. Bazanov et al. 30 vols. Leningrad: Nauka, 1972–90.

Dostoevsky, Fyodor. *The Brothers Karamazov.* Translated by Constance Garnett. Revised and edited by Ralph E. Matlaw. New York: Norton, 1976.

———. *The Notebooks for "A Raw Youth."* Edited by Edward Wasiolek. Translated by Victor Terras. Chicago: University of Chicago Press, 1969.

———. *A Writer's Diary.* Translated and annotated by Kenneth Lantz. 2 vols. Evanston: Northwestern University Press, 1993.

Dumas fils, Alexandre. *Camille (The Lady of the Camellias)* (translator not identified). New York: Signet, 1972.

Durylin, Sergei. "Ob odnom simvole u Dostoevskogo. Opyt tematicheskogo obzora." In his *Dostoevskii,* 163–98. Moscow: Gosudarstvennaia Akademiia Khudozhestvennykh nauk, 1928.

Engelstein, Laura. *The Keys to Happiness: Sex and the Search for Modernity in Fin-de-Siècle Russia.* Ithaca: Cornell University Press, 1992.

Enko, T. F. *Dostoevskii—Intimnaia zhizn' geniia.* Moscow: OOO MP Geleos, OAO BI-GAZ-SI, 1997.

Erofeev, Viktor. "Metamorfoza odnoi literaturnoi reputatsii: Markiz de Sad, Sadizm i XX vek." *Voprosy literatury,* 1973, no. 6:135–68.

Fedorenko, B. V. "Iz rasyskanii o Dostoevskom. 2. Iz tvorcheskoi istorii romana F. M. Dostoevskogo 'Besy.'" In *Novye aspekty v izuchenii Dostoevskogo: sbornik nauchnykh trudov,* ed. V. N. Zakharov, 265–94. Petrozavodsk: Izdatel'stvo Petrozavodskogo Universiteta, 1994.

Feoktistov, F. M. *Vospominaniia.* Edited by Iu. G. Oksman. Leningrad: Priboi, 1929.

Foucault, Michel. *The History of Sexuality*. Translated by Robert Hurley. 3 vols. New York: Vintage, 1990.

Frank, Joseph. *Dostoevsky: The Mantle of the Prophet, 1871–1881*. Princeton: Princeton University Press, 2002.

———. *Dostoevsky: The Miraculous Years, 1865–1871*. Princeton: Princeton University Press, 1995.

———. *Dostoevsky: The Seeds of Revolt, 1821–1849*. Princeton: Princeton University Press, 1976.

———. *Dostoevsky: The Stir of Liberation, 1860–1865*. Princeton: Princeton University Press, 1986.

———. *Dostoevsky: The Years of Ordeal, 1850–1859*. Princeton: Princeton University Press, 1984.

Freud, Sigmund. "Dostoevsky and Parricide." In *The Standard Edition of the Complete Psychological Works of Sigmund Freud*, 24 vols., ed. James Strachey, 21:175–96. London: Hogarth Press and Institute of Psycho-Analysis, 1953–74.

———. "Three Essays on the Theory of Sexuality" (1905). In *Freud on Women: A Reader*, ed. Elisabeth Young Bruehl, 89–145. New York: Norton, 1990.

Frye, Northrop. *Anatomy of Criticism: Four Essays*. Princeton: Princeton University Press, 1957.

Fusso, Susanne. "Maidens in Childbirth: The Sistine Madonna in Dostoevskii's *Devils*." *Slavic Review* 54, no. 2 (Summer 1995): 261–75.

———. "The Weight of Human Tears: *The Covetous Knight* and *A Raw Youth*." In *Alexander Pushkin's Little Tragedies: The Poetics of Brevity*, ed. Svetlana Evdokimova, 229–42. Madison: University of Wisconsin Press, 2003.

Gay, Peter. *The Bourgeois Experience: Victoria to Freud*. Vol. 1: *Education of the Senses*. New York: Oxford University Press, 1984.

Gerigk, Horst-Jürgen. *Die Russen in Amerika: Dostojewskij, Tolstoj, Turgenjew und Tschechow in ihrer Bedeutung für die Literatur der USA*. Stuttgart: Guido Pressler, 1995.

———. *Versuch über Dostoevskijs "Jüngling": Ein Beitrag zur Theorie des Romans*. Munich: Wilhelm Fink, 1965.

Girard, René. *Deceit, Desire, and the Novel: Self and Other in Literary Structure*. Edited by Yvonne Freccero. Baltimore: Johns Hopkins Press, 1965.

Goethe, Johann Wolfgang von. *Faust*. Edited by Cyrus Hamlin. Translated by Walter Arndt. New York: W. W. Norton, 1976.

———. *Faust. Tragediia. Soch. Gete*. Translated by M. Vronchenko. St. Petersburg: Fisher, 1844.

———. *Goethe's Faust*. Translated by Barker Fairley. Toronto: University of Toronto Press, 1970; reprinted 1985.

———. *Goethes Faust: Der Tragödie erster und zweiter Teil. Urfaust*. Edited by Erich Trunz. Hamburg: Christian Wegner, 1963.

Gogol', N. V. *Polnoe sobranie sochinenii.* 14 vols. Moscow: Akademiia nauk SSSR, 1937–52.

Gol'diner, V. "Saltykov-Shchedrin i Dostoevskii ob advokature." *Sovetskaia iustitsiia,* 1961, no. 1:19–21.

Golstein, Vladimir. "Accidental Families and Surrogate Fathers: Richard, Grigory, and Smerdyakov." In *A New Word on "The Brothers Karamazov,"* ed. Robert Louis Jackson, 90–106. Evanston: Northwestern University Press, 2004.

Gounod, Charles. *Faust. A Lyric Drama in Five Acts.* Libretto by Jules Barbier and Michel Carré after the Tragedy by Johann Wolfgang von Goethe. New York: Broude Brothers, n.d. (opera first performed 1859 in Paris).

Gozenpud, A. *Dostoevskii i muzykal'no-teatral'noe iskusstvo.* Leningrad: Sovetskii kompozitor, 1981.

Greenblatt, Stephen. "Me, Myself, and I." *New York Review of Books,* April 8, 2004, 32–36.

Greenleaf, Monika. *Pushkin and Romantic Fashion: Fragment, Elegy, Orient, Irony.* Stanford: Stanford University Press, 1994.

Grimstad, Knut Andreas, and Ingunn Lunde, eds. *Celebrating Creativity: Essays in Honour of Jostein Børtnes.* Bergen: University of Bergen, 1997.

Healey, Dan. *Homosexual Desire in Revolutionary Russia: The Regulation of Sexual and Gender Dissent.* Chicago: University of Chicago Press, 2001.

[Herzen, Alexander]. A. Gertsen. *Povesti i rasskazy.* Moscow: Khudozhestvennaia literatura, 1967.

Holland, Kate. "The Legend of the *Ladonka* and the Trial of the Novel." In *A New Word on "The Brothers Karamazov,"* ed. Robert Louis Jackson, 192–99. Evanston: Northwestern University Press, 2004.

Holquist, Michael. "How Sons Become Fathers: *The Brothers Karamazov.*" In his *Dostoevsky and the Novel,* 165–91. Princeton: Princeton University Press, 1977.

Jackson, Robert Louis. *The Art of Dostoevsky: Deliriums and Nocturnes.* Princeton: Princeton University Press, 1981.

———. *Dialogues with Dostoevsky: The Overwhelming Questions.* Stanford: Stanford University Press, 1993.

———. "Dostoevskij's 'Anecdote from a Child's Life': A Case of Bifurcation." *Russian Literature* 25 (1989): 127–40.

———, ed. *A New Word on "The Brothers Karamazov."* Evanston: Northwestern University Press, 2004.

Jordanova, Ludmilla. "The Popularisation of Medicine: Tissot on Onanism." *Textual Practice* 1 (1984): 68–80.

Kantor, V. K. "Freid contra Dostoevskii." In *Tolstoi ili Dostoevskii? Filosofsko-esteticheskie iskaniia v ku'turakh Vostoka i Zapada,* ed. V. E. Bagno, 197–207. St Petersburg: Nauka, 2003.

Kariakin, Iu. "Khram bez kupola ('Besy' bez glavy 'U Tikhona')." In his *Dosto-evskii i kanun XXI veka*, 319–34. Moscow: Sovetskii pisatel', 1989.

Karlinsky, Simon. "Russia's Gay Literature and History (11th–20th Centuries)." In *Gay Roots: Twenty Years of Gay Studies*, ed. W. Leyland, 81–104. San Francisco: Gay Sunshine, 1991.

Kasatkina, Tat'iana. "Kak my chitaem russkuiu literaturu: o sladostrastii." *Novyi mir*, 1999, no. 7:170–82.

Kashina-Evreinova, A. *Podpol'e geniia: Seksual'nye istochniki tvorchestva Dostoevskogo*. Petrograd: Tret'ia Strazha, 1923; reprint edition, Leningrad: Atus, 1991.

Katz, Michael. "Dostoevsky's Homophilia/Homophobia." In *Gender and Sexuality in Russian Civilization*, ed. Peter I. Barta, 239–53. London: Routledge, 2001.

Kaufman, F. "Dostoevskij a Markiz de Sade." *Filosofický časopis* (Prague), 1968, vol. 3, pp. 384–89.

Kirpotin, V. "Dostoevskii o 'Egipetskikh nochakh' Pushkina." *Voprosy literatury*, 1962, no. 11:112–21.

Kistiakovskii, A. F. *Molodye prestupniki i uchrezhdeniia dlia ikh ispravleniia s obozreniem russkikh uchrezhdenii*. Kiev: V universitetskoi tipografii (I. I. Zavadzkogo), 1878.

Knapp, Liza. *The Annihilation of Inertia: Dostoevsky and Metaphysics*. Evanston: Northwestern University Press, 1996.

―――. "Mothers and Sons in *The Brothers Karamazov*: Our Ladies of Skotoprigonevsk." In *A New Word on "The Brothers Karamazov,"* ed. Robert Louis Jackson, 31–52. Evanston: Northwestern University Press, 2004.

Kogan, G. F. "Iz istorii sozdaniia 'Ispovedi Stavrogina.'" *Izvestiia Akademii nauk. Seriia literatury i iazyka* 54, no. 1 (1995): 65–73.

Komarovich, V. "Dostoevskii i 'Egipetskie nochi' Pushkina." In *Pushkin i ego sovremenniki: Materialy i issledovaniia*, no. 29–30, pp. 36–48. Petrograd: Rossiiskaia Akademiia nauk, 1918.

Koni, A. F. *Na zhiznennom puti: Iz zapisok sudebnogo deiatelia*. Vol. 1. St. Petersburg: Trud, 1912.

Kostalevsky, Marina. "Sensual Mind: The Pain and Pleasure of Thinking." In *A New Word on "The Brothers Karamazov,"* ed. Robert Louis Jackson, 200–9. Evanston: Northwestern University Press, 2004.

Kundera, Milan. *The Unbearable Lightness of Being*. Translated by Michael Henry Heim. New York: Harper and Row, 1984.

Kuznetsov, Sergei. "Fedor Dostoevskii i Markiz de Sad: Sviazi i pereklichki." In *Dostoevskii v kontse XX veka*, ed. K. A. Stepanian, 557–74. Moscow: Klassika plius, 1996.

Langan, Janine. "Icon vs. Myth: Dostoevsky, Feminism, and Pornography." *Religion and Literature* 18, no. 1 (Spring 1986): 63–72.

Laqueur, Thomas W. *Making Sex: Body and Gender from the Greeks to Freud*. Cambridge, Mass.: Harvard University Press, 1990.

———. *Solitary Sex: A Cultural History of Masturbation.* New York: Zone Books, 2003.

Lary, N. M. *Dostoevsky and Dickens: A Study of Literary Influence.* London: Routledge and Kegan Paul, 1973.

Leatherbarrow, W. J. *Fyodor Dostoevsky: The Brothers Karamazov.* Cambridge: Cambridge University Press, 1992.

Levina, L. A. "Nekaiushchaia Magdalina, ili pochemu kniaz' Myshkin ne mog spasti Nastas'iu Filippovnu." In *Dostoevskii v kontse XX veka,* ed. K. A. Stepanian, 343–68. Moscow: Klassika plius, 1996.

Levinton, G. A. "Dostoevskii i 'nizkie' zhanry fol'klora." *Literaturnoe obozrenie, spetsial'nyi vypusk: Erotika v russkoi literature, ot Barkova do nashikh dnei, Teksty i kommentarii.* Moscow: Literaturnoe obozrenie, 1992.

Likhachev, D. S. *Poetika drevnerusskoi literatury.* 2nd ed. Leningrad: Khudozhestvennaia literatura, 1971.

Lipking, Lawrence. *The Life of the Poet: Beginning and Ending Poetic Careers.* Chicago: University of Chicago Press, 1981.

Literaturnoe nasledstvo. Vol. 41–42: *A. I. Gertsen II.* Moscow: Akademiia nauk SSSR, 1941.

Literaturnoe nasledstvo. Vol. 71: *Vasilii Sleptsov: Neizvestnye stranitsy.* Moscow: Akademii nauk SSSR, 1963.

Literaturnoe nasledstvo. Vol. 77: *F. M. Dostoevskii v rabote nad romanom "Podrostok." Tvorcheskie rukopisi.* Edited by I. S. Zil'bershtein and L. M. Rozenblium. Moscow: Nauka, 1965.

Lotman, Iu. V. "O dueli Pushkina bez 'tain' i 'zagadok.'" In his *Pushkin. Biografiia pisatelia. Stat'i i zametki 1960–1990. "Evgenii Onegin." Kommentarii,* 375–88. St. Petersburg: Iskusstvo-SPB, 1995.

Lunde, Ingunn. "'. . . ia gorazdo umnee napisannogo': On Apophatic Strategies and Linguistic Experiments in Dostoevsky's *A Raw Youth.*" *Slavonic and East European Review* 79, no. 2 (January 2001): 264–89.

Macmillan, Malcolm. *Freud Evaluated: The Completed Arc.* Cambridge: MIT Press, 1997.

Martineau, L. *Leçons sur les déformations vulvaires at anales produites par la masturbation, le saphisme, la défloration, et la sodomie.* Paris: Adrien Delahaye et Émile Lecrosnier, 1884.

"Materialy dlia biografii A. Pushkina." *Poliarnaia zvezda. Zhurnal A. I. Gertsena i N. P. Ogareva v vos'mi knigakh, 1855–1869,* bk. 6:132–40. Facsimile edition. Moscow: Nauka, 1968.

Matich, Olga. "What's to Be Done about Poor Nastja: Nastas'ja Filippovna's Literary Prototypes." *Wiener slawistischer Almanach* 19 (1987): 47–64.

Meerson, Olga. *Dostoevsky's Taboos.* Dresden: Studies of the Harriman Institute and Dresden University Press, 1998.

Merzheevskii, V. *Sudebnaia ginekologiia. Rukovodstvo dlia vrachei i iuristov.* St. Petersburg: B. G. Ianpol'skii, 1878.

Meshcherskii, V. P. *Moi vospominaniia*, pt. 2 (1865–1881). St. Petersburg: Tipografiia kniazia Meshcherskogo, 1898.

Miller, Robin Feuer. *Dostoevsky and "The Idiot": Author, Narrator, and Reader.* Cambridge, Mass.: Harvard University Press, 1981.

Modzalevskii, B. L. "Kto byl avtorom anonimnykh paskvilei na Pushkina?" In *Novye materialy o dueli i smerti Pushkina,* ed. B. L. Modzalevskii, Iu. G. Oksman, and M. A. Tsiavlovskii, 13–49. Petersburg: Atenei, 1924.

Morson, Gary Saul. "Introductory Study: Dostoevsky's Great Experiment." In Fyodor Dostoevsky, *A Writer's Diary,* trans. and annotated by Kenneth Lantz, 1:1–117. Evanston: Northwestern University Press, 1993.

———. *Narrative and Freedom: The Shadows of Time.* New Haven: Yale University Press, 1994.

———. "Prosaics, Criticism, and Ethics." *Formations* 5, no. 2 (Summer-Fall 1989): 77–95.

———. "Tempics and *The Idiot.*" In *Celebrating Creativity: Essays in Honour of Jostein Børtnes,* ed. Knut Andreas Grimstad and Ingunn Lunde, 108–34. Bergen: University of Bergen, 1997.

———. "Verbal Pollution in *The Brothers Karamazov.*" In *Fyodor Dostoevsky's "The Brothers Karamazov,"* ed. Harold Bloom. New York: Chelsea House, 1988.

Mosse, W. E. "Imperial Favourite: V. P. Meshchersky and the *Grazhdanin.*" *Slavonic and East European Review* 59, no. 4 (October 1981): 529–47.

Murav, Harriet. "Legal Fiction in Dostoevsky's *Diary of a Writer.*" *Dostoevsky Studies* 1, no. 2 (1993): 155–73.

———. "Reading Woman in Dostoevsky." In *A Plot of Her Own: The Female Protagonist in Russian Literature,* ed. Sona Stephan Hoisington, 44–57. Evanston: Northwestern University Press, 1995.

———. *Russia's Legal Fictions.* Ann Arbor: University of Michigan Press, 1998.

Nazirov, R. G. "Tragediinoe nachalo v romane F. M. Dostoevskogo 'Unizhennye i oskorblennye.'" *Filologicheskie nauki,* 1965, no. 4:27–39.

Neuhäuser, Rudolf. *F. M. Dostojevskij: Die grossen Romane und Erzählungen. Interpretationen und Analysen.* Vienna: Böhlau, 1993.

O'Bell, Leslie. *Pushkin's "Egyptian Nights": The Biography of a Work.* Ann Arbor: Ardis, 1984.

Opochinin, E. N. "Iz 'Besed s Dostoevskim.'" In *F. M. Dostoevskii v vospominaniiakh sovremennikov,* ed. V. E. Vatsuro et al., 2 vols., 2:381–89. Moscow: Khudozhestvennaia literatura, 1990.

———. "Ustnyi rasskaz F. M. Dostoevskogo: Iz archiva E. N. Opochinina," ed. M. Odesskaia. *Novyi mir,* 1992, no. 8:211–17.

Orwin, Donna. "Did Dostoevsky or Tolstoy Believe in Miracles?" in *A New Word on "The Brothers Karamazov,"* ed. Robert Louis Jackson, 125–41. Evanston: Northwestern University Press, 2004.

Paperno, Irina. *Chernyshevsky and the Age of Realism: A Study in the Semiotics of Behavior.* Stanford: Stanford University Press, 1988.

———. *Suicide as a Cultural Institution in Dostoevsky's Russia.* Ithaca: Cornell University Press, 1997.

Perlina, Nina. "Rethinking Adolescence." In *Celebrating Creativity: Essays in Honour of Jostein Børtnes,* ed. Knut Andreas Grimstad and Ingunn Lunde, 216–26. Bergen: University of Bergen, 1997.

"Pervaia russkaia zhenshchina-medik." *Zhenskii vestnik,* 1867, no. 8:82–84.

"Pis'mo A. S. Pushkina k kavalerist-devitse N. A. Durovoi, s poslesloviem barona F. A. Biulera." *Russkii arkhiv* (1872): 204.

Porter, Roy. "Forbidden Pleasures: Enlightenment Literature of Sexual Advice." In *Solitary Pleasures: The Historical, Literary, and Artistic Discourses of Autoeroticism,* ed. Paula Bennett and Vernon A. Rosario II, 75–98. New York: Routledge, 1995.

Pozefsky, Peter C. "Love, Science, and Politics in the Fiction of *Shestidesiatnitsy* N. P. Suslova and S. V. Kovalevskaia." *Russian Review* 58 (July 1999): 361–79.

Pustygina, N. G. "O familii Dolgorukov v romane F. M. Dostoevskogo 'Podrostok.'" *Uchenye zapiski Tartuskogo gosudarstvennogo universiteta: Problemy tipologii russkoi literatury,* no. 645 (1985): 37–53.

Rancour-Laferriere, Daniel. *The Slave Soul of Russia: Moral Masochism and the Cult of Suffering.* New York: New York University Press, 1995.

Ransel, David L. *Mothers of Misery: Child Abandonment in Russia.* Princeton: Princeton University Press, 1988.

Rayfield, Donald. "Dumas and Dostoevskii—Deflowering the Camellia." In *From Pushkin to Palisandriia: Essays on the Russian Novel in Honor of Richard Freeborn,* ed. Arnold McMillin, 70–82. New York: St. Martin's, 1990.

Reed, Natasha. "Reading Lermontov's 'Geroj nashego vremeni': Problems of Poetics and Reception." Ph.D. dissertation, Harvard University, 1994.

Rice, James L. *Dostoevsky and the Healing Art: An Essay in Literary and Medical History.* Ann Arbor: Ardis, 1985.

———. *Freud's Russia: National Identity in the Evolution of Psychoanalysis.* New Brunswick: Transaction, 1993.

———. "Psychoanalysis of 'Peasant Marei': Some Residual Problems." In *Russian Literature and Psychoanalysis,* ed. Daniel Rancour-Laferriere, 245–61. Amsterdam: John Benjamins, 1989.

Richardot, Anne. *"Thérèse philosophe:* Les charmes de l'impénétrable." In *Faces of Monstrosity in Eighteenth-Century Thought,* ed. Andrew Curran, Robert P. Maccubbin, and David F. Morrill. Special issue of *Eighteenth-Century Life* 21, n.s., no. 2 (May 1997): 89–99.

Rodnianskaia, Irina. "Between Kon and Dostoevsky: A Reply to Vitalii Svintsov." *Russian Studies in Literature* 38, no. 4 (Fall 2002): 35–38.

————. "Mezhdu Konom i Dostoevskim: Replika Vitaliiu Svintsovu." *Novyi mir,* 1999, no. 5:213–15.

Rosario, Vernon A. II. "Phantastical Pollutions: The Public Threat of Private Vice in France." In *Solitary Pleasures: The Historical, Literary, and Artistic Discourses of Autoeroticism,* ed. Paula Bennett and Vernon A. Rosario II, 101–30. New York: Routledge, 1995.

Rosen, Nathan. "Breaking Out of the Underground: The 'Failure' of 'A Raw Youth.'" *Modern Fiction Studies* 4, no. 3 (Autumn 1958): 225–39.

————. "The Madness of Lise Khokhlakova in *The Brothers Karamazov*." *Dostoevsky Studies,* n.s., vol. 6 (2002): 154–62.

————. "Style and Structure in *The Brothers Karamazov*." In Fyodor Dostoevsky, *The Brothers Karamazov,* trans. Constance Garnett, rev. and ed. Ralph E. Matlaw, 841–51. New York: Norton, 1976.

Rosenshield, Gary. "The Imprisonment of the Law: Dostoevskii and the Kroneberg Case." *Slavic and East European Journal* 36, no. 4 (1992): 415–34.

————. *Western Law, Russian Justice: Dostoevsky, the Jury Trial, and the Law.* Madison: University of Wisconsin Press, 2005.

————. "Western Law vs. Russian Justice: Dostoevsky and the Jury Trial, Round One: The Kroneberg Trial." *Graven Images: A Journal of Culture, Law, and the Sacred* 1 (1994): 117–35.

Rousseau, Jean-Jacques. *Confessions.* Translated by J. M. Cohen. Harmondsworth: Penguin, 1975.

————. *Emile; or, On Education.* Translated and edited by Allan Bloom. New York: Basic Books, 1979.

Rowe, William Woodin. *Dostoevsky: Child and Man in His Works.* New York: New York University Press, 1968.

Rozenblium, L. M. "Tvorcheskaia laboratoriia Dostoevskogo-romanista." In *Literaturnoe nasledstvo,* vol. 77: *F. M. Dostoevskii v rabote nad romanom "Podrostok." Tvorcheskie rukopisi,* ed. I. S. Zil'bershtein and L. M. Rozenblium, 7–56. Moscow: Nauka, 1965.

————. *Tvorcheskie dnevniki Dostoevskogo.* Moscow: Nauka, 1981.

Rozova, K. "Pervaia russkaia zhenshchina vrach." *Fel'dsher i akusherka,* 1945, no. 3:48–52.

Saltykov-Shchedrin, M. E. *Polnoe sobranie sochinenii.* Vol. 15. Edited by V. Ia. Kirpotin et al. Moscow: Khudozhestvennaia literatura, 1940.

Saraskina, Liudmila. *Fedor Dostoevskii: Odolenie demonov.* Moscow: Soglasie, 1996.

————. *Vozliublennaia Dostoevskogo. Apollinariia Suslova: Biografiia v dokumentakh, pis'makh, materialakh.* Moscow: Soglasie, 1994.

Sazhin, V. "Ruka pobeditelia: Vybrannye mesta iz perepiski V. Belinskogo i M. Bakunina." *Literaturnoe obozrenie, spetsial'nyi vypusk: Erotika v russkoi literature ot Barkova do nashikh dnei. Teksty i kommentarii*, 39. Moscow: Literaturnoe obozrenie, 1992.

Scher, Steven Paul. *Verbal Music in German Literature*. New Haven: Yale University Press, 1968.

Schiller, Friedrich. *Dramen*. Edited by Benno von Wiese. Frankfurt: Büchergilde Gutenberg, 1959.

———. *Five Plays*. Translated by Robert David MacDonald. London: Absolute Classics, 1998.

Sedgwick, Eve Kosofsky. *Between Men: English Literature and Male Homosocial Desire*. New York: Columbia University Press, 1985.

Semashko, N. A. "Na zare russkoi gigieny i sanitarii (F. F. Erisman)." *Sovetskoe zdravookhranenie*, 1944, no. 4–5:26–32.

Semyonov, E. N. *Roman Dostoevskogo "Podrostok" (Problematika i zhanr)*. Leningrad: Nauka, 1979.

Shchegolev, P. E. *Duel' i smert' Pushkina. Issledovanie i materialy*. 2nd ed. Petrograd: Literaturnaia knizhnaia lavka, 1917; reprint ed., Ann Arbor, 1975.

Shmit, Klara. "O prepodavanii v obshchestvennykh shkolakh faktov, otnosiashchikhsia k polovomu voprosu." In *Polovoe vospitanie. Sbornik statei uchitelei, roditelei i vospitatelei*. Moscow: Vil'de, 1913.

Sidorov, I. S. "Eshche raz ob anonimnom 'diplome' i kn. P. N. Dolgorukove." *Moskovskii pushkinist* 1 (1995): 208–11.

Smirnov, Aleksandr. *Pervaia russkaia zhenshchina-vrach*. Moscow: Medgiz, 1960.

Smirnov, Igor' P. *Psikhodiakhronologika: Psikhoistoriia russkoi literatury ot romantizma do nashikh dnei*. Moscow: Novoe literaturnoe obozrenie, 1994.

Sophocles. *Oedipus the King*. In *Greek Tragedies*, ed. David Grene and Richmond Lattimore, vol. 1. Chicago: University of Chicago Press, 1960.

Stites, Richard. *The Women's Liberation Movement in Russia: Feminism, Nihilism, and Bolshevism 1860–1930*. Princeton: Princeton University Press, 1978.

Straus, Nina Pelikan. *Dostoevsky and the Woman Question: Readings at the End of a Century*. New York: St. Martin's, 1994.

Suslova, A. P. *Gody blizosti s Dostoevskim. Dnevnik. Povest'. Pis'ma* (1928). Edited by A. S. Dolinin. Reprint ed., New York: Serebrianyi vek, 1982.

Suslova-Erisman, N. "Iz nedavnego proshlogo." *Vestnik Evropy*, 1900, no. 6:624–73.

———. Review of *O vospitanii detei v pervye gody zhizni*, by Mar'ia Manasseina (St. Petersburg, 1870). *Arkhiv sudebnoi meditsiny i obshchestvennoi gigieny*, 1870, bk. 4: 21–31.

Svintsov, Vitalii. "Dostoevskii i 'otnosheniia mezhdu polami.'" *Novyi mir*, 1999, no. 5:195–213.

————. "Dostoevskii i stavroginskii grekh." *Voprosy literatury*, 1995, no. 2:111–42.

————. "Dostoevsky and 'Relations between the Sexes.'" *Russian Studies in Literature*, vol. 38, no. 4 (Fall 2002): 7–34.

Tarczylo, Théodore. *Sexe et liberté au siècle des Lumières.* Paris: Presses de la Renaissance, 1983.

Tarnovskii, V. M. *Izvrashchenie pologovo chuvstva. Sudebno-psikhiatricheskii ocherk. Dlia vrachei i iuristov.* St. Petersburg: M. M. Stasiulevich, 1885.

Terras, Victor. *A Karamazov Companion: Commentary on the Genesis, Language, and Style of Dostoevsky's Novel.* Madison: University of Wisconsin Press, 1981.

Thompson, Diane Oenning. *"The Brothers Karamazov" and the Poetics of Memory.* Cambridge: Cambridge University Press, 1991.

Tissot, Samuel-Auguste-André-David. *L'onanisme, dissertation sur les maladies produites par la masturbation, par Mr. Tissot, Doct. med.* 8th ed. Lausanne: Franç. Grasset et Comp., 1785.

————. *Onanizm ili rassuzhdenie o bolezniakh, proiskhodiashchikh ot rukobludiia. Soch. G. Tissotom . . . perevedennoe s poslednego original'nogo izdaniia protiv prezhnego znachitel'no umnozhennoe i ispravlennoe. V trekh chastiakh.* St. Petersburg: V tipografii Imperatorskogo Vospitatel'nogo Doma, 1822.

————. *Onanizm ili rassuzhdenie o bolezniakh, proiskhodiashchikh ot rukobludiia, Sochinenie Doktora Tissota. S frantsuzskogo perevel doktor meditsiny Aleksandr Nikitin.* St. Petersburg: V tipografii Iv. Selezneva, 1845.

Toews, John E. "Having and Being: The Evolution of Freud's Oedipus Theory as a Moral Fable." In *Freud: Conflict and Culture,* ed. Michael S. Roth. New York: Knopf, 1998.

Tolstoi, L. N. *Sobranie sochinenii v dvadtsati tomakh.* Edited by N. N. Akopovaia et al. 20 vols. Moscow: Khudozhestvennaia literatura, 1963.

Tracy, Lewis. "Decoding Puškin: Resurrecting Some Readers' Responses to *Egyptian Nights.*" *Slavic and East European Journal* 37, no. 4 (1993): 456–71.

Trenin, V., and N. Khardzhiev. *Poeticheskaia kul'tura Maiakovskogo.* Moscow: Iskusstvo, 1970.

Tschižewskij [Chizhevsky], D. "Schiller und *Die Brüder Karamazov.*" *Zeitschrift für slavische Philologie* 4 (1929): 1–42.

Tunimanov, V. A. "Publitsistika Dostoevskogo. 'Dnevnik pisatelia.'" In *Dostoevskii—Khudozhnik i myslitel': Sbornik statei,* ed. A. L. Grishunin et al., 165–209. Moscow: Khudozhestvennaia literatura, 1972.

Turgenev, Ivan. *Fathers and Sons.* Edited by Ralph E. Matlaw. New York: Norton, 1966.

Tynan, Kenneth. "The Journals of Kenneth Tynan." *New Yorker,* August 7, 2000, 48–59.

Unbegaun, B. O. *Russkie familii.* Moscow: Progress, 1989.

Vetlovskaia, V. E. "Alyosha Karamazov and the Hagiographic Hero." In *Dostoevsky: New Perspectives,* ed. Robert Louis Jackson, trans. Nancy Pollak and Susanne Fusso, 206–26. Englewood Cliffs, N.J.: Prentice-Hall, 1984.

———. *Poetika romana "Brat'ia Karamazovy."* Leningrad: Nauka, 1997.

Vigel', F. F. *Vospominaniia,* pt. 1. Moscow: Katkov, 1864.

Vinogradov, V. V. *O khudozhestvennoi proze.* Moscow-Leningrad: Gosudarstvennoe izdatel'stvo, 1930.

Vladiv-Glover, Slobodanka. "Dostoyevsky, Freud, and Parricide: Deconstructive Notes on *The Brothers Karamazov.*" *New Zealand Slavonic Journal,* 1993, 7–34.

Volgin, Igor'. *Propavshii zagovor: Dostoevskii i politicheskii protsess 1849 g.* Moscow: Libereia, 2000.

Wachtel, Andrew. *The Battle for Childhood: Creation of a Russian Myth.* Stanford: Stanford University Press, 1990.

Wasiolek, Edward. *Dostoevsky: The Major Fiction.* Cambridge: MIT Press, 1964.

Weiner, Adam. *By Authors Possessed: The Demonic Novel in Russia.* Evanston: Northwestern University Press, 1998.

Welsh, Alexander. *George Eliot and Blackmail.* Cambridge, Mass.: Harvard University Press, 1985.

Witte [Vitte], S. Iu. *Vospominaniia.* Edited by A. L. Sidorov. 3 vols. Moscow: Izdatel'stvo sotsial'no-ekonomicheskoi literatury, 1960.

Zakharov, V. N. *Problemy izucheniia Dostoevskogo.* Petrozavodsk: Petrozavodskii Gosudarstvennyi Universitet, 1978.

Ziolkowski, Margaret. "Dostoevsky and the Kenotic Tradition." In *Dostoevsky and the Christian Tradition,* ed. George Pattison and Diane Oenning Thompson, 31–40. Cambridge: Cambridge University Press, 2001.

Zohrab, Irene. "Dostoevsky and Meshchersky and 'Homosexual Consciousness.'" *Australian Slavonic and East European Studies* 12, no. 1 (1998): 115–34.

———. "Dostoevsky and the 'Other' Meshchersky: Refashioning Masculinities on the Pages of *The Citizen* (with a Decoding of a Section from *The Adolescent*)." *Soviet and Post-Soviet Review* 28, no. 3 (2001 [2002]): 333–62.

———. "'Mann-Männliche' Love in Dostoevsky's Fiction (An Approach to *The Possessed*): With Some Attributions of Editorial Notes in *The Citizen*. First Installment." *Dostoevsky Journal* 3–4 (2002–3): 113–226.

Zolotonosov, M. N. "Seks 'ot Stavrogina': Pornosoficheskii kommentarii k 'otrechennoi' glave iz romana 'Besy.'" In his *Slovo i telo: Seksual'nye aspekty, universalii, interpretatsii russkogo kul'turnogo teksta XIX–XX vekov,* 9–78. Moscow: Ladomir, 1999.

Index

Index

Index

Russian Herald (journal), 31, 38–39, 40–41

Sade, Marquis de (Donatien Alphonse François, Count de Sade), 3, 6, 13, 14, 16, 165n13, 167n22
sadomasochism, 9, 78, 168n36
Saltykov-Shchedrin, M. E., 82, 89, 92, 97, 173n35, 188n8, 190n23
Sand, George, 90–91, 105, 189n20
Saraskina, Liudmila, 174n41, 189n15
Sazhin, V., 99
Scher, Steven Paul, 58
Schiller, Friedrich, 109, 195n16, 195n20
Schoenberg, Arnold, 58
Scott, Sir Walter, 167n21
Sechenov, I. M., 89
Sedgwick, Eve Kosofsky, 51–52
sex addiction, 9, 165n12
Smirnov, Aleksandr, 189n12, 189n21
Smirnov, Igor' P., 196n25
Smith, Rebecca F., 184n15
Sophocles, 114
Spasovich, V. D., 83, 84, 85, 87–89, 96–100, 111, 116, 117, 118, 188n8, 192n40, 192n43, 192n45, 195n17, 196n21
Strakhov, N. N., 165n8
Straus, Nina Pelikan, 171n22, 172n29, 196n24
Sue, Eugène, 10
suicide, 31, 36, 77, 78, 105
Suslova, Apollinaria Prokof'evna, xiv, 89–90, 189n15, 189n20, 190n26
Suslova, Nadezhda Prokof'evna, 89–94, 96, 97, 189n12, 189nn17–21, 190n26, 190–91n27
Svintsov, Vitalii, 35

Tarnovskii, V. M., 47–48, 50, 52, 178n25, 179n30
Thérèse philosophe, 13–16, 26–27, 74, 168nn31–32, 171n24, 184n12

Thompson, Diane Oenning, 106–7, 194n11, 196n23
Timmerman (journalist), 3–4
Tissot, Samuel-Auguste-André-David, 77, 94, 95, 185–86n19, 186n21, 191n33, 191n35
Titova (cook in Kroneberg case), 84, 87
Toews, John E., 115
Tolmacheva, Evgeniia Eduardovna, 3–5, 12
Tolstoy, Leo, 53, 103, 183n72
Tuchkova-Ogaryova, Natal'ia, 105
Turgenev, Ivan, 3, 102–3, 193nn2–3, 196n25, 196n27
Tynan, Kenneth, 168n37

Unbegaun, B. O., 176n10

Veinberg, P. I. [Kamen'-Vinogorov], 4, 5, 7
Vetlovskaia, V. E., 185n15
Vigel', F. F., 178n25
Vinogorov. *See* Veinberg, P. I.
Vinogradov, V. V., 188n8
Vladiv-Glover, Slobodanka, 184n15
Voice, The (journal), 82, 84–85, 92, 187–88n6
Volgin, Igor', 176n7

Wachtel, Andrew, 174n1
Wasiolek, Edward, 183n73
Weiner, Adam, 172n25
Welsh, Alexander, 55, 180n42
Witte, Count S. Iu., 45, 176n9, 179n30

Yeats, William, Butler, 67

Zakharov, V. N., 40
Zohrab, Irene, 171nn22–23, 175n4, 176n8, 179n35, 181n48, 183n1
Zolotonosov, M. N., 171n24, 172n27

216

About the Author

Susanne Fusso is a professor of Russian language and literature at Wesleyan University. She is the author of *Designing Dead Souls: An Anatomy of Disorder in Gogol* and the translator and editor of *A Russian Prince in the Soviet State: Hunting Stories, Letters from Exile, and Military Memoirs* by Vladimir Sergeevich Trubetskoi.